authentic
relationships
from the
inside out

D0281408

authentic
relationships
from the
inside out

sarah abell

HODDER &
STOUGHTON

First published in Great Britain in 2009 by Hodder & Stoughton
An Hachette UK company

1

A CIP catalogue record for this title is available from the British Library
Unless indicated otherwise, Scripture quotations are taken from the
Holy Bible, New International Version.
Copyright © 1973, 1978, 1984 by International Bible Society.
Used by permission. All rights reserved.

ISBN 978 0340 979891

Printed and bound in the UK by
CPI Mackays, Chatham ME5 8TD

Typeset by Hewer Text UK Ltd, Edinburgh

158.
2

Hodder & Stoughton policy is to use papers that are natural, renewable
and recyclable products and made from wood grown in sustainable forests.
The logging and manufacturing processes are expected to conform to the
environmental regulations of the country of origin.

Hodder & Stoughton Ltd
338 Euston Road
London NW1 3BH

www.hodder.co.uk

contents

vi

In memory of Nicholas

To Mum and Dad for giving me roots and wings
and to David for joining me on the big adventure

a few thanks

The problem with trying to thank people is that once you start it is hard to know where to stop. Probably everyone I know has contributed in some way to this book whether they realise it or not – so please everyone consider yourself thanked.

But there are a few people who deserve a special mention. First of all, thanks to the team at Hodder, particularly to Wendy for having faith in me and to Julia my editor for guiding me through the process and encouraging me when I wasn't sure what on earth I was doing.

Over a thousand people completed my rather long survey and some gave me further stories to use. If you were one of those – I want to thank you for your time and for your honesty.

I am very grateful to all those who took the time to read through the manuscript and feed back their wise comments: Cheryl, David, Jane, Janet, Jo, Katharine, Lise, Luke, Martin, Michelle, Nicky and Rachel. Without you I would probably be embarrassing myself an awful lot more than I am! And I want to express my gratitude to Rob Parsons, Harry Benson and Simon Walker for sparing the time and allowing me to ask lots of questions.

To Andy, Connie, Jo, and Marika, I want to give you credit for seeing this book in me before I saw it myself. And to Patrick for enabling me to take the first step.

When it comes to the content of this book I am aware that I am standing on the shoulders of giants – many of whom I have quoted throughout these pages. I am indebted to you for going first and for inspiring me with your own research, books and resources.

And finally, on a personal note I want to thank the people who have helped me put into practice the lessons that I write about in these pages. To Mum and Dad for all your love and encouragement, to Frank and Victoria for being fab in-laws, to my Kona friends for letting me be me, to Amelia for being a constant, to Amanda for asking questions, to my Friday morning group, to Michael and Mary-Clare, to Nick and Sarah for your continual support and to all my family and friends for being you. And a huge thank you goes to Nicky and Sila Lee who have taught me so much and for making it such fun along the way.

And last and most importantly – the biggest thank you goes to David for not only pushing me to do this book but for making it possible through your love, help and encouragement ... (I promise I will do some cooking now!).

how to use this book

When I read a book I tend to wolf it down as if it is a rather tasty Krispy Kreme donut. If I ever have to stop to do something else I'll turn down the corner to mark my place. If the book contains any quizzes or questionnaires, I'll have no qualms about reaching for my pen or pencil (whichever is nearest) and filling them in. I'll also underline any quotes that I think are helpful.

My husband David, on the other hand, takes much longer to read a book, hates to find dog-eared pages, never fills in a quiz (unless I make him) and gets annoyed if he sees me marking anything up.

When it comes to books we all like different things. So with this one – I just want to say do what you like . . . it is your book to use as you want.

You can read it cover to cover in one sitting.

You can read a chapter a day or one a week.

You can just dip in to the bits you think might be interesting.

You can read it with someone else and discuss the questions as you go along.

You can skip all the questions and quizzes if they aren't your thing or you can give them all a go.

You can keep it looking pristine or you can scribble your comments, thoughts, and questions all over it.

You can use it as a basis for a group discussion. Go to www.hodder.co.uk website for some recommended questions.

Or you can read just one page and decide it would be a great book for propping up your computer monitor!

The choice is yours.

taking stock

1. pause for thought – how are you doing?

I love mankind: it's people I can't stand.
LINUS, *PEANUTS* CHARACTER

Life is relationships; the rest is just details ... Everything in life that truly matters can be boiled down to relationships.
DR GARY SMALLEY, *THE DNA OF RELATIONSHIPS*

Love is the most important thing in life. You cannot live without love.
ANNABEL, AGED EIGHT

a moment to reflect

We all relate. It is like breathing or eating – it is what we humans do. Whether we are at home, at work, in the gym, down the pub, shopping, visiting the doctor or doing anything else that we might do during the day – we are relating to others. Even when we're on our own we are often interacting with people online, in our thoughts or in our dreams. Whether we like it or not there's no getting away from relationships. But how do we know whether we're any good at them?

What's the measure of success? How many friends we have on Facebook or numbers on our mobile? How busy our diary is, the number of people we think would turn up at our funeral or the fact that everyone at work or at the local shops knows our name (and we know theirs)? Perhaps we measure it by the number of times we've been asked to be best man, bridesmaid or godparent, the number of dates we've been on (if we are single), the fact that someone chose to marry us and is still with us (if we are married), or that our grown-up children (if we have any) are still talking to us?

Or maybe we don't measure by quantity but by quality. Do we have people we could count on in a crisis? Who would be pleased to see us if we turned up at their door uninvited? Who do we know who would sort through our wardrobe with us, practise headers with us, throw a surprise party for us or laugh at our jokes (even the bad ones!)? Do we know people who would still love us if we told them our most embarrassing or awful secret? Who will look after us when we are too old to look after ourselves or who would visit us if we did something really bad and ended up in prison? Would anyone donate their bone marrow if we needed a transplant or give us a bed if we were homeless? How quickly would people notice if we suddenly died in our home alone? (OK, so that's a little morbid but I doubt that I'm the only person who has ever thought about that.)

Or turn all that on its head and maybe some of us measure how well we're doing in relationships by how much we are giving out to others. How good are we at helping people through a crisis? Do our family and friends feel loved and supported by us? Are there people at work (or in some other area of life) that we have invested in, helped and mentored? How much of our time, skills, effort and money do we give to charities, voluntary organisations or people in need? Are we generous, patient, loving, forgiving and kind? Would people be able to trust us to keep our promises? Is our home a place where people feel welcomed, loved, safe and looked after? And when people spend time with us do they feel energised and encouraged?

However we decide to measure it, the question is, do we? Most of us will probably take time to review how our careers are going (if we are working), whether our diet is succeeding, the performance of our favourite football team if we have one, how our finances are doing, and whether our car, home and body need mending or improving. But many of us don't stop and ask ourselves how we are doing at the important business of relating. And that is strange when you think about it, because relating is probably the most important thing any of us do in life.

need to get real

And that's why it is good to get real about our relationships.

Getting real means pressing the 'pause' button and asking yourself that question – 'How am I doing'?

Are your friendships as genuine or strong as you'd like them to be? Have you got a relationship or relationships that you are struggling with at the moment? Or maybe you are generally happy with how things are with your family, friends, neighbours and work colleagues but know that there's always room for improvement?

Perhaps you long for more time to spend with your loved ones or for loved ones that you would want to spend more time with? Do you wish you didn't lose your temper so much or that you could express your emotions more? Would you love to be understood more or be able to understand those around you better?

Sometimes it takes a huge life event to get us to stop and think: an illness, a bereavement, a redundancy or some other crisis. I know, because that is what happened to me.

my story

I was twenty one when I first realised I wasn't 'doing relationships' very well. On the surface things looked pretty good: I had more than 250 people on my Christmas card list (not sure how I afforded the stamps on my student grant), an endless stream of party invites and was never short of a boyfriend. But just before I was about to start my final year at university, my bubble burst. My only brother, who was four years older than me, died suddenly. I realised then

5

the truth of the statement, 'It isn't the friends you can count that matter but the friends you can count on.' I can remember to this day the four people who were there for me during those first couple of weeks and I can also recall what it was like when people whom I thought were my friends crossed the road to avoid me.

It was during that time I slowly realised some difficult home truths:

- My friendships weren't as close or as deep as I had assumed
- Quantity is no substitute for quality when it comes to friendships
- I wouldn't have been any better if something similar had happened to a friend of mine
- I wasn't any good at discussing my true feelings with anyone (and didn't actually know how to access them)
- Life is short and precious and really – when all is stripped away – relationships are what matter.

In the eighteen years since that horrific event and the subsequent wake-up call I have been on a quest to discover how to be better at relationships, and how to love authentically and invest in others. In the last eight years I've even had the privilege of turning that quest into a job. It has been a fantastic, hard and exciting journey and one that is still continuing. I have learnt so much from so many people of all ages and nationalities, many of whom are further ahead in the journey than me, and I am still learning and hope I never stop.

What I do know now is that it is possible to change, to grow and to learn to love better – and we can start from where we are.

There's a great little bit I love in *Winnie the Pooh* by A. A. Milne … which is normally accompanied by a picture of Christopher Robin dragging poor Pooh down the stairs: 'Here is Edward Bear coming down the stairs now, bump, bump, bump on the back of his head. It is, as far as he knows, the only way of coming down the stairs but sometimes he feels there really is another way if he could only stop bumping for a moment and think of it.'

And it is the same with relating; sometimes we just can't see another way of doing it but the great news is we don't have to settle for things as they are at present. There is another way. We can learn to have more authentic relationships and that is what this book is all about.

the great relationship survey

To help with research for this book, my husband David and I compiled a survey, which was completed by over a thousand people. Some were friends and some were friends of friends but most were friends of friends of friends. We had replies from men and women of all ages, from sixteen years and above, and from many countries around the world. It wasn't meant to be an academic study or a highly accurate, representative sample. We just did it because we wanted to see what other people thought and felt about their relationships.

I'll be quoting from the results throughout the book but here are just a few of the findings as a taster:

64 per cent don't think they give enough time to their close friendships.
33 per cent often feel lonely.
63 per cent agree that they regularly feel stressed and/or tired.

how are you doing?

Which brings me back to you. How would you rate your relationships and your relationship skills at the moment? This simple questionnaire may help you think more about that. Be as honest as you can.

Rate the following statements and how they apply to you by assigning a number:

5. I strongly agree
4. I mainly agree
3. I neither agree nor disagree
2. I mainly disagree
1. I strongly disagree

- I am a really good listener and completely focus when someone is telling me something important ☐
- I am good at expressing my feelings (both negative and positive) ☐
- I have a good work–life balance ☐
- I find it easy to make new friends ☐
- I am happy with the time that I give to my closest relationships ☐
- I have (or had if she is no longer alive) a good and healthy relationship with my mum ☐
- I find it easy to live with other people and share my space ☐
- I am able to control my anger and only use it constructively ☐
- I have good boundaries and find it easy to say 'no' when needed ☐
- I am easily able to tell people when they have hurt or upset me ☐
- I have (or had if he is no longer alive) a good and healthy relationship with my dad ☐
- I find it easy to understand and appreciate people who are very different from me ☐
- I am able to admit when I am wrong, say sorry and ask forgiveness ☐
- There are people in my life whom I know I can turn to and trust if I am in trouble ☐

- I am a good and trustworthy friend to my close friends ☐
- I find intimacy easy and have people in my life who really know and understand me ☐
- There are people in my life with whom I can share my deepest fears ☐
- I enjoy working in a team ☐
- I have a good understanding of what it takes to make a good marriage (even if you are not married yourself) ☐
- I have a good understanding of what it takes to be a good parent (even if you are not a parent yourself) ☐

Add up your scores: *Total =*

If you scored 80-100

You are probably pretty satisfied with your relationships and how you relate to others. You have a good understanding of what it takes to make a relationship work and you believe that you are doing many of those things. It may be worth checking that others agree with you – try asking a good friend to answer the questions for you and see if they come up with the same score. The fact that you are reading this book probably means that there is some area you would like to improve or you would like to help someone else improve.

If you scored 50-79

You probably think your relationships are pretty good although you know there are some relationships that could definitely be better. You are quite aware that you are not perfect. Hopefully this book will help you to look at some of those difficult relationships and will also give you some ideas and tips as to how you can improve your interaction with others.

If you scored 10-49

Relationships are probably not easy for you. Perhaps there is a particular relationship that is causing you grief at the moment or perhaps you have a general dissatisfaction with many of your relationships.

9

You are aware that you aren't always the easiest person to get on with and you would like to be better at relating. The good news is that being aware of your issues is the first step to changing them.

room for improvement?

The truth is that we can all improve our relationships. In the survey only 2.5 per cent of people strongly disagreed with the statement: 'My relationships could definitely be improved.' This book is for the other 97.5 per cent!

We asked: 'What would you most like to improve about your relationships?' The majority of people mentioned they wanted more time to spend with people, better communication and deeper relationships. Here are just a few of the other answers they gave:

'Openness ... we tend to talk about the easy stuff but not always the hard stuff'

'More spontaneity, less blame, less bickering'

'Not getting on the defensive when I'm criticised'

'Courage to be vulnerable, again'

'I wish that I had the ability to express negative feelings to others (close friends, outside of my family) when I'm upset with them. I tend to put all the blame on myself or avoid conflict rather than taking the risk of saying, "I'm upset with you for x"'

'More patience with some people who annoy me'

'To be able to talk without arguing'

'To put friends before my work life and tiredness/laziness'

'Difficult. It's tempting to say everyone else should change, but that would be very arrogant. So I'd like to grow in my ability to understand others so that I could find out what makes them tick'

'I would like to meet a partner'

'I would like my family to listen to my opinions and not dismiss them'

'I want to feel like I belong'

'I would like to hold my temper better'

'I want to be better at expressing frustration/anger i.e. not people pleasing!'

'More sex'

'I want to be more focused on other people, rather than projects'

'Be able to be completely real with people'

'I would like to feel able to be myself more of the time, to be more open and trusting'

'I would like to have a smaller group of friends that I see more regularly and spend quality time with, rather than a larger less intimate group'

'I hate the "let me check my diary and see if I can squeeze something in" culture that we have. We make our friends feel like a business appointment ... I love diaries but I'd like my relationships to feel a bit more special than a meeting'

what about you?

What would you most like to change or improve about your relationships? Try and think of 5 things:

1. ....

2. ....

3. ....

4. ....

5. ....

what brings us to the point of change?

Becoming aware of how we want things to improve is a great first step. It is hard to change unless we know how we want things to be different. But just being aware isn't enough.

We have to really want things to be different. We need a vision of how things can be; like the couch potato who looks at his athletic friend and thinks, 'I want to be like that.' We need to want our vision enough to do something about it! We can't just keep on doing the same things over and over again and hope that things will change. We actually need to be proactive and try another approach.

I'm not going to pretend that change is easy. Often, it isn't. But if our vision is a good one then we may be prepared to sacrifice some effort and discomfort to get there. If the couch potato really wants to get fit he'll have to put in the hours down the gym or running around the park. It will probably be very uncomfortable and painful at times, but if he pushes through he'll reap the benefits.

The American author Marilyn Ferguson once said: 'It's not so much that we're afraid of change or so in love with the old ways, but it's that place in between that we fear ... It's like being between trapezes. It's Linus when his blanket is in the dryer. There's nothing to hold on to.'

I hope this book *will* be something you can hold on to. It will help you to explore how things can be different and also how you can take practical steps to make the changes you want. It will look at how we can:

- Build deeper relationships where we can be 'ourselves' with others
- Make more time for our most important relationships
- Learn to be great listeners and really understand others
- Say what we mean and mean what we say
- Discover the impact that we have on others
- Deal with tricky situations and have the difficult conversations (we'd rather avoid)
- Be the friend we've always wanted
- Be a leader worth following
- Thrive (not just survive) with our families
- Date like we mean it (for those that are wanting to find a partner), and
- Make a marriage that matters (for those who are married).

authentic relating

When I looked through the surveys what I read again and again was a desire for relationships where people can be real … where they and others can be 'themselves' – loved, accepted, respected and understood for who they are. They want their relationships to be deeper, genuine and more meaningful than they are at the moment. They are searching for something more AUTHENTIC. And whether we are conscious of it or not, that is probably something many of us want.

In *Affluenza* Oliver James writes: 'Authenticity is being real: as actual, hard, durable and densely weighty as stone. Like art historians authenticating pieces for auctioneers, the authentic individual labours to distinguish the true original from the false, searching for the impenetrable and the autonomous in human existence.'

But if we want to be authentic it must start with us. Authenticity isn't something you can make up or pretend to have. You become it. It comes from the inside out. It is a way of being, a way of relating.

Being authentic won't always be easy. You may find yourselves swimming against the tide.

As Oliver James points out: 'The authentic go back to basics, seeking something that is true in all times and places, not subject to fashion, making the natural and the unfashionable good places to look. The consequent Being is often at odds with received, habitual, convention.'

We have a choice. We can carry on as we are or we can change.

The couch potato can remain unfit or he can start to exercise.

We can follow the crowd or we can find a better way.

We can become authentic from the inside out.

And that is the great relationships challenge.

2. the great relationships challenge

"What is REAL?" asked the Rabbit one day, when they were lying side by side near the nursery fender, before Nana came to tidy the room. "Does it mean having things that buzz inside you and a stick-out handle?"

"Real isn't how you are made," said the Skin Horse. "It's a thing that happens to you. When a child loves you for a long, long time, not just to play with, but REALLY loves you, then you become Real."

"Does it hurt?" asked the Rabbit.

"Sometimes," said the Skin Horse, for he was always truthful. "When you are Real you don't mind being hurt."

"Does it happen all at once, like being wound up," he asked, "or bit by bit?"

"It doesn't happen all at once," said the Skin Horse. "You become. It takes a long time. That's why it doesn't happen often to people who break easily, or have sharp edges, or who have to be carefully kept. Generally, by the time you are Real, most of your hair has been loved off, and your eyes drop out and you get loose in the joints and very shabby. But these things don't matter at all, because once you are Real you can't be ugly, except to people who don't understand."

MARGERY WILLIAMS, *THE VELVETEEN RABBIT*

in search of authenticity

The Skin Horse knew what it was to be authentic. It wasn't about having a 'stick-out handle', buzzy things inside or all his hair. It was about being real and being known and loved for who he really was. He didn't become like that overnight. It was a long process that was painful at times.

What does it mean for us to be REAL? We asked those we surveyed what they thought authentic relating meant, and whether they experience it in any of their relationships. These are some of their answers:

'Authentic relationships always require vulnerability and always the type of vulnerability that at times may feel deeply uncomfortable. Being known and seeking to know others truly. There's a cost in that but that is why there's a value.'

'Spending time with a person and really being able to listen to each other. Sometimes the clutter of life can make us unable to hear each other because we are so busy thinking of the next thing we have to do in the day …'

'I think authentic relating is when you say the same thing about someone when they're with you as you would when they're not with you. I think it's also not changing who you are with different people – something I've had to learn and something I'm still learning.'

'Authentic relating is the ability to be with other people and not use a mask to protect yourself. It requires a great deal of courage to be able to present one's weakness and one's strengths without diminishing either one for fear of judgement.'

'Although authentic relating is generally associated with intimate relationships of best friends, family and lovers, I also think authentic relating can be done with people we only meet once or twice. It is about us being true to ourselves … through the attitude of our heart, our words and our actions.'

'Authentic relating requires people who are brutally honest with themselves and each other. It requires a huge amount of self-awareness, laying down of pride, and stripping bare. It also requires a good level of self-esteem (to feel confident to be vulnerable) – this is why authentic relationships are rare!'

'Being really honest and cutting the crap. Listening and accepting people as they are without judgement and biased expectation – this is easier said than done. I experience it with some of my closest friends, and would like to experience it more with people I am not so close to, e.g. colleagues, 'polite acquaintances' – I would like to practise it more myself too.'

'Being able to be "naked" emotionally and as a person. I only completely experience this with my wife. But I'd "strip to my underwear" with a few other close friends!'

getting naked!

Do we really want to get 'naked' (emotionally that is, not literally) and 'strip to our underwear'? Some of us will read that and think 'no way'! We don't like the idea of being vulnerable and exposed. We don't like the idea of being unprotected, of having nowhere to hide. We fear that others may not approve of what they see (all our lumps and bumps and bits we don't like) and that they may laugh at us, reject us or attack us. We may even have tried a little bit of stripping in the past but found it a bad experience and we're determined now to keep well and truly covered up.

But just maybe there's a part of us – deep down – that thinks there is something appealing about this real relating idea. We want to be able to be ourselves and to be known and loved for who we are. And we don't want other people to feel they have to pretend or cover up with us. We want to get to know them and relate to them without their masks and with their defences down.

Probably the truth for many of us is that we want it both ways. We want the deep connection but we also want to keep protected. We don't like the idea of being hurt.

17

a prickly dilemma

It reminds me of the hedgehog's dilemma.

On a cold and frosty day, a hedgehog will search out other hedgehogs to huddle up with to keep warm. But because of the prickly spines on his back (and the others' backs) he is forced to make a choice. Get close, stay warm and get stabbed; or keep away, stay safe and freeze.

In 1851 German philosopher Arthur Schopenhauer came up with the 'Hedgehog's Dilemma' (I paraphrased it a little) to describe how as humans we often face the same predicament. We long for strong and intimate relationships but we also fear getting hurt and do all we can to protect ourselves from others.

When it comes to a picture of human relationships in our twenty-first-century society Schopenhauer was spot on. We long for connection but at the same time we fear the pain and hurt that can come from close relationships.

Our search for connection

Closeness comes at a price – the risk of getting hurt or hurting others. We all have our 'spikes' and when we connect with others there's a chance that we will cause damage or be damaged. The closer we get the more potential there is for hurt.

Dr Sue Johnson in *Hold Me Tight* writes: 'We are all vulnerable in love; it goes with the territory. We are more emotionally naked with those we love and so sometimes, inevitably, we hurt each other with careless words or actions.'

For some of us, our desire for connection is so strong that we will do anything to get it – even if it does mean getting wounded or wounding others in the process. For example:

- The young teenage boy who joins the local gang because he longs to belong
- The twenty-five-year-old woman who is so desperate for love that she has lost count of how many men she has 'hooked up' with
- The high-flyer who will go to any lengths (and step on anyone's toes or head) to be accepted by the board and promoted to 'Director'.

Or it can be more subtle, as when we:

- Break a confidence because we want others to be interested in what we have to share
- Say 'yes' to a request (even though we really want to say 'no')
- Tell people we like skiing (when we don't) because we want to be invited on the group holiday.

Our desire for protection

Like the hedgehog that retreats and curls up into a spiky ball to keep others at bay, we also have ways of protecting ourselves. During our lifetime we will have developed ways of trying to keep ourselves safe. We may hide away bits of ourselves that we don't want others to see, we may pretend to be something we're not, we may attack others or we may just decide to stay away altogether.

For some people, their fear of getting hurt is so great that they'd rather avoid connection. Often, they will not be aware of their behaviour. For example:

- The office bully who attacks, criticises and puts people down because she wants to be able to reject others before they have an opportunity to reject her. Rejection is what she fears most in life and what she experienced as a child.
- The husband who has a good lifestyle but whose wife and children feel as if they don't really know him because he struggles to express his feelings or thoughts to them.
- The young teenager who withdraws from friends and family, spending all his spare time in his room playing computer games on his own because he feels he can be in control with the characters on the screen in a way that he can't with people in reality.

But this also occurs in more subtle ways, as when we:

- Won't tell our friend the real reason we are upset with them
- Make ourselves too busy doing things to spend time with a family member or
- Won't admit to our work colleague that we messed up.

The naked hedgehog

As I write this in my study there is a postcard in front of me with a drawing by the Dutch artist, Leendert Jan Vis. It is one of my favourites. On the front are two hedgehogs sitting down having a chat. To the side of them is a coat rack where they have hung up their prickly coats. They are naked. The words on the card read, 'A friend is someone you can be completely at ease with.'

Isn't that the answer to our own and the hedgehog's dilemma? If we want to get close without hurting each other we need to get 'naked'. We need to be real and authentic.

We won't want to do that with everyone, especially if they are hard to trust. And we won't want to suddenly strip bare in front of everyone tomorrow. As the Skin Horse said, 'it takes a long time' – it's a process.

Some of you will be further along on the journey than the rest of us and that is fantastic. You can show us the way and be the safe people with whom we can learn to be naked hedgehogs. That is a great gift you offer us.

But the rest of us will have to learn step by step.

the long-term view

Those steps won't always be easy. Sometimes we'll get despondent or hurt and we'll wonder if it is worth it. That's why it is important to keep remembering the goal: to be real and have authentic relationships.

We may have more specific goals. Yours may be different to mine. These are a few possible examples of goals (some may apply to you, others may not):

- I want to be a great friend to my friends. I want them to be able to share the good, the bad and the ugly with me and I want to be able to be myself with them.
- I want to be true to myself with everyone I meet. I don't have to reveal everything but that which I chose to reveal I want to be real. I want to be open to learning about others and understanding what it means to be them.

- I want to be a good boss. I want to have a positive impact on those that I lead and I want to be open to feedback and prepared to change when I need to. I want to have integrity and be a person worth following.
- I want to be a great parent. I want to love my children for who they are and not for what I want them to be. I want to be able to model authentic relating to them through what I say and what I do and more importantly through who I am with them.
- I want to be authentic with my own parents and family. I want to love them not for what they can do for me but for who they are. I don't want to pretend to play a role that may be expected of me – I just want to be me and I want to allow them to be them.
- I want to be a great husband/wife. I want us to be 'naked and unashamed' together – free to be ourselves without judgement, criticism or rejection. I want to be my partner's greatest supporter – encouraging them to be all that they can be and I want our marriage to be a safe place where we can have fun but also where we can give and receive comfort, assurance and love. I want us to explore together what it means to be an 'us' and for that 'us' to have a positive impact on those around us.

your goal

Think of your own goal and try putting it into words:

I would like to be ...

....

....

How do we get there?

We know where we want to get to. The question is, how do we get there? It will happen as we take steps to trust more, to be open more, to learn more and to let our guard down more with people we feel safe with. It will happen gradually.

Dr Henry Cloud writes in his book, *Integrity*:

> Incredible things happen when two parties 'let down their guard' with each other. They get open, creative, take risks, learn from each other, and deliver fruit in whatever their endeavour to a much more leveraged degree than if they were in the protected mode. This happens in personal relationships, such as marriage, friendship, or parenting, and in business as well. To get to everything that can come from two people's hearts, minds, and souls, you have to get to openness and vulnerability. You have to have *access*. And access is only given as trust increases.

Where are the hurdles?

During the process of becoming more authentic we're bound to encounter hurdles both from inside ourselves and from outside. There's likely to be resistance and distractions from ourselves and from others. There'll be times when the status quo seems more appealing and less hard work.

It can help if we keep reminding ourselves of the goal and if we are aware of the things that are preventing us from reaching it.

identifying your hurdles

What do you think are the greatest threats to your relationships at the moment?

What things do you think are standing in the way of you having more authentic relationships?

We asked our survey respondents what they thought were the greatest threats to their relationships. This is what some of them said:

'Fear – of not being loved if I reveal my true self. Anxiety about not even being able to uncover an authentic self.'

'Time, distance, pace of life, over commitment!'

'I've been alone for a while, and I have to learn to trust more, and open up.'

'Losing the impetus to keep driving forward; taking the time and effort to challenge and go deeper; settling for a status quo.'

'I find it very hard to trust men – my father had lots of affairs – and I have had a series of relationships with men that have been negative (issues of control). Whatever the relationship, I need to know that I can trust someone – that they are kind to others and won't trample on people.'

'Time and prioritising who to spend time with. And too much to do on the "to do" list!'

'For me the greatest threat is isolation: I'm a single person of forty, who lives alone. Most of my friends are married and have children. The isolation of coming home to a silent, empty house; of another evening/weekend alone; cooking yet another meal for one and the TV for company. The isolation of going to a party alone, of being the only single in a room full of couples and having no one to go on holiday with. Isolation – that feeling of being a spare part, the odd one out, the one that doesn't fit. Isolation – one learns to live with it but it isn't easy.'

'Time (not enough) + children (third on the way) = tiredness and busyness.'

'When I'm having a bad time I either get very needy and want to be with people all the time or I hide away. So people might not understand me and think I'm messing them around.'

'Trying to fit too many people in. Not seeing friends enough so that we never get past the "catching up phase" and actually just "hang out". I want to live my life with my friends, not just tell them about my life when I see them!'

Keep on keeping on

Sometimes we'll be tempted to think it is too much like hard work and to reach for our cosy prickly jacket once more. If that happens to us it may help to remember the naked hedgehog and our desire for authenticity. And for those of us who live life at full speed, we may need to slow down sufficiently in order to identify and make the changes we really want. Taking our foot off the accelerator is the subject of the next chapter.

3. why a slower day isn't coming

There is more to life than increasing its speed.
GANDHI

You never heard anyone say on their deathbed: 'I wish I'd spent more time at the office.'
STEPHEN R. COVEY

On average I work 55 hours a week, which is slowly destroying my relationships. My social life is non-existent and I am suffering from permanent tiredness as a result.
SAL FROM THE UK ON THE BBC WEBSITE

our fast-paced world

Have you ever wanted life to stop moving long enough for you to get off and have a rest or at least long enough for you to catch up? If you have, you're not alone.

In the survey:

75 per cent agree that there is never enough time to get
through the things they need to do each day.
36 per cent agree that they do not have a good work–life balance.
27 per cent work more than 45 hours a week.

By the way, if you are one of the lucky few who doesn't live life at 100 mph don't stop reading this chapter. The speedaholics in your life need your help.

The need for speed

Living in today's fast-paced world is a little like being on one of those conveyor belts (travelators) at the airport that take you from A to B. You can't stop. The belt is always moving you forward and your only choice is how quickly you go with it. Do you stand still and let it carry you or do you decide to go faster by walking or even running?

In his book, *In Praise of Slow*, Carl Honoré highlights some of the dangers of living in the fast lane of our 24/7 world. These include increasing impatience, stress, road-rage, the need for stim ulants and sleeping pills, poor diet, superficial relationships, and lack of time for community, family and friendship. He writes:

> In this media-drenched, data-rich, channel-surfing, computer-gaming age, we have lost the art of doing nothing, of shutting out the background noise and distractions, of slowing down and simply being alone with our thoughts. Boredom – (the word itself hardly existed 150 years ago) – is a modern invention. Remove all stimulation, and we fidget, panic and look for some-thing, anything to do, to make use of the time. When did you last see someone just gazing out the window on a train? Every-one is too busy reading the paper, playing video games, listen-ing to iPods, working on the laptop, yammering into mobile phones.

Carl Honoré offers an antidote. He urges the speedaholics among us to slow down, to savour the moment, to stop clock-watching, to learn patience, to work fewer hours, to give our relationships the time they need and to become more like the tortoise and less like the hare. And he has a point.

We can't have great relationships if we are too stressed, tired or busy. We can fool ourselves that children only need *quality* time, that a slower day *is* coming, that busyness is an OK excuse for not seeing our friends, that our spouse (if we have one) will understand if we are too tired (again) to have sex or that we'll feel better once we've had a holiday. But the truth is life isn't going to change unless we make the choice to do things differently. If we want real and meaningful relationships we need to invest in them. We need to give them our time and we need to make sure the time we give the people closest to us isn't the dregs ... the little bit left over once everyone and everything else has had a piece of us.

So what is the answer? Firstly, we need to be honest about our own approach to time. Are you a speed addict or are you actually a speed rebel – keen to waste as much time and go as slowly as possible? Or have you got the balance just right – knowing when to move and when to stop? And are you aware of the impact your approach to time has on the other people in your life?

The engine and the anchor

I confess to being a speedaholic, a spinner, a human doing (rather than simply a human being) and I'm the daughter of one too. My mum's diary is so crammed full of appointments that it is virtually impossible to see any blank space unless you look five months ahead (and she's retired).

David and I don't disagree much but during our first couple of years of marriage any arguments we did have were about how to spend our time. He wanted to do less, to have week nights at home and to spend evenings watching DVDs with me next to him on the sofa. And after a busy day at work he wanted to relax first and then do anything that needed doing afterwards. I wanted to do more – to be out seeing people and doing stuff. I didn't want to waste a moment. If we had jobs to do – I wanted to do them first and then relax (although to be fair to David my 'to do' list was so long we would never have had any rest).

A full week's diary filled me with delight and him with horror. On holidays I wanted to plan trips to do and see things ... and he wanted to rest and eat. You get the picture.

I'm not sure we said it to each other but both of us thought the other's way of approaching time was a bit unhealthy. And the thing is, we were both right – we both *did* have unhealthy attitudes as to how to spend our time. We only really understood that when we attended a weekend course on leadership run by a friend of ours, Simon Walker. The aim was to help us (and the people we were with) to look at the impact our behaviour and our leadership style has on those around us. At one stage after talking to David and me on our own he sent us off to find an object around the house where we were staying that represented our internal world as we saw it. In the bathroom I found a little plastic sailing boat on the windowsill. 'Ah, that's it,' I thought. 'That is just like me, moving with the wind ... sometimes fast and sometimes slow.' (Yeah, right! Who was I kidding?) I went to pick up the little boat and then I spotted something I hadn't seen at first. Fixed to the underneath of the boat was a little rocket-propelled engine – now that was more like it!

When I showed David we finally got what was going on for us. I was the engine that never switched off (except when it ran out of power and then came crashing to a halt). And David was the anchor. The more the engine went – the more he wanted to hold the boat back, dig the anchor in and stop it. We both knew something had to change. He wanted me to switch off the engine and I wanted him to lift the anchor.

Are you more like the engine or the anchor? Or are you a graceful sailing boat able to be led by the wind? Try these next questions to find out.

QUIZ

1. If you wanted to book an evening with a friend would you:
    a. have to look several weeks in advance in your diary to find a free date
    b. find it fairly easy to find a space sometime in the next two weeks
    c. have most of your evenings free but you would want to choose a day when your favourite team isn't playing or TV programme isn't on?

2. If a relative asks you to help them do something is your immediate thought:
    a. Yes, of course
    b. It depends
    c. No?

3. Do you find you have:
    a. too little time to spend with all your friends and family but you try and fit everyone in
    b. to make deliberate choices about spending time with the important people in your life and find you have to say 'no' to some others
    c. plenty of time to do the things you want to do?

4. If you are given a project to do with a tight deadline do you:
    a. work all hours and give it everything you've got until it is finished
    b. negotiate to take extra time off after the project is finished and/or ask for help to complete it
    c. insist on only working your set hours even if that means the deadline won't be met?

5. Do you find it hard if you have to:
   a. sit still or relax if there are lots of things to do
   b. be either frantically busy or totally inactive for long periods of time
   c. be constantly on the go?

If you answered mostly As

You are an engine. There is no stopping you. You are very self-motivated and 'boredom' wouldn't be a word in your vocabulary. You may need to stop (long enough) to find out what impact your constant spinning is having on those around you. Would you or they benefit from a few quieter moments? Do you find it hard to delegate or let others help you? You may need to cut back on what you do and share the load with others. Relaxing may not come easily to you. If you know any 'anchors' you may want to let them show you how to kick back and smell the roses.

If you answered mostly Bs

You are more like the sailing boat. You understand the times for hard work and busyness but you also know when to go at a slower pace, enjoying life and those around you. You probably have quite healthy boundaries. You can say 'no' when you have to but you are also quite happy to say 'yes' to people when you know you have the time to give.

If you answered mostly Cs

You are the anchor. You prefer to take life easy. Do the people around you ever try and get you to do more? If you have any 'engines' in your life they may perceive you as lazy and passive. For their sake, and your own, you may want to see if there are times when you could do more to take the initiative or lend a hand. However, on the plus side you can help them to slow down and enjoy the pleasures of life a little more.

navigate a new course

It has really helped me to hold that image of the sailing boat in my mind. I love the fact that a sailing boat can go really fast when the wind is up, slower when the wind is gentle and just has to stay put bobbing on the water when everything is still.

But how is it possible to live like that?

That is the question I grapple with constantly. How do I switch off the engine and know when to move and when to slow down? I can't pretend I've nailed down the answer to that one. But there are a few questions I have learnt to ask myself, which are certainly helping. Let me share them with you as one or two may be a help to you too.

1. People vs process

Mick worked long hours in the office. He wanted to succeed, do well and make enough money so he could retire well. He dreamed of the time when he could spend time with his wife travelling around exotic countries. Every time his wife complained when he came back late, missed his dinner or worked at the weekend he would tell himself it was worth it. One day they would have all the time in the world. But his wife didn't see it quite the same way and when they'd been married twenty-five years she'd had enough, packed her bags and walked off into the sunset with another man, who gave her the attention and time that she craved. Mick was left with his regrets. Regrets that he hadn't focused on the person who was most important to him when he had the opportunity.

Mother of two, Martina, also found herself putting tasks before people:

> I used never to be that interested in tidiness. Pre children this
> didn't bother me too greatly and we would get by with the mess.
> When I had my daughter I gave myself carte blanche to make the
> most of her every waking moment. But gradually the weirdest

thing happened and I turned into a tidy freak – I became conscious of the mess and began to strive more and more for that 'unlived in' look that abounds in glossy magazines. Moving house four times in three years probably didn't help, but by the time my son arrived I had changed from someone who happily spent whole afternoons doing art and craft activities, to someone who starts to tidy up an activity while it's still in progress and who usually refuses to join in the latest game because she is too busy clearing up all traces of the previous one. Our house is still not tidy because it's like fighting the tide. There is always more to do. The truth is, I don't regret a single moment of the time I spent with my daughter in her early years but I very much regret, however, how *little* quality time I have spent with my son. I am endeavouring to change – to keep things clean and tidy but not at all costs and to prioritise what really matters. Besides, playing with the children is much more fun – I think I'd just lost sight of that.

Have you ever missed an important moment because you were too focussed on a task that you were doing?

Have you ever ignored a bid for time from a loved one because you were too busy doing something else?

Have you ever been annoyed, short or unresponsive with a work colleague, child, friend, partner or parent because they interrupted you in the middle of something?

What does it say to those close to us if our 'to do' list comes before them? If our work keeps taking us away from them? Or if we are too busy to notice when they just want us 'to be' with them? Whether we want it to or not, it is saying that what we have to do is more important than our relationship with them.

Is that we want? We need to be honest and ask ourselves what is most important in our lives – people or processes?

Will you get to the end of your life and wish you'd finished everything on your 'to do' list, got the next pay rise, or sealed the next deal or will you wish you had invested more time in your relationships?

2. Important vs urgent

Let's face it, the 'to do' list will never be empty, the work will never be finished and our home will never be perfect. And we'll probably never see all the people we want to keep up with either.

The problem is that time is a limited resource. We only have twenty-four hours a day and some of that needs to be spent asleep. The issue is how we spend the other hours. Are we using the time on the important or the urgent?

I went to a seminar once given by the American author Stephen R. Covey – he had a great way of illustrating how we prioritise our time. It went something like this: imagine you have a bucket, a small pile of rocks, some pebbles and lots of sand. The bucket represents your day, the rocks are the most important things in your life, the pebbles are the fairly important things and the sand represents the unimportant. If you fill the bucket up with sand first, then there will be no room for the pebbles and the rocks. The way to do it is to make sure the rocks and the pebbles go in first and then the sand can be fitted in around them.

What or who are your rocks? Are you carving out time for these in your life? Are you making them a priority? If your rocks are your relationships with children or your closest friends or your spouse, are you making deliberate time to be with them each day or each week? Or is there so much sand in your bucket that you can't fit them in?

pause for thought

Think about which are the five most important relationships in your life.

1. ....

2. ....

3. ....

4. ....

5. ....

How much time do you give each one of these relationships a week?

Do you feel that is enough?

If not, what could you change to make sure you are investing more time in these relationships? What pebbles or piles of sand could you shift to make more room in your schedule?

3. Planning vs spontaneity

If we really want to be deliberate about spending time with our loved ones and the most important people in our lives, we need to plan it. If we wait until we (or they) have a free evening or a quiet moment we may find we're waiting a long time.

Planning allows us to know that we have a definite window to spend specific time with that person or group of people. It could be having:

- Dinner together once a fortnight with flatmates
- A date night once a week with a spouse or partner
- A family night once a week with your children
- A regular slot with your parents or extended family where you have a meal together (or speak on the phone if you live far away)
- A monthly catch-up with a particular friend or group of friends (perhaps to play sport, go to the pub or do a group activity such as a book club, belly dancing lessons, praying, playing in a band or volunteering).

These planned times are an opportunity to touch base with each other, to connect and to build memories with the people who matter in our lives. Planning them means writing them in our diary, making

35

them a priority and sticking to them even when a better offer comes along.

If you're married or in a long-term relationship a regular date night is a chance to keep the romance alive and to have fun together. It is not the time to pay the bills, clean the carpet or discuss the children's education. It is a date just like the ones you probably had when you first met and fell in love.

For those with children, family nights are a great way to ensure there's at least one evening a week when everyone is spending time and eating together. It can be fun to allow the children to take turns deciding what food you'll have or which activity you all do that week.

Planning to spend time with people may seem contrived or lacking in spontaneity but it is an effective way of guaranteeing that the hours, days, weeks or months don't slip by without us spending quality time with our favourite people.

4. Quality vs quantity

While carving out quality time for our relationships is vital, I've learnt that it is NOT a substitute for 'quantity time'. Somehow in our speed-obsessed, stressed, time-poor culture we have come to believe that if we spend quality time with our lover, children or friends we can make up for the fact that we don't see them the rest of the time.

If we believe that, we are kidding ourselves aren't we? It may suit us to believe it – it may even assuage our guilt – but is it true? Isn't the truth that relationships need time as much as plants need water? They need feeding regularly, especially if the roots are going to grow deep and strong.

Think about your deepest relationships – the people who know you best and whom you know well. The chances are that at some stage in your life you spent regular periods of time with them. I don't think it's a coincidence that many people's closest relationships are with people that they had or have sustained contact with: family, childhood, school or college friends, neighbours, work colleagues, other parents at the school gates, team or flat mates etc.

I've known Amelia since I was a baby. Our mums are great friends and we virtually grew up together. We hung out with each other, our families took holidays in the same place in Devon every summer, we often stayed the night at each other's houses, we went for walks in the parks, to swimming, Brownies, tennis and our first disco together. I don't think we even liked each other until we were fourteen but we knew each other pretty well! And as we grew up we became great friends – we saw each other through good and bad times, we shared our secrets, dreams and hopes; we knew the boys each other fancied and we tried to cheer each other up when relationships went pear-shaped.

When we were nineteen we backpacked around the world together for five months, living out of each other's pockets. We were bridesmaids at each other's weddings and I'm godmother to her eldest child. But then three years ago she moved with her husband and children to San Francisco and I only see her once a year now. I found it hard when she went and it's definitely not the same now that she doesn't live in the same city. But the great thing is that when we do see each other we can pick up our relationship straight away. Why? Because for thirty-six years we spent 'quantity' time with each other. Our relationship has firm foundations, which will hopefully enable our friendship to last a lifetime.

There are no short cuts. Our most important relationships need an investment of our time.

David Thomas writing in the *Daily Mail* said, 'Good friendships, similar to good cooking, require time. But these days, time is the one thing that none of us has. We fall back all too easily on instant food and instant friendships. They may look the same, but they aren't.'

Ella, a nineteen-year-old friend of mine, was explaining to me how she has to be deliberate about the people she spends time with. She knows literally hundreds of people and is linked to many more through Facebook. She realised that she had a choice. She could see a different friend every day during her summer holiday from university or she could choose a few friends and just hang out with them every day. She chose the latter:

The holidays are an interesting time as returning to London means that there are so many people around – friends from home, old friends from school and new friends from university and friends of friends who I haven't yet met. The pace of London life can easily make me feel that if I am not doing something all the time – going somewhere/ seeing someone/ doing something – then I am boring or anti-social or missing out.

Therefore the temptation is to flit about – not in a purposefully superficial way – but just trying to be everywhere and see every-one and in the meantime missing the point. In one sense I feel satisfied as I can place big ticks by the proverbial 'to do' list – I've seen that person and that person and that person. However, at the same time it is deeply unsatisfying when I realise that I haven't really managed to spend proper time with anyone and that all my evenings and weekends are being spent just 'catching up'.

It's definitely a choice: whether to see lots of people and be busy, or to hang out and go deeper with a few people. I think I'm still working at that balance but it was better this last holiday when I spent most of my time just hanging out with the same small group of friends and then occasionally meeting up with others. I've learnt it is about focusing on the people I am with and not constantly looking over my shoulder for the next bit of fun and wondering if there is somewhere else I should be.

And while there are no such things as instant friendships, there are no shortcuts to parenting either. Children need time and lots of it from their parents – especially when they're young. Quality time is good but it is no substitute for that daily contact.

In her book *Toxic Childhood*, Sue Palmer writes:

In order to forge a viable family, the 'adults in charge' have to be physically present for a reasonable amount of time every week. This means sorting out their work–life balance so that, even if they work full-time, they still spend plenty of time at home. A recent snippet of Internet wisdom put the case rather well: 'If

you died tomorrow, the company that employs you would fill
your place within a week or so; your family would miss you for
ever.' Indeed, in many cases they're missing you already, and toxic
childhood is the result.

5. Stillness vs activity

To find quality and quantity time for our relationships we may
have to put our foot on the brake and take life at a slower pace ...
(certainly some of the time). That's a difficult challenge for the
'engines' among us.

According to a recent survey by Virgin Media a third of Brits
spend less than twenty minutes having sex. And almost half finish
their dinner in less than fifteen minutes. Psychologist Honey Lang-
caster-James said, 'The question we have to ask ourselves is, where
is this going to end? ... There is a real danger people are heading
for meltdown unless we slow down and realise that there are only
so many hours in the day in which to get everything done.'

Some of us will be busy because we have to juggle too much in
our lives. We may need to stop and ask if we *have* to be involved
in everything we are doing. Could we delegate more or cut down
on some things?

Others of us (and I would count myself here) like being busy
because we find stillness uncomfortable. We aren't quite sure what
to do if there's nothing happening. We probably don't realise it but
we are allowing our busyness to stop us from thinking or feeling
about what is really going on inside. If you are like me, you may
need to ask yourself, 'What is my busyness doing for me? What
thoughts or feelings am I trying to escape from?'

I've watched many people with better balance in their lives than
me and I have noticed that what they have is rhythm. They don't
sprint through every day and week at high speed but rather they
pace themselves. Like the sailing boat – there are times when they
are completely still and other times when they go quickly. Their
lives aren't filled with a constant stream of activities but rather

they are punctuated by times of stillness when they can gather their thoughts, rest, contemplate life, hang out with others, read a book, listen to music, stare out of the window, pray, meditate, go for a walk, study a work of art or do absolutely nothing.

I've noticed that the people I know who do any or all of the following are the least stressed people I know:

- Go for daily walks
- Start their day in prayer or in silent contemplation
- Take their full lunch hour
- Make sure one day a week is spent 'not working', and
- Take all their holiday allowance.

They are also, interestingly enough, the people who seem to get the most done when they *are* active. No doubt their relationships are healthier too.

It's a lesson many of us could do with learning before we reap the results of our whirlwind lives.

6. Yes vs no

In the end, how we spend our time comes down to choice. It is a choice as to what we say 'yes' to and what we say 'no' to.

For some of us that means learning to say 'no'. That may be a hard word to say. But there will be times when we need to say 'no' to some of the demands and requests that we are faced with.

If we say 'yes' all the time ... we will burn out and melt down. We only have limited resources of time and energy to give away.

Clive, who has a large family and runs his own business, has worked out that if he wants to focus on the important things in his life he has to be intentional about what he says 'yes' and 'no' to:

I try and take a step back and ask myself the question 'where do
I want to be in ten years' time?' That helps me to be clear about
my goals. Is what I am doing now helping me to get to that
place, whether that is a good relationship with my children or a

certain objective at work? And then once a year during my summer break I sit down and evaluate what my priorities are for the next twelve months. I think of it a bit like gardening and pruning a tree. I cut back the branches and then I think which branches will represent new growth this year and which ones will be dead ones? The growing branches are the ones that I will give my focus to, my time and my attention. I then say 'no' to everything else.

I am also trying to be more deliberate about my friendships. My wife and I wrote down a list of people we want to see this year and we went through the diary and found some free dates. It has been my job to then phone the people up and book them in. We are finding this is really helping us to keep our friendships alive. I know for myself that if I am not intentional or deliberate about these things; time slips by and they just don't happen.

But if we are someone who finds our security in what others think of us, if we don't like letting others down, if we are people-pleasers, if we fear rejection then we will find it very hard to say 'no'.

How often do we say 'yes' to something but inside we are screaming 'no' … and then maybe we try and find excuses later to get out of it?

If saying 'no' is a problem for you then you may find it useful to delay your response. If someone asks you to do something, say, 'Can I let you know in a couple of hours?' and then go away and think about it. Think about what is motivating your response – is it fear, flattery, guilt or a genuine interest in doing whatever it is?

If, after thinking about it, our answer is 'no' it's important we don't make false excuses and aren't swayed by manipulation, threats or pleading. We need to let our 'no' be a 'no'. And if someone knows that is our answer they can go off and look for someone else to help them, to invite on holiday, to baby-sit, to do the presentation or whatever it is. If we delay our response for too long or make excuses late in the day they have less time to sort the issue out and find someone else.

Equally, while some of us need to say 'no' more there are some others who may need to say 'yes' more. If your tendency is to avoid helping out, taking the initiative or making a commitment you may find saying 'yes' more improves your relationships.

But when we say 'yes' we need to try and stick to it. I know I get upset when someone backs out of something they said they'd do because something better has come along. It's even worse when they lie. When our yes means yes and our no means no we demonstrate integrity and our relating is authentic.

Tips: how to take a chill pill (for those looking to unwind and slow down)

Make space. Book at least one evening a week in your diary when you don't go out (no one needs to know you're staying in and if anyone asks – just say you're busy). Take a work and technology break one day a week and try doing without your computer, work phone, blackberry, TV, iPod etc. And try living without any of them in the bedroom.

Get creative. Take photos. Cook a meal from scratch. Paint a picture or a wall. Make and paint a model. Wear something you wouldn't normally wear – just because you can. Build something with wood. Make your own cards. Join a creative writing or art class.

Get back to nature. Get outside whatever the weather. Go for walks. Go fruit picking or kick leaves with children. Plant herbs in the garden or in a pot inside. Visit a farm. Go on a boat or have a swim. Go snorkelling or have a surfing lesson. Feed the ducks.

Have a good laugh. Kick back with your favourite comedy show or a funny film. Hang out with a five-year-old and see who can be the silliest. Jump in puddles, go skinny dipping, make angel shapes in the snow or play childish games.

De-stress. Have a massage or a long bath (did you know that wine glasses float in water?). Read a good book or flip through your favourite magazine. Stay in your pyjamas until midday and catch up with friends and family on the phone. Rip up your 'to do' list (or try and live without it for a week). Go for a run, pummel a punch bag or do some exercise.

Go slow. Try switching off the TV when you're eating and not eating lunch at your desk. Walk all or part of the journey to work. Leave your watch behind when on holiday. Spend five minutes a day in silent contemplation or prayer. Take time to memorise a verse or a poem.

Get into culture. Visit a museum or gallery (or just meet a friend there for coffee). See a film or play. Go to a concert or listen to music you don't normally listen to. Ask a friend to recommend a good book or join a book club.

tuning in to others

4. why we're made with two ears and one mouth

A good listener is a good talker with a sore throat.
KATHARINE WHITEHORN QUOTED IN *THE WEEK*

Listening is when you switch your ears on and your mouth off.
TARA, AGED NINE

Everyone should be quick to listen, slow to speak and slow to become angry.
THE BIBLE

my confession

I used to think I was quite good at listening. After all I'd been trained as a TV reporter and knew how to ask insightful questions and not talk over the answers. But as I became more aware of my own behaviour I realised that while I was proficient at nodding and looking interested I wasn't actually any good at listening ... really listening ... what I would call *authentic* listening.

There were several issues at play. The first problem was that I was multi-tasking and not focusing. At the same time as nodding and pulling appropriate faces I was having a full-on conversation with myself inside my head:

Did she just give me the sound-bite I need? ...
Perhaps I should try asking the same question a different way ...

47

Haven't got long though ...

We really need to leave here in five minutes if we're going to get
back to edit this in time ...

This answer is too long-winded ...

I wonder if that siren outside is too loud ... yes, I think we need to
do this one again.

And so it would go on. In the fast turn-around, stressful world of
TV news being able to multi-task like that can be very useful but
it definitely wasn't so productive when I used the same technique
in my everyday conversations with loved ones.

David: Hi, I'm back.

Me: How did it go ... did you win?

My head: *I hope they did win otherwise he's going to be grumpy*
tonight and we're seeing Paul and Emma later ...

David: Yes, 2 - 1.

My head: *... and I must remember to take the chocolates out of the*
cupboard ... did he just say he won? Thank goodness for that ...

Me: That's great ... did you score?

My head: *I wonder who else is going tonight ... perhaps Rob and*
Claire will be there. Oh no I've still got Claire's book on B and
Bs in Ireland ... Now where did I put it? ...

David: Yup – got them both ... the first was a brilliant header
from the edge of the box just as we started the second half –
really deep cross from the left and I popped up between two
defenders and POW! ... But then they equalised two minutes
later. It shouldn't have been allowed – one of their players was
off-side but the ref claimed he didn't see.

My head: *Shame we never booked that trip ... perhaps we could go*
for a long weekend next month ... not sure what is in the diary ...

Me: ... oh ...

David: And then we got a penalty just two minutes before the final
whistle. And guess who stepped up to send the keeper the wrong
way? (*He does little victory shuffle in the middle of the room.*)

Me: Oh … that's great …

My head: *Although … November might be a bit cold and wet in*
Ireland … perhaps we should wait until it is warmer …
Anyway, we will need to check the budget – I wonder if we've
saved enough yet for those window repairs … that reminds
me I must phone Matthew to see when he can come and
quote …

David: How was your day? Are you OK? You seem a bit quiet.

I needed to learn to switch off the dialogue in my head.

Another problem with my television interviewing technique was that I often ignored all that was unsaid. I wasn't taking the time to pick up on the verbal and non-verbal clues that can tell us so much about what is really going on *inside* the person. In my haste to get the interview over I was just skimming the *outside* and taking what I could. However, my best interviews were often the ones where I did take more time, where I was more flexible and made the effort to really listen to and watch the person and follow up any leads I heard or observed. In these instances the interview would often change direction and would end up being far more interesting than my preconceived idea of how it should be. I needed to learn to tune in to the other person.

And the third problem was that I was listening with an agenda. I wanted a certain answer, of a certain length, said in a certain way. I wasn't really interested in hearing anything else. I was using them for my own end, to get the best quote for my news story. That may be understandable (although not excusable) in this context but too often I would find myself doing something similar in my personal relationships. The classic and rather sad example from my single days was when I would talk to someone I was attracted to, listening for clues that he liked me too. I would filter out the negative and only listen for anything he might say that would fit my agenda (not a great tactic). The problem here was my attitude – I needed to learn to engage and focus more on the other person than on my own desires.

I had many more bad listening habits (I'll come to those later) – but the important thing is that it *is* possible to change. We can all be good listeners if we know how. We need to learn to switch off (our distractions), we need to tune in (to the other person) and finally, we need to engage our heart in the listening process. I'll be looking at how we do that in the rest of this chapter.

your favourite listener

Who would you say is the best listener in your life?

Think for a moment about how you feel when you are talking to them.

Can you identify what it is that makes them so good?

Now think about an incident where you didn't feel listened to by someone.

How did it make you feel?

How did you know they weren't listening?

the importance of listening

Really listening is one of the most powerful things we can do for someone. It helps us to build connection and it is vital for authentic relating. When we set aside everything going on around us (and inside us) and totally focus on the person speaking we are in effect saying, 'I care about you, you matter to me and what you want to communicate is important.'

When we listen like that, we are offering a gift of our time and our attention. We are putting aside our own agendas, our own desires, our own judgements and we are making ourselves available to the other person. There is an element of sacrifice on our part. But this kind of listening helps us to see inside the other person and it also helps them learn more about themselves.

recognising our own bad habits

Before we can improve our listening it can be a help to discover what kind of listener we are at present. Try the following questions and find out.

Rate the following statements and how they apply to you by assigning a number:

1. I strongly agree
2. I mainly agree but not totally
3. I neither agree nor disagree
4. I mainly disagree but not totally
5. I strongly disagree

- I often find myself finishing other people's sentences ☐
- I pride myself on my ability to listen while doing many other things ☐

- I tend to interrupt people when they are speaking to me ☐
- I believe if someone is telling me a problem, they must want my advice ☐
- If I've had a similar experience to someone, I'll always tell them ☐
- If someone is upset I am keen to cheer them up as quickly as possible ☐

Total score =

If you scored 22 to 30
I expect you are probably the kind of person whom people love to talk to. They feel valued when you listen to them and you build connections with others easily.

If you scored 14-21
You probably aren't too bad at listening but you have a few bad habits that stop you being as good as you can be. The good news is that with a bit of awareness and practice you can get better.

If you scored 6-13
Honestly? People probably find you rather frustrating and annoying to talk to. Most conversations seem to be more about you than the other person. You will probably find that if you work on your listening skills you'll see a marked improvement in the quality of your relationships.

how to get good at listening

In order to be a good and authentic listener we need to learn to switch off, tune in and engage. If we can do these three things, the person speaking to us will feel heard and understood by us. We will have made a connection with them.

1. switch off

It helps if we can be good at listening in all our conversations but realistically we may not be able to stop and focus every time someone says something to us. But the important thing is to realise the times when it would be really helpful if we did. Examples of this could be when:

- A work colleague comes to your desk and asks, 'Have you got a minute?'
- Your husband/wife/flatmate comes in looking frustrated and tells you work was a bit tricky today
- A child asks a provocative question or says something out of the ordinary like, 'If I have a tummy ache do I have to go to school today?' or 'Wayne said that Gramps has gone to hell'
- Or a friend calls you on the phone clearly upset and crying.

In all the above examples the other person is making a strong bid for connection. They want our focus and our attention. They are inviting us into their world. We have a choice. Do we ignore the invitation, keep on with what we're doing and shut them out or do we stop what we're doing, turn towards them and give them our time? If we make the choice to move towards them, we need to switch off everything that may distract us from really hearing what they're saying to us.

Stop

We need to stop what we're doing. If we're distracted from hearing properly because we're watching the TV, looking at our computer, cooking the dinner ... we will need to turn it off or turn away. If what we're doing can't wait ... it may help to suggest a better time:

(With work colleague) 'I'm really sorry, but Jake wants this report on his desk in twenty minutes so I need to get it done now. However, I'm free for lunch later if you want to go out and chat over a sandwich?'

53

(With husband/wife/flatmate) 'I want to hear all about it. Let me just finish these potatoes and then let's sit down with a drink before Cheryl arrives.'

If you are face to face with the person you are listening to it can really help too to turn off your phone (or put it on silent). If you are having the conversation on a phone then make sure your surroundings aren't a distraction to you. No one wants to be discussing their deepest worries with someone who can be overheard paying for their shopping or typing on their laptop. Suggest a better moment if you're out and about or in the middle of doing something else.

Get comfortable

It is very hard to listen if you are uncomfortable, too cold, too hot, too tired, thirsty, hungry or dying for the loo! Sort yourself out first before you sit down and listen, even if that means delaying it until a better time.

For example, I've learnt with David not to try and get him to listen to something important when he's hungry. Another friend of mine can't listen to anyone early in the morning. It helps to know what times are bad for you or for those close to you.

Be present

This means being in the moment with the person speaking and doing all you can to focus on them and what they are saying or trying to say. It means turning off the conversations in your own head. That can be hard if you're anything like me. I've found it helps to keep checking myself and bringing my thoughts back to the person if my mind is wandering.

Interrupting people when they're trying to talk is also a habit I've had to learn to break. And apparently I am not the only one. Recent research shows that the average person waits just seventeen seconds before interrupting. That means there are a lot of us who need to learn to bite our tongues. Practice is the best thing – next time someone is telling you something, try listening for a minute before saying anything. If you are a habitual interrupter or a sentence-finisher it will seem like a very long 60 seconds!

It is important to remember that this moment is about them, not you. That means doing all you can to lay down your own opinions, prejudices, experiences or emotions about what they're saying. That can be hard but if we don't these things will prevent us listening properly.

Opinions. I'm one of those people who is naturally quick to give advice. If someone is telling me something I'll be thinking of what they should be doing, what I'd do if I was them and what would fix whatever is worrying them. Sometimes I don't just think it – I tell them! However, if I am working out solutions in my head I am no longer listening to them. If I do actually share my pearls of wisdom with them I may be preventing them from working out their own thoughts, opinions and solutions about the issue. It took me a while to realise that most people have the answer to their own problems and don't actually need me to solve them!

I've found a golden rule is: *Wait to be asked for your opinion or advice and then only offer it very tentatively.*

Prejudices. If we're honest there are all sorts of things in life that we don't feel neutral about: we have either negative or positive thoughts or beliefs about them. Perhaps we don't trust men in glasses, or we have a particular fondness for old people; maybe we believe all fat people are lazy or posh people are stupid. Prejudices like these are not based in fact and are often driven by our own fears, limited experience or preferences. It helps to work out what our prejudices are and to make sure they don't cloud our ability to listen.

Experiences. It can be very tempting to compare other people's situations to our own. If we've been through something similar then we may assume that we understand exactly what they are feeling or thinking. But just because we have also been through break-ups, problems at work, struggles about being single or arguments with a parent, it doesn't mean their response will be the same as ours. We need to resist the temptation to hijack the conversation and start telling them all about our story. Let them talk through what they want to say first – focus on them. The time to share our story may come later.

Emotions. Our feelings can also get in the way of listening properly. Think about what happens when a good friend starts telling you about how upset they are with you because of something you did. As they are talking you may start feeling angry, defensive, sad or remorseful depending on whether you agree with them or not.

Or it may be that they're telling you about something that triggers a memory in your own life and connected feelings start to surface. Or perhaps you have a strong feeling about what they are saying or where you feel the conversation is going. Like Mark and planes for example:

> I *hate* flying and if my boss starts talking to me about something
> that involves the possibility of getting on a plane I start to feel
> anxious and then I try and think of all the different ways that I
> could travel so that we don't have to fly. The problem is … I am
> no longer listening to what my boss is talking about … she's
> moved on to something else and I'm still working out how long it
> would take in a boat to New York!

Or maybe we find it hard to deal with the feelings of the person speaking. Have you ever been upset and someone has tried to shut you down by either reassuring you or telling you to get your act together? The person listening to you was probably uncomfortable with the feelings you were expressing.

Difficult as it is, we need to try and set aside our own feelings for the moment. It may be appropriate to share them later. Otherwise we'll find them distracting us from what the other person is trying to communicate.

Switching off is the first step to authentic listening and the second is to tune in.

2. Tune in

When we tune in to someone we are doing everything we can to understand what they are trying to communicate to us. We do this through listening to what they are saying and how they are saying it as well as by observing the ways they are communicating to us without words (non-verbal communication).

Gary Smalley, in his book *The DNA of Relationships*, writes:

> Effective communication comes down to listening and speaking with your heart. When people feel understood emotionally, they feel cared for. This is very different from listening to someone from the head – that is, looking merely for the content of the person's words, without paying attention to the emotion. The goal of effective communication is to understand the emotional message of the speaker. You have to ask yourself, 'What is this person feeling?'

I remember during my training as a journalist someone mentioned that *only* 7 per cent of what we communicate actually comes through the words we speak. That doesn't seem very much. Thirty-eight per cent comes from our tone of voice – in other words how we express what we want to say. And then an amazing 55 per cent comes from our body language. So we actually say more by not saying anything at all.

Therefore if we are going to be good listeners we need to tune into all three.

What they say

What is the person trying to express to us? What feelings are they describing? What thoughts or opinions are they sharing? What story are they telling? What problem are they airing? What is the most important thing they are saying?

How they say it

You can pick up a lot about what is going on for the person through the tone of their voice. How do they sound to you? Are they speaking very quickly or slowly, loudly or quietly? Is their pitch higher or lower than normal? Do they sound angry, frightened, worried, happy, excited, anxious etc?

Does what they are saying match how they sound? A mismatch between the two can tell you a lot. For example, someone in an interview tells you that they are highly confident but their voice sounds very tense and nervous. Or someone tells you they are really excited but they sound monotone to you.

What they say without speaking

This requires us to listen with our eyes. What are we observing as they speak? How are they sitting? Are they looking relaxed or tense? What are they doing with their hands? What are their eyes doing? What do their facial expressions tell you about how they are feeling?

Reflect back to them

If we are actively listening to someone we can act like a mirror – helping the other person understand themselves more clearly. Used well, 'reflecting back' can be an amazing tool. If you aren't used to doing it, it can seem very contrived at first but once you've tried it a bit you may be surprised to see how effective it is. This is especially true when someone is discussing an issue or problem they are struggling with.

What do you do? Well, as you listen you feed back what you are hearing and sensing about what the other person is saying. So you might say … 'Let me just see if I've got what you are saying …' and then you paraphrase in your own words what they have just said. You then check with them if that is right. They may then correct you or expand on what they said. This is helping them to work out what the problem is and what they are feeling about it. If they have mentioned feelings or metaphors as they were speaking you may want to feed those back too … 'It sounds like you are really anxious and that you feel as if you are drowning under all the pressure.' Or you can feed back what you are observing. So if they say, 'I am really thrilled about that … ' but don't look it, you could say, 'You say you are really excited about it – but you don't look very excited. Is there something that is worrying you about it?'

Holding a mirror up like this helps the person to process and tune into what is really going on for them inside.

If the problem is about you then you may find it very difficult to listen without defending yourself or clarifying your position. Try not to. Hear them out first and try to see the issue from their point of view. That will mean setting aside your own agenda for the present. It won't be easy but it will help you to understand the other person better.

Get to the heart of the matter

It may be that as you spend time listening and reflecting back to the other person you find out that what they started talking about isn't the real problem and there is something deeper going on. The more you reflect back, listen and gently probe the more you may discover of the root of the problem.

For example, someone may be over-reacting to a situation. You have heard what has happened but it doesn't seem to justify their reaction. You may want to try saying, 'You sound very angry about it. What do you think is the thing that is making you so annoyed?' or if you suspect there is something else going on you could ask, 'Have you been in a similar situation to this before? What does it remind you of?'

Listening and reflecting back like this will take time. Don't rush them and don't be nervous of silences. Sometimes a silence can be very powerful as the person works out in their mind or heart what they are thinking or feeling. Don't be too quick to fill the gap. The same with tears. It can help to cry but sometimes we are so quick to shut someone down and cheer them up that we don't give them the space to feel their emotions.

Help them work out the solution

Once they have identified the problem and their thoughts and feelings about it, the final step is to help them work out a solution or the next course of action. The idea is not to do this for them but to help them get there themselves. Again, gentle questions can help. 'What would make this better for you?' or 'What do you think you could do now?' or, if you are part of the problem, 'What would you like me to do?' Help them to find a way of moving forward – even if it is a very small step. 'Is there someone else who could help you with this?'

By the end of the conversation the other person may be feeling vulnerable or exposed. Assure them that you care for them and that you are really pleased, honoured or privileged that they have shared this with you. If they are your partner, child or close friend you may want to give them a hug and tell them that you are there for them and that they can come and talk to you about it more at any time. It is also important to reassure them that you can be trusted to keep anything told to you in confidence. (An exception to this would be if they tell you about anything that involves them harming themselves or someone else, in which case you may need to encourage them to get help; if they won't then you will have to tell them that you cannot keep it a secret.)

3. Engage

The difference between being a good listener and an authentic listener can be found in your attitude. You can learn the right techniques and work through your bad habits but if your attitude isn't right then your listening will appear hollow and insincere.

Your work colleague, child, partner or friend will soon pick up on it if your heart isn't in your listening. They might not be able to put their finger on why, but they may feel that you are not really connecting with what they are trying to say to you.

Think about it for a moment: who would you rather listen to

you – someone who is clearly interested in you and totally 'for you' but who interrupts a little too often or someone who has no obvious bad habits but doesn't seem to be engaging with what you are trying to say?

You probably chose the first person. There is something fantastic about being listened to by someone who is really listening, who is seeking to connect with us and wants the best for us. But when someone – however nice they are – doesn't seek to engage with us, we are left feeling detached from them.

Dr Henry Cloud, in his book *Integrity*, writes, 'Detachment is about not crossing the space to actually enter into another person's world through the curiosity and desire to know them, to understand them, to be "with" them, to be present with them, and ultimately to care for them. Sadly, a lot of loving and nice people are detached in this way, and their relationships suffer for it.'

If we want to have authentic relationships we need to set our hearts towards people and take a step into their world.

5. saying what you mean and meaning what you say

The greatest kindness I have to offer you is always: the truth.
JOHN POWELL, AUTHOR

Is what I am saying loving, compassionate, kind, empowering, or insightful?
RHONDA BRITTEN, FOUNDER, FEARLESS LIVING INSTITUTE

*'Then you should say what you mean,' the March Hare went on. 'I do,'
Alice hastily replied; 'at least I mean what I say – that's the same thing
you know.'*
LEWIS CARROLL, *ALICE'S ADVENTURES IN WONDERLAND*

what are you talking about?

Being a great listener is only half the story. For us to be able to
communicate authentically with others we also need to be able to
say what we mean and mean what we say. That may sound fairly
straightforward, but how easy is it to do in reality? Think for a
moment about how your friends, work colleagues and family express
themselves. We probably all know people (may be even ourselves
included) who do one or more of the following:

- Struggle to express what they are feeling
- Seem unable to censor anything that comes out of their
  mouth

- Say one thing one minute and then say the opposite even more passionately the next
- Use hinting or manipulation rather than saying directly what they want
- Hurt others with their unkind words, put-downs and criticism
- Use flattery and false praise to win approval
- Speak unkindly of others behind their backs
- Make promises that they don't keep
- Tell white lies
- Talk in riddles, use long words or jargon that is hard to understand
- Never seem to talk about anything meaningful
- Permanently talk about themselves
- Refuse to talk about themselves.

When we communicate clearly, honestly and effectively we are offering people a window through which they can see who we really are. We are inviting them to know us, to understand us, to connect with us. But when we do any of the things listed above we make the window harder to see through. We may secretly want others to work it out for themselves and to just 'get us', to see through the frosted pane of glass … but most of the time they don't. Instead they paint their own picture of us, based on the assumptions which they draw from the limited evidence that we have given them. If those assumptions are wrong we can be left feeling unknown, misunderstood or alone.

If we want to relate authentically – to be known from the inside out and to know others – we need to use our words effectively; words that will help build up connection rather than break or damage it.

levels of communication

In reality we are unlikely to throw open the window to everyone we meet (and with good reason). What we choose to share with the shop assistant we've never met before will be different from what we reveal and say to our best mate. How deep we go depends on the level of trust, acceptance, intimacy and openness that exist in the relationship and our willingness to risk rejection.

There are five levels we can choose to communicate at:

1. surface to surface.

This is general chit-chat – small talk – the stuff that we use in an opening encounter with a stranger or with people we don't know very well. It can also be the warm-up act in a conversation with people we do know better. Talking about the weather is a classic example (and one the British are particularly good at). Others might be asking, 'How are you?', 'Have you ever been here before?' or 'Have you worked here for long? Or commenting on your surroundings or what is happening in the moment: 'This is such a lovely flat', 'When did you change the display, it looks great?', or 'The traffic is awful today, I don't know what is going on.'

And then there are introductions: 'Hi, I'm Sarah, I'm a friend of Jane's – we used to be at school together', 'Hello, I'm Brian Peters, the Press Officer … we spoke on the phone. I hope you managed to park OK?' or 'Do you know each other? This is Claire, my friend from art class … and this is Ali who is also very creative; she takes amazing photos.'

Some people hate small talk. They find it tedious, superficial and a waste of time. And if that was all we did every day – I could understand their point. But small talk has its uses: it is a great way to put someone at ease, to connect with strangers, to start off a conversation and to extend ourselves to others. And it's important. People will form their first impressions about us pretty quickly through how we act and what we say in those first few minutes. So, we need to make sure we are transmitting the messages we really want them to receive.

For example, a warm smile conveys that we are friendly, open and warm. Making introductions shows we are interested, talking about topics people can join in with helps them feel safe around us, and asking questions and showing interest in what the other person is talking about shows we value what they have to say.

Inviting and allowing others to speak helps them to know that we are trying to connect.

Conversely, if we don't smile, but look as if we'd rather be somewhere else, or if we look over their shoulder to spot someone we know, then people may well perceive us as disinterested, closed off or rude. If we stand around and wait to be introduced they may think we are passive or aloof. Opening with a topic that is a bit off the wall or provocative may make people think we are unsafe. Dominating the conversation is likely to lead people to conclude that we are self-absorbed or boring. These may or may not be the messages we wanted to convey, which is why it helps to be aware of how we come across.

a first encounter

How do you tend to act when you meet someone for the first time?

What worries you (if anything) about a new situation or starting a conversation with someone you don't know? What is the worst thing that could happen?

What, if anything, helps you to feel more confident, relaxed and 'yourself' in the situation?

Ask someone you know well how you come across in a social or work situation where you are meeting strangers or people you don't know very well? Are there ways you could improve your approach?

I'd rather eat slugs! If we are shy we may find small talk and unknown situations particularly hard or painful. Avoiding situations in which we may have to initiate conversation may be one option, (although not a very practical one). Avoidance will only limit our abilities to grow, to make new contacts and meet people who may be potential new friends, business contacts or even a date (if you are single). It is important not to let our shyness isolate us and hold us back from connecting. Better options may be:

- To realise that lots of other people find it hard to talk to new people. Even extroverts can feel shy sometimes. My friend Jonathan is an extrovert and the last person you would expect to be shy but he has to brace himself to go to a party.
- To smile, unfold your arms and watch your posture. People will be friendlier to you if they think you look friendly. Another friend who is shy said it helped her when she took small steps. Every time she entered an office, a meeting or a gathering she would make herself smile and say 'good morning' or 'hello'. The more she did it the easier she found it.
- To take the focus off how you feel and your discomfort and instead turn your attention onto someone else. Make it your mission to discover two or three interesting facts about them.
- If you get a negative reaction or the brush-off from someone don't take it personally. Ninety-five per cent of the time it will be their issue not yours and for the 5 per cent when it is because of something you did, count it as a learning experience and make a note to try not to do it again. And remember it is your behaviour, not you, they are rejecting and that's good news because you can do something about your behaviour.
- Practise and keep practising, especially in situations that you find less threatening. It will get easier.

2. sharing facts.

At this level we are talking about things we know about or we are discovering about things we don't. We are still not revealing much about ourselves, other than perhaps our level of knowledge.

Topics we are discussing may include things like news events, current affairs, a film we've seen, something we've read, celebrity gossip, stories about people or things we have in common, TV programmes, sports or trivia.

Carl remembers being given some good advice by one of his teachers at school:

> Mr Baldwin was one of those people who seemed to know every-
> thing. He used to tell us that if we wanted to get on in life we
> should always make sure we were up to speed on current affairs.
> He recommended that we read at least the front and back page of
> a 'quality' newspaper every day (he was a *Times* reader himself) –
> that way he reckoned we would never be short of conversation
> and we'd have some clue as to what others were talking about.
> I've always tried to do that and the great thing now is that with
> the Internet and publications like *The Week* it is even easier.'

3. sharing opinions.

By this level I am revealing more of myself to you and with that revelation comes a greater risk of rejection. I am telling you some-thing of who I am: my ideas, my opinions, and my beliefs – what I think about a certain topic. You may not agree with me or you may see my thoughts as stupid, ill-informed or wrong. But that is the risk I take. And my hope is that you may not reject my thoughts. Perhaps you'll agree with them or find them interesting or be excited about the opportunity to engage in a friendly debate about our differing points of view.

As we open up and explore each other's thoughts and opinions we learn more about each other and how we think and see the world. A temptation at this level can be to:

Make assumptions. This is when we jump to conclusions about the other person based on their opinions or beliefs. For example we might think, based on our own negative prejudices:

- He's a Tory – so he must be rich, thick and traditional
- She's a Christian – she must be narrow-minded, prudish and boring
- They think rambling is a great way to spend a weekend – they must be odd, dull and unimaginative.

If we are quick to write people off, put them in a box or assume we know what they think about something, then we are narrowing our own experience of others. We are missing opportunities for growth and connection.

Tailor the truth to your audience. Is it just me, or have we all done this at some time? The classic is the job interview or the first date where you answer a question in a particular way because you think that is what the other person wants to hear. Or you exaggerate just that little bit extra because you think they'll be impressed. Or you change or delete some details about your past that you think might come across as unfavourable. This may or may not make us feel better about who we are in the short term but the trouble is it isn't authentic. We aren't painting a true picture of ourselves and we are building our future relationship with them on weak foundations. Better to be ourselves and get the job or the next date because they like what they see in us than get it because we were pretending to be something we aren't. The truth is likely to find its way out at some stage.

Take it personally. Just because someone doesn't agree with our political, spiritual or economic beliefs or doesn't like our favourite team, celebrity, book, film or band doesn't mean they are rejecting us. Life would be very dull indeed if we all agreed with each other all of the time. Take time to learn from the other person and understand where they are coming from and why they like what they like or believe what they believe. And when it is our turn to speak it helps if we can share our own personal opinion – not one we read somewhere or heard someone else say once. If people understand our story and how we got to our point of view it is harder for them to discount our experience or tell us we are wrong!

Bert discovered this approach in the first few years of his relationship with his partner:

> It would appear to an outside observer that Mia and I are at opposing ends of the political spectrum. We have often talked about issues such as the welfare state, immigration, social housing, or the benefits system and ended up in disagreement. However, we have realised that if we have good evidence and examples to back up what we are saying, the conversation is much more fruitful and doesn't lead to an argument, but instead we look at our own opinions and why we have them.
>
> If we are not careful, discussions on contentious issues could easily descend into name calling, but if we take care to keep informed and not just be reactionary, we can learn a lot about the way the world works and why we feel like we do about things.

It helps if we don't see the discussion as a competition or an argument to be won. And even if we are really passionate about a topic we need to try not to get too fanatical or dogmatic about it, especially with some poor person we've only just met. It is likely to put them off us and the topic and they may end up feeling like a project we are trying to win over rather than a person with their own valid views and opinions. Now is the time to practise our listening skills. Hear what they have to say, let them speak and really try and understand their point of view.

It also helps if we can keep hold of our sense of humour. If we don't take ourselves too seriously and can have a good laugh, particularly at ourselves, we will find it a lot easier to diffuse or survive a heated debate.

4. sharing emotions.

This is when I move beyond just telling you what I think to sharing how I feel. The window is opening even wider now as I tell you about my reactions and my emotions. I am revealing more of who I am to you and I am trusting you to accept me and all that I feel.

But I may be worried that you'll disregard my feelings, that you might trample on them or that you'll be too hurt, shocked or overwhelmed by them. The temptation may be to keep them hidden but if I do that I conceal part of myself from you. I stop relating authentically with you and I retreat back behind the frosted window.

5. sharing deeply with each other.

This is where we experience the greatest level of intimacy. It is when both you and I can be vulnerable and open with each other. We can share not only our feelings but also our disappointments, hopes, fears, desires, failures, worries, joys, sorrows, anger, guilt and inadequacies, doubts and dreams etc. with each other.

In order to share like this with you, I probably know you well and we trust each other. Perhaps you are my spouse, a great friend or a close family member. I care about you deeply.

At times it will be really difficult to tell you what I feel because it may involve you and I don't want to upset you or make you think badly of me. But if our relationship and intimacy is to grow then I know I need to take a risk and tell you what I really mean. Only by taking that step will I be able to have the depth of relationship with you that I long for. And by taking that courageous step myself I am encouraging you to take one too.

John Powell, in his book *Why Am I Afraid to Tell You Who I Am?*, writes:

> It is certain that a relationship will be only as good as its communication. If you and I can honestly tell each other who we are, that is, what we think, judge, feel, value, love, honour and esteem, hate, fear, desire, hope for, believe in and are committed to, then and only then can each of us grow. Then and then alone can each of

us be what he really is, say what he really thinks, tell what he really feels, express what he really loves. This is the real meaning of authenticity as a person, that my exterior truly reflects my interior. It means I can be honest in the communication of my person to others. And this I cannot do unless you help me. Unless you help me, I cannot grow, or be happy, or really come alive.

you and the 5 levels

Think about and come up with an example of someone you talk to at each level:

1. Surface level: ....

2. Sharing facts: ....

3. Sharing emotions: ....

4. Sharing feelings: ....

5. Sharing deeply: ....

Which level do you prefer talking at? Why is that?

....

When do you find it appropriate to share at level 5? (When might it not be?)

....

How often are you sharing with people at level 5?

....

If this isn't as much as you would like it to be what could you do to change the situation?

....

fear of disclosure

Some of us will find it hard to communicate past level three, especially if we're not used to doing so. For us, talking from the heart about feelings and emotions is about as appealing as stripping off naked in a supermarket! It makes us feel awkward, exposed, embarrassed and vulnerable. We can't see or understand the appeal even if we 'get' the benefits intellectually.

In our survey, 19 per cent of people said they strongly or mainly agreed that they find it hard to express emotions.

So what is preventing some of us from wanting to bare ourselves emotionally?

Big boys don't cry

Perhaps open communication wasn't done or even allowed in our families as we were growing up. It could be that we were encouraged to be 'strong' and control or hide away any emotions.

You won't like me

For others it could be our personalities – some of us are worried about being misunderstood or laughed at. Or perhaps we fear the reaction we may get and don't want to upset the other person. We believe that it would be safer and more harmonious if we suppressed any negative feelings.

My feelings aren't important

Or possibly we believe that what we feel doesn't matter. It is OK for us to care and worry about other people's emotions but we don't want to bother people with ours. It may be that at some stage in our lives we have had to look after someone or be in close contact with someone who was very emotional. We may have taught ourselves that our feelings are less important and no one would be interested in them.

No one will hurt me again

If we've had our trust broken in the past or we're fearful about rejection, we might not want to take that risk again and instead we frost over the windows of our hearts.

I don't know how

Or there may be some of us who just don't know how to share our feelings because we aren't really sure what it is we *are* feeling. Maybe emotions aren't something we 'do' and even if they were we wouldn't know how to express them.

my own frosted window

I definitely used to find it really hard to speak about my feelings … even now it doesn't come all that naturally to me.

When I was eight I went away to a boarding school that had about thirty girls and one hundred and fifty boys. It was a very competitive school where the emphasis was on success, being strong and overcoming difficulties. During my first term there I was miserable. I was the only new girl and I missed home dreadfully. The first few weeks I felt abandoned, angry and very upset. I would cry myself to sleep most nights. But it wasn't the done thing to be showing all those emotions and I was encouraged to pipe down and get on with it. I soon realised that I wasn't going to escape from Alcatraz and so I did what most of the other pupils seemed to be doing: I bit my lip, stuffed down my emotions and made the best of a bad situation. I focused instead on making friends and doing well.

As I look back I can see that I then took those learned behaviour patterns into adulthood. On the outside I seemed pretty normal, confident and capable but try and venture inside and you wouldn't get very far. I would avoid confrontation, never showed anger and kept my fears hidden. Even when my brother died, I found it hard to grieve and share my feelings with anyone else.

73

When I was twenty-four I moved back to live in Bristol (where I'd been at university) to start my first job with the BBC and some friends of mine suggested that I got in touch with a friend of theirs who'd also just moved to the city. At that time I hadn't ever encountered anyone quite like Amanda – someone who really wanted to get to know me, to understand me, to work out what made me tick. Well, perhaps I had, but no one who persevered like she did. As we got to know each other she really helped me to open up.

She would ask me questions. Lots of people ask ,'How you are?' and then barely listen to the response. But Amanda took a different tack. If she heard me mumble 'OK' or 'Fine, and you?' she would come back at me with a 'Yes, but how are you *really*?' and she'd wait for a more accurate reply than my first attempt.

If I told her about something that was happening in my life at the time, or about a past event, she would ask questions to explore what I was feeling about it. Most of the time I didn't have a clue myself, but the questions helped me stop and think about it. And if I said or did something which she didn't think quite rang true she would gently challenge it by reflecting back to me what I had just said or done. For example, she'd known me quite a few months before she found out my brother had died (and I don't think she even discovered that from me). Next time she saw me, she mentioned it and said she thought it was strange that I hadn't said anything about what must have been a major event in my life, especially when we'd both shared quite a lot about ourselves with each other.

When she reflected back to me like that it helped me to see and understand how my actions came across to others. She was acting like a mirror – showing me the bits of me that I didn't normally get to see or that I avoided looking at.

i'm feeling what ... ?

If you're like me and you find it difficult to talk about your emotions, these are a few things that you might want to try.

First, identify which emotions you experience and how easy it is to talk about them. Take a look at the list on page 76 of some common feelings and work out how often you feel each emotion. Is it hardly ever, sometimes or often? If there are some you hardly ever feel then maybe there are reasons you can think of for why this might be. Then, think about whether you find it easy or difficult to express or talk about all the emotions. If you find any difficult, why might that be?

Second, it may help to journal – to write how you're feeling during the day. Try to use 'I feel' statements, instead of 'I think', and then, as you feel more courageous, you may try sharing more emotions with a close and trustworthy friend. Perhaps start by explaining to them why you find it so difficult.

Third, it helps to try to put feelings into context, so not just, 'I feel angry' but 'I feel angry because of what you said to me earlier' or 'I feel upset because you didn't turn up to meet me when you said you would and it felt as if you didn't care.' This helps us not only to express what we're feeling but why we're feeling it, and that helps in our understanding of each other.

The final thing is practice. Just like learning a language or a musical instrument, it's only as we practise that it starts to feel less forced and more natural. And if you're good at speaking about your emotions but have a friend who struggles in this area, take time to listen to them and draw them out.

emotion	I feel it ...			expressing the emotion is ...		why is this?
	hardly ever	sometimes	often	easy	hard	
fearful						
happy						
scared						
joyful						
angry						
relaxed						
guilty						
frustrated						
appreciated						
annoyed						
amused						
miserable						

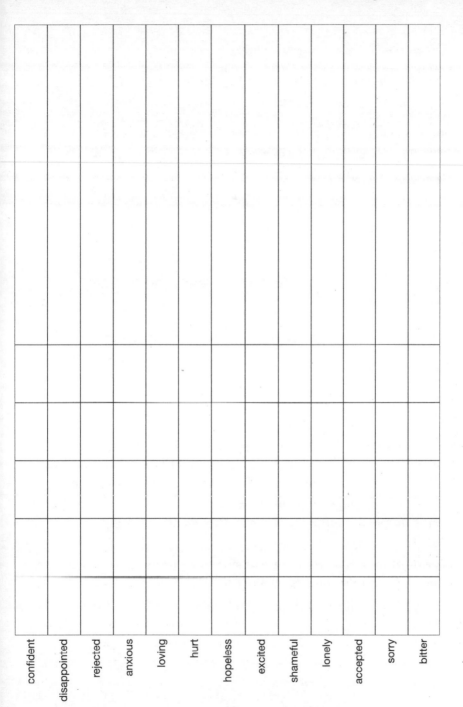

confident

disappointed

rejected

anxious

loving

hurt

hopeless

excited

shameful

lonely

accepted

sorry

bitter

you and your feelings

How do you find talking about your feelings and emotions?

....

If you find it hard why do you think that is? What or who do you think could help you overcome some of your issues? What one step could you take today?

....

If you have a close friend, spouse or family member who struggles to express feelings can you identify the cause? How could you help them in this area?

....

avoidance

What happens when we resist intimacy or resist talking about our feelings? We can end up playing games with others, or we can find ourselves nagging, manipulating, hinting, deflecting or being sarcastic and not being honest about how we feel.

For example, Sumit is a master of the art of deflecting:

If someone starts asking me questions about myself, I will cunningly turn the conversation around so it became about the other person. A rather crafty technique because it means that I came across as all concerned about the other person but what I am probably doing is avoiding intimacy. I am genuinely interested in finding out about the other person – it's just I am not so keen on them finding out about me.

Or we can suppress our feelings and get ill. It's impossible to completely bury our emotions and get away with it. If we try, we'll often find them leaking out in other ways, sometimes physically. Not surprisingly, when I was younger and struggling to acknowledge negative emotions I would suffer from severe headaches, stomach aches and chronic fatigue. My body was finding an outlet for all those buried feelings.

John Powell writes: 'We do not bury our emotions dead; they remain alive in our subconscious minds and intestines, to hurt and trouble us. It is not only much more conducive to an authentic relationship to report our true feelings, but it is equally essential to our integrity and health.'

when to keep a lid on it

It may sound as if I am suggesting that we say everything that is going on in our hearts and minds. But that isn't the case. There will be times when it will be much more helpful and conducive to our relationships if we hold back and don't say everything we are feeling or thinking.

In an article called 'Yours Sincerely' in *Psychologies* magazine, philosopher Julian Baggini writes:

> Too often we think sincerity and authenticity are just a matter
> of doing or saying what we feel like, forgetting that some of the
> things we value – such as thoughtfulness, tact and patience –
> require us to control as well as express ourselves. Someone who
> does not even try to control what they reveal of their thoughts
> about others is not a model of sincerity, but of emotional
> incontinence.

If we don't want emotional incontinence, we need to understand the times when it would be better to put a lid on it or count to ten – anything that will actually stop us saying something we don't really mean. For example, when what we want to say is:

Untrue

We may tell lies for all kind of reasons: to make ourselves look better, to try and protect the other person from the truth or because it is easier or more convenient than dealing with the actual facts. Perhaps we tell ourselves they are just little 'white lies' and they are harmless. But are they? When we tell white lies we are avoiding an opportunity for true connection; we are eroding our integrity and damaging trust.

If a work colleague is always telling lies then how easy will you find it to trust them? If a parent uses white lies or idle threats then how will the child know when they really mean something? If the person we are dating, or married to, avoids telling us the truth about how they feel, or if they habitually lie to us, how can we really get to know them?

Telling the truth isn't always that easy but if we want to be authentic it is an important way to build trust with the people around us.

Unkind

Wherever did that daft nursery rhyme come from: 'Sticks and stones may break my bones; but words can never hurt me'? Harsh and cruel words can and do hurt, especially when spoken by those we care about and love. The truth is that words have great power. We can do horrendous damage to others when we misuse them. We can probably all remember something horrible that someone said to us as a child. The wounds of insults, put-downs, harsh criticisms and cruel words can run deep and the scars can remain for years. Unkind words will erode intimacy and may eventually kill a relationship.

The thing is, we probably don't really *mean* what we are saying if we think long enough about it. Our unkind words are often just a front for what we really mean but find it hard to say. Take the example of the woman who shouts at her husband and says: 'You're a lazy slob. I can't bear seeing you sitting around the house day after day on your big fat arse. I hate the sight of you. I must have been *mad* to have married you.' That is what she is saying but what she actually means may be something more like: 'I'm feeling really frustrated because it feels like I do all the work around here. I'm really tired and I long for you to help me and to take more responsibility for some of the jobs that need doing. When we got married I really hoped we'd work as a team but at the moment I feel as if I am in this alone and you don't care.'

What if she had said what she *really* meant? Instead of alienating and hurting her husband she might have found that he actually responded positively to her openness and vulnerability. He might have explained what was going on for him, perhaps he would have apologised for his passivity and maybe he'd be able to understand more about the impact his behaviour was having on her. He might not do any of those things, but if she never reveals the truth or tries the authentic route she won't know if things could be different. However, if she carries on being unkind it is likely their relationship will just get worse and her husband is more likely to respond with harsh words and accusations as well. Then they'll find themselves in a dangerous downward spiral.

We are most likely to say unkind things when we are upset, hurt, annoyed, angry or feeling a surge of any strong negative emotion. But while saying something spiteful, unkind or hurtful may help us feel better in the short term the pay-off will be the damage we will have done to our relationship. Is that a risk we want to take?

If we are prone to lashing out and saying unkind things then it may help to press the 'pause' button and remove ourselves from other people until we've calmed down enough to think and speak rationally. Just popping to the next door room for a glass of water or walking the dog round the block can give us the few minutes we need to compose ourselves.

Unclear

Where do we get the idea that those closest to us can mind read? (I think this is particularly true for many women.) We hint at something or say nothing at all and expect our friend, parent, partner, work colleague or whoever to just 'get it'. And then, when they don't, we get upset, frustrated, hurt or feel misunderstood.

81

If we want someone else to understand something or to do something it is up to us to be clear.

A man won't always guess that when his wife says: 'I'm shattered and there's so much to do before Jim and Kath arrive,' that what she really means is: 'I would really like it if you could tidy the room, put away the pile of papers, light the fire and open the wine.'

And a new work colleague won't necessarily understand that when his manager says: 'We need to get our customer Christmas cards out,' he means: 'I would like you to check with the printers that the cards are ready, then update our contacts list and then get all the senior directors to sign each one by hand. You then need to make sure you've sent them all out by second class post by Friday at the latest.'

Unhelpful

If what we are going to say isn't going to be helpful to the other person, why say it? Sometimes we can just come out with a judgement, a criticism or an opinion that was uncalled for and is unhelpful.

Chelsea still remembers the time she went away with a boyfriend for the night to stay with his best friend:

> That evening we had just got ready to go out and I appeared in a
> new top. My boyfriend took one look at it and said it was horri-
> ble and that I looked dreadful in it! It was the only one I had
> with me and so there was nothing for it but to wear the 'horrid'
> top all evening. You can guess I felt great in that. I wish he had
> waited until we got home before telling me that it wasn't his
> favourite.

We really don't need to say everything on our mind. We don't need to tell our son that his girlfriend is dreadful; we don't need to tell our child that she has ugly feet; we don't need to tell our mother-in-law that we hate her new curtains and we don't need to tell our colleague that his presentation was hopeless two minutes before he has to do it again! Stop and think: is this going to be helpful? Can they do anything about it? If not, resist the urge to share your opinion. And if they ask you for one? You don't have to answer but if you do make sure you sandwich any negative feedback in the midst of something more positive. So, for example, with the colleague who has just done the presentation you might say:

> You covered lots of good points. However, I wasn't really sure
> about the joke you told about greedy lawyers – I don't think it
> got quite the laugh you were hoping for. Maybe you could drop it
> this time? I like the way you used the stage and how you asked
> those great questions at the end. That was really good. Good luck
> – I hope it goes really well.

Unedited

Some of us think aloud, especially if we are extroverts. But we need to be sensitive to the people around us and to the situation we are in. Not everyone will want every silence filled, want to know every detail of our thought process or want a running commentary on anything and everything.

It can be particularly hard for others if we make all our decisions out loud. One minute they think we mean one thing and the next it has changed! I remember doing that with a friend of mine when we were planning a trip once. I would get excited about all the different destinations. One day I'd feel passionate about going somewhere but the next day I felt equally passionate about going somewhere different. My friend found it very hard to keep up as he thought what I'd said one day was my final decision and was already making plans. He couldn't understand what was going on when it was all changed the next day! When we saw it was causing a problem we found some ways of dealing with it. I would say, 'This isn't my decision yet … I am just brainstorming various ideas. I will let you know when I have come up with the final two options.' I would then try and do some of my thinking and decision-making on my own and would then offer him the edited highlights and we discussed those. That proved a lot better.

83

Sometimes we need to hold back and do some editing in our heads. What do I really think or feel about this? Is that really my decision? We need to check that we are meaning what we say. Meanwhile, if you are an introvert you may need to be encouraged to share more and say more of what you mean. David is an introvert and a lot of the time has much better ideas than I do – the trouble is that too often they just stay in his head. I try and get him to share a little more of his thinking process with me so that I get a bit more of a discussion and not just the conclusion! Who said communication was easy?

meaning what you say

Which do you struggle most with: to say what you mean or to mean what you say?

What do you think holds you back and what would it be like if you could overcome this?

How often do you say things that are: untrue, unkind, unclear, unhelpful or unedited? What causes you to do that and what do you think would happen in your relationships if you stopped doing this?

What steps could you take this week to improve the way you communicate with those around you?

---

6. real to real – building connection

You can make more friends in two months by becoming genuinely inter-ested in other people than you can in two years by trying to get other people interested in you.
DALE CARNEGIE, *HOW TO WIN FRIENDS AND INFLUENCE PEOPLE*

Ultimately the bond of all companionship, whether in marriage or in friendship, is conversation.
OSCAR WILDE

To refuse the invitation to interpersonal encounter is to be an isolated dot in the centre of a great circle ... a small island in a vast ocean.
JOHN POWELL, AUTHOR

building bridges

What does it mean to connect with people? It is more than just making contact. I can go through a day – rub shoulders with dozens of people on the bus, sit through meetings, poke a few friends on Facebook, send and receive plenty of texts, speak to people on the phone and even attend a party – and still *not* actually connect with anyone.

Connection is about building a bridge between us. It is when something of the real me touches something of the real you.

85

It isn't about distance or proximity

You can live on the other side of the world but if we can write, Skype or phone and share something of ourselves with each other then we can still connect. Conversely, two people can live in the same house, share the same bed and yet fail to connect. Sadly, there are plenty of married couples who feel lonely.

In fact, loneliness is a big issue for many people today. In our survey 22 per cent of those who are married and 59 per cent of single people who are not in a relationship said they often feel lonely. An article in a recent Sunday supplement highlighted the problem:

> Increasing numbers of people are finding modern life very isolat-
> ing, either because they are living alone, or because today's
> demanding pace leaves no time to enjoy the company of loved
> ones, or because they've grown apart from their families and
> simply cannot relate to them any more. Tellingly, many of today's
> lonely people don't fall into the expected categories of the old, the
> ill, the divorced or the widowed, but tend to be young, successful
> people with jobs in glamorous cities.

The antidote to loneliness is connection

We don't have to settle for a life of loneliness, and we don't have to let those in our lives settle for one either. We can choose to build our bridge towards them and we can notice when they build theirs towards us. That will mean relinquishing any desire to be totally independent.

That can be a challenge for many of us who are used to being self-sufficient. In our Western society independence is something that is prized and encouraged and it is what many of us seek to achieve. We get a job to pay our way, we live on our own, we do our own cleaning, accounts, washing, shopping, DIY and cooking (even if that is only warming something in the microwave). We take that same independent behaviour into our relationships and we're keen not to be a burden to anyone. In the survey, 43 per cent of people said they would rather sort out their problems on their own than ask for help.

But I am not sure that is how we are made to function. Of course, there will be people who prefer their own company (23 per cent from the survey) but even the introverts among us could do with others in our lives whom we can care for and know and who can know and care for us. There are proven psychological benefits from having at least one or two close relationships in our lives.

Instead of independence it is much healthier to live *interdependently*. When we are interdependent we are prepared to ask people for help and to help people when they need us. We open ourselves up to others and allow others to open themselves up to us. We walk through life together rather than on our own. We build bridges to each other's islands. We learn from each other, we encourage each other, we support each other, we care for each other, we have fun together, we build memories together and we help each other to grow. We realise we are stronger and better as two or more than we are on our own.

Interdependence isn't the same as dependence. Dependence is when we *have* to have someone in our lives whatever the cost. It is when we need other people to function and to feel ourselves. Just like independence, it isn't a healthy way of living. Other people will never be able to meet all our needs or desires and expecting them to do so will only leave us disappointed. The more we cling to others and demand that they love us the more likely we are to lose their respect and our connection with them.

Connection is an amazing and precious thing. It is given freely and taken freely. It cannot be forced, demanded or manufactured. And we cannot expect our connections to just happen and to endure. We have to be prepared to make deposits in our relationships. That means giving of our time, putting in the effort, giving of ourselves and also being generous with our money and possessions. It means sharing our most precious commodities with others.

We can use our time, effort and money to build bridges or we can use them to build a bigger and stronger fortress on our island. Which will it be?

your connections

Think about your relationships. How often do you feel that you are really connecting with people?

_____

Are there times when you feel lonely? If so, can you identify what causes that feeling?

_____

Would you say your tendency is to be more independent, dependent or interdependent in your relationships? What would it take to be even more interdependent?

_____

how to build bridges

What would make someone want to build a bridge to your island or allow you access to theirs? If you think about it there are probably plenty of people you meet every day but not all of them will be people you want to connect with or become friends with. And yet there are others whom you would love to spend time with and get to know better.

Whether it is a quick encounter or a lifelong relationship, how can we be the kind of people that others want to connect with? I realise there are probably lots of answers to that question but I just want to mention seven ways in which we can be bridge builders.

1. Warmth

You can't fake warmth. And warmth isn't about being fake or trying to be larger than life. It is about being relaxed, honest and not taking yourself too seriously. (If you are too self-absorbed you probably don't have it.)

Warm people smile. They show interest, they listen, they empathise, they laugh and people feel brighter about life for just being around them.

Warm people aren't prickly, aloof, self-protected or critical and they leave you feeling energised not drained.

taking your temperature

Think about someone you know who comes across as warm. What do they do or say that makes them appear warm? How does their behaviour make you feel?

Think about someone you know who comes across as cold or aloof. What do they do or say that makes them appear cold? How does their behaviour make you feel?

Would you say you come across as more warm or cold? Are there ways you could increase your warmth?

2. Curiosity

Whether we have just met someone or have known them all our lives it helps to be curious. Curiosity isn't about just asking lots of questions or being nosey. It is about being genuinely interested in the other person. It is about learning about who they are, how they see the world, what they like and don't like and what they think and feel about things. It is about focusing on them and finding out what the world looks like through their eyes.

We often find this easier with people we've recently met. When we've known people a long time we can become complacent. We can assume we know all there is to know and that we can predict what they are feeling or thinking. But people aren't static – they will change and develop over time. Whether it is our parent, old friend, child or spouse, we must never stop taking the time to learn more about them.

It is an added bonus if we remember what we've been told. I always love it if someone remembers things I've told them. If a stranger remembers my name the next time I meet them, if a friend remembers to ask me how my interview went, or if a work colleague asks how my holiday in Devon was. It can help to make a mental note of the things people tell you. (Write them down if you have a bad memory. I remember one relative of mine would walk around with a little note book and after he'd met up with someone he'd scribble some things down about what they'd said and next time before he saw them he'd have a look in his book. People could never work out how he recalled so much about their last encounter.)

3. Kindness

If anything is going to make me reach for my prickly coat again it is someone who is unkind; whether they're unkind to me or unkind to others it doesn't matter. If someone is unkind to others I can only assume that before long they will be unkind to me too.

If someone puts others down, is hurtful, hard or critical, or if they score points, bully or tease someone who hates being teased, then others will want to avoid them, protect themselves or fight back. No one wants to be vulnerable with someone whom they think is going to hurt them.

If we want people to want to connect with us we need to be kind. Being kind means being caring, compassionate, safe, understanding and sensitive.

4. Reciprocity

Our connection won't last long if only one of us wants it and is prepared to work at it. It takes two to connect.

It isn't enough to care. Caring is great but if you only give to me and won't receive from me then we are not really connected. We both need to be able to be open to each other — giving and receiving.

We both need to be able to take responsibility for our relationship. That means both of us being proactive. If one of us always takes the initiative we are not enjoying a mutual connection.

Reciprocity also means that we grow the connection together. Difficulties can arise if one person has greater expectations or desires for the relationship than the other. This can often happen in romantic relationships but it can happen in friendships too. One person wants more intimacy than the other and is keen to meet up more often than the other would like.

Cathy is in her thirties. She has had to relocate three times in the last four years and she is aware that she often expects too much too soon from new friendships:

> I think I have a tendency when I meet new people, whom I'd like
> to be friends with, to sort of 'idolise' them – to see only their
> good points, and focus on how wonderful they are. I'm excited if
> they want to be my friend and subconsciously I'm thinking, 'Oh,
> everything about this person is fab. They are my best friend
> ever.' Of course, everyone has faults and then, at some point, their
> failings become obvious or they let me down or they are just
> somehow human and then I am disappointed. 'Oh they're not so
> perfect and great after all.'

Cathy has had to learn not to let her hopes and expectations for a friendship run too far ahead of reality.

It won't always be easy but it can help to try and match each other's input and desire for connection. Take things gradually. Respect the speed of the slowest participant. Think of it as going for a walk with someone. It helps to go at the same pace as the other and while the fastest one can try and encourage speed from the other they cannot force it.

But there will be times when the other person doesn't want to connect with us at the level we would like. Perhaps the colleague at work turns down our invitations for coffee or the person we like romantically doesn't feel the same. Perhaps a parent or a teenager doesn't want to talk to us about their feelings or a friend doesn't give the same level of importance to our relationship as we do. We can build our bridge and make a bid for connection but if they won't or can't allow us in then we need to respect their position. We can hope the situation may change in the future but for the moment all we can do is accept the relationship for what it is now.

Sometimes, with someone close like a partner or a child who is reluctant to communicate, it can help to do things with them that they enjoy. During or after the activity they may feel more connected to us and more willing to open up. Some people find it easier to connect through actions and activities rather than words. For example:

- A teenage girl is being moody and uncommunicative but after a day out shopping with her mum she is more willing to chat when they sit down for a cup of tea.
- A man isn't responding well to his partner's incessant pressure to talk about their relationship. Both of them are feeling disconnected but when she takes time to go for a walk with him and make love with him she notices that he is much more responsive and willing to talk. And she feels less need to have the 'big chat' because she feels he is closer to her again.

Over time we will be building new connections in life as we meet new people and become involved in new situations and life stages. Equally, there will be some connections that become weaker, perhaps because one of us moves away, our situations or our priorities change, the things we have in common are no longer there or we just drift apart.

But it can be particularly painful if a relationship ends when we don't want it to or we are not expecting it. Paul and Gary were great mates at college. They were part of the same small group of close friends but the summer after they left Paul didn't hear from Gary (and neither did the others). They phoned and left messages for him and once they even went round to his parents' house and left a note. They wondered if they had done something to upset him or whether something bad had happened, but they never heard from him. Years later they were able to Google him and they discovered what he was up to. At least they knew he was alive, but they never did find out why he didn't want any contact with them any more.

In those situations where we have tried all we can to reach someone there isn't much more we can do. When it has happened to me I have tried to keep the door open by sending a Christmas card or the occasional text. This gives them the option to reconnect if they want. But in a few cases I have had to grieve the end of the friendship. Grieving helps me to let go of any false hopes of being in a relationship with them now and allows me to celebrate the good memories I have of them from the past.

5. Trust

Trust is the foundation of real connections. Just like the naked hedgehog who is willing to take off his prickly coat, we need to reveal our real self to others. Of course, you may reject me, hurt me or dislike what you find but I have to believe that it is a risk worth taking.

If we fear taking risks we can start with small ones. We can look for safe people whom we can trust and count on. And we can also help others take risks by being safe people whom they can trust and count on.

Are we someone who is loyal? Can we keep secrets? If we say we'll do something will we keep our word, even if we get a better offer? Do we reveal our real self to the other?

6. Grace

If trust is the foundation of real connection then grace is the oil that keeps relationships running smoothly. Grace means that you don't have to be perfect. It means I will like you or love you for who you are and not for what you can do for me. It means I won't try and change you. It means I will forgive you when you mess up and I will work through problems with you when we encounter them.

Grace enables you to be you and hopefully your grace will allow me to be me.

7. Understanding

Understanding means appreciating our differences. It means celebrating our uniqueness and learning from each other. It means that my world will expand because I know you and yours will hopefully expand from knowing me. We know different things, we behave differently, we think and feel differently, we have had different experiences and we believe different things. And so when I take time to understand you I am saying to you that you are worth getting to know. I am saying that who you are matters to me.

bridge builders

Look at the seven ways in which we can be bridge builders. How well do you think you display those traits?

1. Warmth
2. Curiosity
3. Kindness
4. Reciprocity
5. Trust
6. Grace
7. Understanding

If there are any you would like to improve, how could you do that? And how would your relationships be different if you did?

being deliberate with our connections

There is obviously a limit to the number and depth of connections that we can maintain on a regular basis. As we saw in Chapter 3, we only have so much time in our day or our week to spend on our relationships. So how do we make sure that we are spending the time on the people who are most important to us and, when we do give them time, that we are connecting at the level we would like?

Prioritising our efforts

Professor Dunbar, an anthropologist from Liverpool University, discovered that on the whole humans have the brain capacity to cope with a social network of up to 150 people. These are 150 people whom we know, relate to and would be happy to join for a drink if we bumped into them unexpectedly in a bar.

Social networking sites such as Facebook and MySpace enable some people to have hundreds if not thousands of 'friends'. But the reality is probably that once we pass the 150 mark many of these are acquaintances whom we have little more than a passing and superficial relationship with (if at all). It is impossible to maintain great friendships with 1000 people. I should know I used to try. In my early twenties my social network was probably about 400 people (in the days before the Internet) and what I found was that many of my friendships weren't as deep as I would have wanted because my time was spread so thinly. Over the years I have learnt that while I will probably always enjoy connecting with lots of people (because I am a natural networker), I have to make sure that I am deliberate about nurturing a few close relationships at the same time.

In the survey 25 per cent of people said they have more than 100 friends while 18 per cent have fewer than 20. The rest chose a figure somewhere in between the two.

95

There are likely to be even fewer names on our list of closest relationships with best friends and family because we can only care deeply for a finite number of people. In the survey 42 per cent said they have five or fewer close friends and 53 per cent have between six and twenty. Only 5 per cent claimed to have more than twenty close friends.

Malcolm Gladwell, in *The Tipping Point*, says that if you made a list of all the people whose death would leave you truly devastated most people would come up with around twelve names:

> Those names make up what psychologists call our sympathy group. Why aren't groups any larger? Partly it's a question of time. If you look at the names on your sympathy list, they are probably the people whom you devote the most attention to – either on the telephone, in person, or thinking and worrying about. If your list was twice as long, if it had 30 names on it, and, as a result, you spent only half as much time with everyone on it, would you still be as close to everyone? Probably not. To be someone's best friend requires a minimum investment of time. More than that, though, it takes emotional energy. Caring about someone deeply is exhausting. At a certain point, at somewhere between 10 and 15 people, we begin to overload ...

The difficult thing, if we find that there is too much pressure on our time, is to prioritise those closest relationships over the others in our life. Jon and Zara lived in the city and realised with their busy schedules that they were spreading themselves too thin when it came to their friendships:

> We had an amazing group of friends – but we hardly saw anyone regularly. It felt like we didn't have any real community or any sort of deep, true, significant friendships with anyone. So we wrote a list of about 6 people and agreed that they would be the people whom we would really like to spend time with. We kind of sheepishly let them know what we were thinking (as it's

an unusual thing to do) and asked if they'd like to get together more frequently etc. They were all really touched and there was a resounding 'yes'! Friendships take time (which is really tricky in the big city) but we now see them more often and have great friendships which flow two ways in both the good and bad times.

Remember the illustration of the bucket with the rocks, the pebbles and the sand from Chapter 3? Jon and Zara were making sure their rocks and pebbles were being looked after first.

We may not want to be quite so prescriptive but we may still need to be deliberate about making the time for our most important relationships. If we don't, we may find we are not spending the time with the people we care about the most.

your top ten or twenty

Who would appear on your sympathy list?

....

....

How do you feel that you are doing with prioritising these relationships?

....

How much time do you give to each of these relationships a
week? Do you feel this is enough?

....

If you feel any aren't getting enough of your time or energy what
could you do to change this?

....

Using technology to help, not harm, our relationships

The fantastic thing about technology is that we don't have to be in the same location as the people with whom we want to maintain and build connections. Which is just as well as more of us are now living away from family or friends. In the survey 49 per cent said their family lived too far away and 19 per cent said that their nearest close relative lived over six hours away.

It is great that we can now see and chat to people on the other side of the globe. This means we don't have to wait for a visit in person to see how a child is growing, what our friend's latest hairstyle or new partner is like, or to catch a glimpse of the newest arrival (baby or pet) – we can see it all with the help of our computer. It will never be the same as seeing or being able to touch people in person but it does mean that we are able to keep the connection growing even when we are far apart.

Hannah is our lodger, and her fiancé Ben lives in Singapore, so they chat online most evenings. On the weekend when they have more time they will often just hang out with each other. They turn on their webcams, potter around or do chores in their room while they chat, just as they would if they were in the room together:

> It is a great way of keeping connected when we're so far apart. It's hard to imagine how we would sustain our relationship without Skype – no doubt we would – but I think technology nowadays helps to create a more natural relationship even when distance is involved. Relationships are complicated enough but being able to communicate like this helps to minimise misunderstandings or where there are any it provides a forum to address them.

But while technology can help us to keep connected, it can also become a way of hiding from authentic relationships. I am as guilty as the next person at sending an email to a work colleague who sits at the next desk, sending a text to a friend because I'm feeling a bit too lazy to call or sending an e-card because I haven't made the effort to buy a real card in time. I find that if I am not careful I can suddenly find that days have gone past without me having voice contact with anyone outside of my home.

Some people definitely take electronic forms of connecting too far. I read recently of a teenager from Florida who sent and received 35,463 texts in one month. If she slept for an average of eight hours a night that is the equivalent of about seventy-four messages an hour. And apparently she isn't even the record holder. That dubious title is held at the moment by a man from India who sent and received 182,689! I can't work out how they have time to live when they are so busy texting.

It is good to keep asking ourselves whether we are using technology to bring us closer to people or to keep them at a distance.

Making choices that impact our connections

Every day we make choices that affect the level of our connections. Some of those choices will be small, such as whether to pick up the call when someone rings or whether to accept the invitation to coffee. Others, however, will be big, like deciding to take a job miles away from our existing home or to marry someone from a different country.

Do we stop and think about how our choices will impact those ten to fifteen closest relationships? Who will look after our parents if we move country? How will my time with my family be reduced if I take the job with really long or anti-social hours? What will happen to my friendships if I marry someone who wants to live abroad? In some cases we may feel we don't have a choice but if we at least stop to weigh up all the costs and benefits of our decision we can be aware of the sacrifices we are making. We will never be able to have it all. We can't please all of the people all of the time (or even some, some of the time) but we can try and make sure that we aren't unnecessarily weakening or breaking connections for someone or something if they aren't as valuable to us as our closest relationships.

I remember just after I turned thirty sitting down and re-evaluating how I was living my life. As I mentioned, I am a natural engine. This is partly because my mum is one and because I am not very good at being still. But it is also because I am a high achiever and feel driven to do things well ... or preferably perfectly. For years I found my significance in my job as a TV news reporter. However, the combination of my perfectionism and the demands of the job meant that I regularly got exhausted. Every day I had to perform and to produce a story to a tight deadline. Every day I wanted to do better than the day before. I was living on adrenaline and junk food and working thirteen hour days. I was hardly ever free in the evenings and on my days off I wanted to see my friends, whom I hardly ever saw, but I also wanted to sleep!

I loved my job; it was interesting and exciting and no two days were the same but after seven years I knew something had to give. My health and relationships were suffering. I was single and prone to bouts of chronic fatigue. Whenever I *did* see friends I sounded like a broken record. 'How are you?' they would ask and my reply would be the same: 'Really busy and really tired.' I decided to take a year's sabbatical and spent the time volunteering for a charity abroad. It was just the break I needed. I slowed down, I enjoyed helping others and I built great relationships. It was good to be known and liked for being me and not as 'Sarah who works for the BBC'. And I met some amazing people of all ages from all over the world. Those friendships really helped me to take stock and re-evaluate what was important to me. I came back after the twelve months and quit my job!

I decided life would be different. I took a pay cut, found a great job working in relationship education (which I realised I was passionate about), sold my car, cut back my spending and got a lodger. To try and protect my health and my time I opted to work only four days a week. I also resolved to spend more time on building good friendships. Sometimes I watch former work colleagues presenting on TV and think about what could have been, but I don't regret the decision I made. For a start I wouldn't have met David on the counselling course we did together (before I quit I would never have had time to do a course like that).

I didn't have dependants, which probably made my decision a lot easier. But the principle is the same for everyone – how can we make our lives work so that we can still give time to the people we really care about? When children are involved it can often mean finding a compromise which works for everyone involved, as my friend Tara has found. She lives with her partner and has two children and three stepchildren and works part time in a very busy and stressful environment:

For three days a week at work I get to use my professional skills, enjoy being with colleagues and bring in vital income, but I also get to walk my children to school and enjoy some quality time with them on the other four days. I nearly always get home to bath them and read them bedtime stories, even if I have been at work. We talk and have a cuddle and tell each other why we love each other every night. That really matters to me.

Having said that working part-time is a good solution, I think it is common for us mums to still feel guilty because we are not giving quite enough time to either work or home. I feel guilty rushing out of the office to pick up my children and guilty not seeing them every day after school. I have many friends who have chosen to work full time or stopped working altogether and no one ever thinks they have exactly the right balance. I think being a parent is a compromise and you just have to accept that there is no perfect answer.

My partner and I make sure we get quality time together several nights a week. We try to go out once a fortnight, even if it is just to the local pub to chat over a pub meal. Even if we don't get out, we put the kids to bed by eight and cook and sit at the table to eat together every night. We listen to each other and discuss our day. We talk about everything – what is worrying us, and what made us laugh. We love this time as a couple and know how important it is to protect it.

time and relationship audit

Write your name in the middle of the blank page (page 105).

Then write down all the things that take up time in your life.

Put the things that take up the most time nearest your name and the things that take the least time, furthest away. *For example, if you look at Fred's example, his work takes up a lot of his time so he puts 'work' near his name while he doesn't get to spend much time playing sport with his friends so this would be towards the edge of the page.*

Then when you have written everything on your page take your pen and underline the things that you love doing, that energise you and/or are a positive influence on your life. *For example, Fred loves reading. He also realises spending time with his family and spending time reading are positive things in his life.*

Then circle the things that you dislike, that drain you and/or are a negative influence on your life. *For example, Fred hates work at the moment. He is working long hours and difficult relationships with his colleagues mean the time he spends there leaves him feeling drained. He also goes to the gym but finds this draining too.*

The words you haven't underlined or circled are things that are neutral – you don't see them as negative or positive.

Some things may be positive and negative. *For example, Fred realises that while going to the pub generally energises him, too many drinks can be too much of a good thing and when he does have one too many it leaves him feeling drained (and hung-over).*

Then look at the questions at the end. *When Fred does this he realises that he isn't happy with the amount of time he spends with his family and decides to visit his parents more regularly, especially as his mum isn't very well. To claw back some time he decides to give up TV or DVDs for a month, and also decides to limit his computer gaming to two hours a week. Fred also chooses to give up going to the gym and to jog to work instead as he prefers jogging and it will also mean he saves money. He also decides to start looking for another job. He knows his existing one is making him miserable, which is having a negative impact on him and all his relationships. He decides to only go to the pub at the weekend and to try and do other things with his friends on weeknights, such as going to the cinema, playing tennis or inviting them round for a meal. He hopes his new regime may also allow him time to go on a few dates (something he hasn't done for a while).*

making changes

Look at the things that are taking most of your time. How many of these are positive and how many negative? Are you happy with this balance?

Where are your various relationships and friendships in the illustration? Do you feel they get the right amount of your time?

Are there ways in which you would like to change the way your illustration looks? How could you do that?

going out
on dates

time with
family

watching TV
and DVDs

gym

cinema

chores
and food
shopping

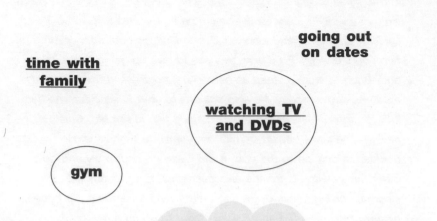

fred

work

pub

computer and
console gaming

playing sport
with friends

reading

Your time and relationship audit

Tips: how to avoid winding people up (for those who find they do)

Keep it down. You may love your music but others may not – so please don't make us listen to it through your headphones or at two in the morning. And if you are the sort of person who has those 'guess what happened last night' calls within ear shot of others, stop and think whether you really want us to know all those things about you.

Remember to say 'please', 'thank you' and 'sorry'. Our mums were right. These three words are important and you can't use them enough.

Switch off. If you are with someone (be it a friend or a shop assistant) switch off your iPod and try not to speak to someone on the phone at the same time. One of the most flattering things you can do is to give someone your full attention – and it may only take a minute.

Play fair. Being competitive is one thing but if you like to cheat at games or sport you may soon be playing alone. Do yourself a favour and accept defeat with grace – no one likes a poor loser.

Get out of the spotlight. You may think you're fascinating but we may not agree. Try not to let the subject of 'you' dominate any conversation. Get interested in others and they in turn are more likely to get interested in you.

Don't ask. Try not to ask a single friend whether they've met someone nice yet, or a married friend when they're having babies ... they may be sick of being asked and if they want to they'll tell you anyway.

Dial it down. No one wants to watch a couple getting, shall we say, overly amorous in front of them. We're thrilled that you're so happy – but we are right over here and it isn't always a pretty sight.

understanding the 'you' factor

7. why an apple doesn't fall far from the apple tree

The shadow cast by the family tree is truly an astonishingly long one.
MAGGIE SCARF, AUTHOR

In my family I've learned that it's much nicer to have a brother and sister than to be lonely and have no one to talk to. Although if I didn't have them more money would go to me instead!
JEMIMA, AGED NINE

Remember, as far as anyone knows, we're a nice normal family.
HOMER SIMPSON

taking a look inside

In the next three chapters I want us to take a journey inside to find out how who we are impacts on how we relate. Our character, our experiences, our upbringing and our past relationships will all have an effect on how we connect with people in the here and now.

There'll be some of us who would rather not look back or inside. Perhaps we are scared of what we may (or may not) find. Perhaps we don't want to revisit any hurtful or bad memories. Perhaps we think it isn't good to navel gaze – that any introspection is self-indulgent and unnecessary. Perhaps we think it would be disloyal to some of the people who were involved in our past. Or perhaps we feel that our history is no longer relevant to the person that we are today. I can relate to all those sentiments because that is exactly what I used to think.

I was at least twenty-five before I took my first look inwards and I didn't relish the idea. In many ways I still don't! But I've learnt that the more self-aware I am and the more I understand where my responses come from, and take responsibility for them, the more authentic I can become. Whether I want it to be the case or not, how I relate on the outside is determined by what is going on in the inside. And how I am on the inside has a lot to do with the past. That will be true for most of us.

In the next chapter I'll look at some of the other things that may have influenced us along the way but in this one I will just concentrate on the family that we grew up in.

the relevance of the apple tree

I once interviewed some people on the street about their views on marriage and relationships. One of the questions was: how does your upbringing affect your marriage or relationship today? A German lady answered: 'The apple doesn't fall very far from the apple tree.' In other words, she was saying that the family we came from helped to shape who we are today.

If you are over thirty-five you can probably testify to the truth of that statement (I say thirty-five because sometimes it can take that long before you really start to notice). There comes a day for most of us when we suddenly catch ourselves saying or doing something that reminds us of our mum or dad. You see something of them in you and it is then you realise that, 'Oh dear, I'm an apple too.' (I say 'Oh dear' because we are normally more aware of the negative traits that we've picked up than we are of all the positive ones.)

No other relationships shape us as much as those with our families, and in particular the relationships we have (or don't have) in our first seven years. These set the foundation and the blueprint for how we see and do relationships for the rest of our lives. We pick up much more than just our genes from our family. Our home is the first classroom where, either consciously or subconsciously, we learn about relating. We learn: whether relationships are safe or not; about how others respond to us and our needs; how we should respond to them and their needs; about relating skills, such as how to communicate, resolve conflict, deal with failure and show love; and what kind of feelings it is OK to express. We also lay down emotional memories that are likely to influence our ability to make and sustain relationships today.

(There may be a few people reading this chapter whose parents separated before you were seven and you may have spent your time divided between two families. If that is your situation you may want to reflect on both families and the impact they had on you. And for anyone who didn't grow up in a family, you may want to think about the main carers who looked after you – the ones you can remember being around the most.)

Presents before or after lunch?

Have you ever gone to someone else's family for Christmas and been amazed at how differently they behave and do things compared to your family? Each family unit is unique ... with their own identity, relating styles, rules, values and traditions ... and often these patterns will become our natural 'default'. These patterns can become very evident when we live with others, get married or have children.

Let me give a couple of trivial examples. In my family we are big on writing thank-you letters but in David's family they say a big thank-you at the time and they don't tend to write. We had both inherited our parents' way of doing things and thought that was 'normal'. We came to realise that neither way was right nor wrong – just different – and together we had to work out how we were going to do things.

And then there's the kissing. In David's family all the men kiss each other on the cheek when they greet, in true Spanish fashion. My family is English and less demonstrative. One day, David kissed my dad and was told later that 'we don't do that!' That hasn't totally put David off trying. He is determined to get another kiss out of him one day!

Your family will probably be very different to mine. And, even within yours, how you experienced it may be very different from how your siblings (if you have any) or other family members perceived it. Sometimes siblings can have been parented very differently depending on what was going on for the parents and the birth order of the children. (For example, they may have been stricter or more cautious with the first one and more relaxed with the second.) This chapter is therefore primarily about you and your own personal experiences.

family environment

Every family will have some kind of collective identity that is greater than any of the individuals within it. In other words, if I could get into a time capsule and go back and visit you when you were seven how would I experience your family (as an insider not just as a guest)? What kind of family environment would I discover? Would I find your family on the warm side or the cold? Would there be much structure and discipline or would people be left to do their own thing?

Psychologists often identify four broad patterns of parenting styles (based on the work of Diana Baumrind). The styles are determined by how warm the parents are and how controlling their parenting is, as you can see from the diagram on the next page.

Different parenting styles

It is unlikely your parents (or main carers) will fit neatly into one particular category and your parents may well have differed from each other or may have changed over time, but as you read the descriptions try to identify which one *most* represents how your family seemed to you.

Just before you do that it is worth mentioning that the object of

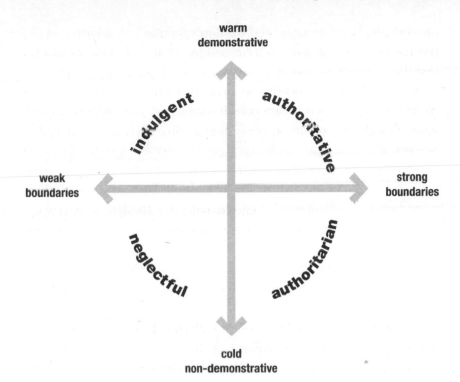

doing this is not to judge our parents or to lay the blame for any of our dysfunction (if we admit to having any) at their door but rather to help us to understand more about the impact that our family home had on how we relate now.

The truth is that despite their best hopes and motivations *no* parent is perfect – certainly not 100 per cent of the time. And for reasons that may be to do with the influence of their own family background or with other circumstances, which may or may not have been within their control, their parenting style may not have fitted the ideal of the first category even if they had wanted it to.

1. Love and limits (Authoritative)

In this first type of family there is lots of warmth and closeness among family members. Parents are loving but not self-indulgent. They monitor their children but don't interfere if they don't have to. Feelings and opinions can be expressed and are listened to by others. There are also clear boundaries. Children know what is expected of them and there are explained consequences for anyone who misbehaves. Children, as they grow, are increasingly encouraged to learn self-control, to mature in the way they express emotions and opinions, to take responsibility for their own actions and to appreciate the needs of others.

People growing up in a home like this usually develop a healthy self-esteem, are articulate, happy with themselves and generous with others. They are self-motivated, do well at school and make friends easily. Of the four categories they are the least likely to get divorced, to suffer from depression, to develop an addiction or to get involved in crime.

From our survey 28.6 per cent of those over the age of forty had families who fitted into this category. For the under-thirties that increased to 42.5 per cent.

2. Do whatever you like (Indulgent)

In this family there is also warmth and openness. When it comes to feelings, children are encouraged to 'let it all out'. Children are rarely taught how to control their emotions or to think about the consequences of their behaviour. There are few limits and not much discipline. Parents prefer to be liked by their children and would rather avoid conflict. The children often get their own way and others looking in on this family may think the children are spoilt and over-indulged.

Children who have grown up in this kind of environment are likely to be impulsive and may find self-discipline hard. As adults, they may be immature and find it hard to accept blame or take responsibility for their actions. They are often dependent on others and are demanding in their relationships. They find it hard to submit to authority. They may be prone to addictions and may find it hard to maintain a relationship or to hold down the same job for a long period of time.

From our survey 3.4 per cent of the over-forties said their families were good with feelings but weak with boundaries. For the under-thirties that had increased to 9.4 per cent.

3. We who must be obeyed (Authoritarian)

The stereotype of this family would be the traditional pre-1960s household with strict parents and children who are seen and not heard. Angry outbursts or crying are met with disapproval. Personal problems are not really discussed and there isn't much demonstrative warmth among family members. However, there is a lot of structure. Everyone knows what is expected of them and a lot is expected of them. There are firm rules and boundaries and definite consequences for overstepping them. Love is definitely conditional on good performance and behaviour in this family.

In more recent times, the modern trend for 'helicopter parenting' would fall under this category where parents micro-manage their children, organising every minute of their day, signing them up for every class, group and activity, refereeing their fights and hovering over them as they work and play. These parents are often reluctant to allow their children to 'just play' and spend their free time doing what they want (especially if there is too much mess or any risk involved).

People who grew up in this kind of home may suffer from low self-esteem and are likely to hear their parents' instructions, and their critical and negative comments in their heads (even when they are no longer about). In turn, they can be critical of others even if they never voice it. Some will be perfectionists, driven to achieve but never feeling they are good enough. Others may under-achieve and stick to safe jobs that they know they are able to do competently. They may struggle to build intimate relationships and find it hard to open up to people. They like control and may lack spontaneity (finding it hard to 'let go'). They may be prone to depression. In some cases, children in a home like this may react against their parents and rebel.

From our survey 54.4 per cent of the over-forties said their families were not good at showing emotions but did have strong boundaries. This fell to 36.2 per cent for the under-thirties.

4. No one to care (Neglectful)

In the fourth type of family there is neither a great deal of warmth nor many boundaries and this may be because the parents are unable to be like that or because they aren't around a great deal. There isn't much focus or consistency for the children in this household. Parents are more concerned with their own needs than with their children's needs. One of the parents (or both) may be emotionally or physically absent, either through choice or through circumstance (illness, alcohol or drug addiction, long hours or time away for work or because of a divorce etc.). Their parenting is therefore unpredictable, with the child never sure how their parent is going to react or what is going to happen to them next. In extreme cases their parenting may be very neglectful and children may be humiliated, screamed at or even abused.

Children growing up in this sort of household may be angry and resentful of their parents. They may as a result turn this anger onto others. As adults they may find it harder to empathise or to build healthy relationships. They may seek control in relationships and may struggle to trust others but will be loyal to those whom they know are loyal to them. People are often either 'in' or 'out'. Some people who have grown up in this kind of home may go on to become care-givers – keen to meet the needs in others that they didn't have met themselves and which they find it hard to admit they have. But others are more likely to seek out short-term pleasures. They may be susceptible to drug or alcohol addictions and prone to sexual promiscuity. In extreme cases they are also more likely to be involved in criminal activities or to become abusers themselves.

From our survey 13.5 per cent of the over-forties said their families weren't demonstrative and didn't have strong boundaries. This fell slightly, to 11.9 per cent, for those under thirty.

General trends

As I mentioned, these categories are generalisations and within each one I mentioned the extremes. Not every child brought up in each type of family will definitely grow up to behave in the ways expressed. Some will buck the trend. It may be that other factors, people or events will increase or decrease the positive or negative impacts (we'll look a bit more at those in the next chapter).

(It was interesting to note from the survey that the general trend seems to be that parents are becoming warmer in their styles as shown by the difference between the over-forties and the under-thirties. Perhaps less encouraging is the trend that families are increasingly becoming weaker with their boundaries. If our survey is at all indicative of society as a whole that would suggest that we will be creating more immature, irresponsible and impulsive adults.)

reject or accept?

We won't all want to emulate the environment that we grew up in. Some of us will deliberately reject it – being determined to do things differently.

In our survey we asked people how they were now at demonstrating emotions and at being self-disciplined and imposing boundaries. Were they the same as their families or different?

Of those who grew up in an 'authoritative' home, 86 per cent were good at expressing their feelings and 64 per cent had good boundaries.

Of those who grew up in an 'indulgent' home, 88 per cent were good at expressing their feelings and 43 per cent had good boundaries.

Of those who grew up in an 'authoritarian' home, 54 per cent were good at expressing their feelings and 60 per cent had good boundaries.

Of those who grew up in a 'neglectful' home, 61 per cent were good at expressing their feelings and 40 per cent had good boundaries.

you and yours

Think back to your own childhood. Where would you put your family on the four quadrants? (See p.113)

Mark an 'X' at the point where you think your family would have been. How did it feel growing up in that family environment?

What impact do you think it had on how you are now?

Think of other people you know and try to think where they might appear on the quadrant and the impact this has had on them. You may want to try and think of your parents' families and what these were like (if you know).

If you are married or in a long-term partnership, where would your partner's original family appear on the quadrants? Mark them on it too.

What impact do you think that had on how your partner is now?

If you are a parent where do you think your own family will appear on the quadrant? If you are not a parent (but would like to be one day), mark where you would want your family to appear.

family relationships

As young children we will have learnt most about relationship skills from observing others in our home: how our parent(s) related to us; how they related to each other (if they were both present); how they related to our siblings (if we had any); how they related to other family members and others in our lives; and how all those people related to us.

Parents with you

In the survey 61 per cent agreed that their parents had a positive effect on how they relate today, while the other 39 per cent felt the effect was negative.

For the majority of us these will have been the most influential relationships in our early years, particularly the one with our mum (or dad if he was the main carer) before the age of three. According to the attachment theories of the UK psychoanalyst John Bowlby, and others since him, this was the time when we developed our expectations of how others will behave and respond to us. We learnt if people could be trusted and whether it was safe for us to bond or attach to them.

As a baby, was our mum's love consistent or inconsistent? Did we receive conditional or unconditional love? Was she emotionally responsive or emotionally withdrawn? If we can answer in the positive then we will have learnt from an early age that people can be trusted and depended on and we are likely to grow up building healthy and close relationships with others. However, if our mum was unable (for whatever reason) to give us the love and care we needed we may have subconsciously learnt that people can not be trusted or that we are unlovable. Consequently, we may have had a harder time building secure and healthy attachments as we grew up.

Louis Cozolino, in *The Neuroscience of Human Relationships*, explains it like this: 'If we learn *not* to fear in early relationships, we will enter subsequent relationships assuming that others are trustworthy, caring, and dependable. If early relationships are problematic, we connect with others in a tentative way, anticipating that what has occurred will happen again.'

According to psychologists it is in these formative years that our brains set down neural pathways – our emotional wiring. We learn to remember the emotions we like feeling and the ones we would rather avoid. We develop ways of keeping ourselves safe and protecting ourselves from any perceived danger. These patterns (this wiring) that we establish will then inform the way we view others and different events as we grow up.

That is why two different people can experience the same event and react to it very differently. Take, for example, two guys who grew up in very different families. Johnny grew up in an authoritative household. His mother was attentive but not over controlling when he was little. He learnt that people could be trusted and were generally 'for him'. However, Luke grew up in a neglectful home. His dad had left when he was very young and his mum was unpredictable in her care. Sometimes she was loving and attentive but most of the time she was unable to look after his needs. She was an alcoholic and he was never sure of how she would react. Her boyfriend, who came and went, was also unpredictable and could be abusive after too many drinks. Luke learnt to be very wary of trusting anyone.

Now imagine that both Johnny and Luke experience the same event. They are meant to be meeting a friend for lunch but she is half an hour late. Her phone is off so it impossible to contact her. How do they react? Johnny feels mildly irritated but he is also a little concerned. He runs through the reasons she could be late in his head. It is unlikely that he thinks she has just stood him up (his wiring tells him that people generally do what they say they'll do and anyway she has never done this before). He therefore concludes that she is probably stuck in traffic or on the underground (which may explain the phone not working). He hangs around for another ten minutes and then when she doesn't turn up he leaves a message on her phone explaining that he had to go and that he hopes she is OK and to give him a ring when she picks up his message. He then goes back to work a little concerned but not overly worried.

When the same thing happens to Luke he feels himself getting increasingly angry and uncomfortable. He doesn't like how he is feeling (his emotions are familiar ones that he experienced many times and his wiring tells him these are ones that he should do his best to avoid). He assumes she has stood him up or that she has forgotten. It just confirms that people can't be trusted and he realises he was a fool for thinking she was a nice girl. After ten minutes he leaves a rather annoyed message on her machine demanding to know where she is. Five minutes later, she still hasn't arrived and the feelings inside are getting more uncomfortable. He is not really conscious of it, but under the anger he is feeling the fear of abandonment and of being out of control. He's had enough. He phones her again and leaves a message saying he doesn't care why she is late and he doesn't want to see her again.

We have two different people, the same event and two different reactions. They are interpreting today's event through their own emotional wiring. One believes that he can trust people and the other believes that he can't. One feels mild emotions appropriate to the facts he has at the time, while the other over-reacts, feeling intense feelings because his past experiences tell him to be hyper-sensitive to any unpredictable behaviour. His solution is to cut off the relationship before he gets hurt.

We'll look more at how our past impacts on our reactions in the next chapter, but now I want to look at the effect of other family relationships on us.

Parents with each other
If we lived with both our parents, we will have learnt a great deal about relating from viewing their relationship with each other. Did they show love to each other or were they unkind to each other? Did they resolve conflict effectively or did they sulk or explode? Did you see them apologise and make up or did they bear grudges?

Did they communicate well or just grunt at each other from behind the paper? Did they enjoy being together or did they lead very separate lives? Did they solve problems together or did they keep arguing about the same things?

Our attitudes to marriage will have been heavily influenced by our parents' relationship or lack of one. Did marriage look like an attractive proposition or something to be avoided at all costs? Were we able to see what it takes to make a lifelong commitment?

The actress Halle Berry has blamed her bad relationship with her late father Jerome for her own disastrous love life. Her father left the family home when she was four. After going through two divorces herself she decided that she had to work through her psychological issues, otherwise she might never find lasting love. The magazine *Teen Hollywood* quoted her as saying:

> I think being without a father has made a dramatic difference in
> my life. I used to think it really didn't matter because I had such
> a strong, wonderful mother and that was enough. But as I've got
> older I've seen a pattern repeating itself over and over in my
> life … I think not having a strong male figure has affected the
> way I relate to men. It's also affected what I think I deserve
> when it comes to a man. My mother had a lot of failed relation-
> ships, and I think on some subconscious level that's what I
> expect for myself.

Research shows that children of divorced parents are more likely to get divorced themselves than those whose parents stayed together. Of course, that doesn't have to be the case and thankfully it isn't for many people but it makes sense that a child who experienced their parents' break-up may be more wary of commitment and if they do commit they may struggle with conflict and how to resolve it effectively.

your mum and dad

What was your parents' relationship like?

What do you think you picked up from them about how to build strong relationships (or from any other relationships they had if one parent died or they divorced)?

Which aspects of the way they relate do you hope you've picked up and which do you hope you haven't?

If your parents divorced or separated (or one of them died) what impact do you think this had on you as a child? And what impact do you think it has on you and your relationships now?

Siblings

For most of us families aren't just about us and our parents – there's the other one or the other lot too. If we had brothers or sisters or both then we will have learnt a lot about relating (and no doubt about a few other things) from them too.

When there is more than one child you learn how to share. You will have to share your parents' love and attention (which may or may not be evenly distributed), you share space and you often have to share things (even if it is only the TV remote control). You learn whether life is fair or not. You learn what it is like to live with people who aren't the same as you. If you have a sibling of the opposite sex you learn about how boys and girls are different. You learn how to resolve conflict and discover what seems to work and what doesn't. You learn to give and take. You hopefully learn to have fun together and you build and share memories together.

Where you came in the birth order may have an impact too. Were you the responsible eldest or the eldest rebel who broke all the boundaries first (as in my brother's case)? Were you the baby who never grew up or the youngest that grew up quicker than everyone else? Lily grew up in a house with three big brothers:

I also had an older sister but she went off to university when I was three and left me alone with these brutes. On Saturdays, or actually almost any day, my mother would have to go off to the supermarket to do a big shop.

The words that filled me with fear were, 'Boys, watch your sister while I run to Kroger.' I knew what was coming – not always but most of the time. Within five or ten minutes of my mother leaving, my brothers, being boys, would want to go outside and play – ride bikes, wrestle, play ball, sling rocks at birds in trees – all things I had no desire to do whatsoever. I wanted to play Barbie, thank you very much.

Now my brothers had a basketball hoop like most boys in 1960s America. It was nailed to the front of our house over the garage. It was affectionately known by them as 'the babysitter' and it was the place where I was headed when I heard my name being called.

They would lift me up and drop me, butt first, into the hoop so that I couldn't get out – my knees and my armpits stopped me from falling through – and they were free to go off and play. I would stay there for ages, sometimes hours. Well, it was probably no more than fifteen minutes but to a five-year-old stuck in a hoop it certainly seemed like a long time.

They had this amazing sixth sense of knowing when my mother was coming home and would always drag me down in time and threaten me within an inch of my life if I told. I finally did, three years ago. When I was thirty-eight.

For only children there will have been an impact as well. David didn't have any siblings so he had to learn to keep himself amused and play on his own when his parents weren't about. He was more spoilt than some of his friends but equally there were times when he had to be more mature than them – making polite conversation with adults or always having to keep his room tidy (as there was no one else to blame the mess on).

Who was who?

In families we often take on a role. We subconsciously give each other labels and then expect people to play their part. Were we the comedian, the carer, the beautiful one, the brain-box, the fixer, the bad egg, the charity case, the mediator, the attention seeker or something else?

Those roles can stay with us into adulthood. We may find ourselves playing them with others or we may find ourselves reverting to them when we get together with our family – assuming our traditional role as soon as we walk through the door of our old family home or meet up with parents or siblings. Sometimes it can be hard for us and for our family if we want to lay the role down. (If you want to check out this theory then the next time you are together as a family try behaving in the opposite way to how you normally are with them and see how others react.)

Gender too may have played a role in how we were treated. Were girls treated differently to boys? What did we pick up in our home about the roles of men and women? How was sexuality expressed (or not)? What did we see modelled by our parents and our siblings?

you and the others

If you had brothers or sisters what was your relationship like with them? What do you think you learnt from them?

What did you learn from the way your parents treated you all?

Where did you come in the birth order? What effect did this have, if any?

If you were an only child, what impact do you think this had on you?

What role do you think you played in the family? Do you still find yourself playing that role now and, if so, with whom?

How did your gender affect the way you were treated in the family? What did you learn about what it means to be feminine or masculine? How was your sexuality encouraged or not?

Grandparents and others

As well as parents and siblings you may have had other family members, family friends or carers who played a big part in your family life and also had an influence on the way you relate. This may have been your grandparents, or one of them, a close cousin, an uncle, aunt or godparent you saw often, an au pair or a carer who looked after you.

Tim grew up in a large family with five siblings. There wasn't much one-to-one time at home but he had a great godmother who would look out for him:

> She always remembered my birthdays and Christmas which when you come from a big family is a nice treat. But best of all she invited me to stay with her for a long weekend every school holiday up in London. She would take me to the cinema, to McDonalds, for pizzas and to play computer games. I loved having that one-to-one time and someone who was interested in me. It was great to be treated as an individual – and not just one of the

boys. It made me feel special and meant I didn't have to compete for attention for a while.

If one or both of your parents remarried, there may have been step-parents and half brothers and sisters as well. The children may have been there all the time or only part of the time. These relationships will also have had an impact.

family rules

As well as being affected by our family environment and learning about relationships from watching and interacting with the others in our home, we will also have been exposed to our family's rules and values.

Rules can be spoken or unspoken. In my family, my dad's rule of 'not kissing men hello' was an unspoken one (although it soon became vocalised when David overstepped the line!), and 'always remember to say "please" and "thank you"' was a firm rule, as was 'it is rude to be late' and a favourite of my grandmother's was 'always ask permission before you get down from the table'.

The rules in your home may have been to do with manners, or they could have been to do with other things like how to treat people (as in 'ladies first'), how things should be done (cutlery pointing up or down in the dishwasher) or what behaviour or feelings were acceptable ('don't rock the boat').

Here are a few other examples of possible family rules:

- Don't express ... (anger, sadness, envy, fear)
- Don't talk about ... (sex, religion, politics, mad Auntie Betty!)
- No topic is ever taboo
- Don't air our dirty laundry in public (i.e. family secrets stay in the home)
- No swimming for at least an hour after eating
- Children should be protected from painful experiences (death, funerals, etc.)

127

- Always put the loo seat down
- Don't talk to strangers
- It is not OK to fail
- Do your homework before watching the TV
- Family comes first.

In Nikki's house she learnt that 'normal' was to never confront:

> I grew up in a house with a strict dad and soft mom – which had interesting effects on the way my siblings and I felt we could stand up for ourselves or make our opinions be heard. If we ever did this, my dad would tell us to 'stop being cheeky', accompanied by the cold shoulder for a couple of hours. This would upset us, which would upset my mom, which would upset us further. So we learned not to argue back, or express contrary views because mostly it would not be accepted well by my dad. As a result I'm no good at confrontations and I want to run a mile if I see I'm headed for conflict. Interestingly, the topic of us being accused as 'cheeky' when we were younger came up recently with my parents and my dad, who has since mellowed considerably, flatly denied ever saying this to us! In fact it rather upset him. Ironic, really. It was quite a revelation to me that something that can forever shape one person can be completely erased from the other person's memory.

your family rules

Think back to your family. What were some of the unspoken or spoken rules in your home?

Which ones have you accepted or rejected yourself?

family values

As with family rules family values can be expressed or left unsaid. Values are the things that your family believed were important. They were the foundations on which they would have made decisions as to how to spend money, time or energy.

For example, if they thought success at work was an important value then your parents may have spent a great deal of time and energy on their jobs or careers and they may also have invested money (if they had any spare) in your education or encouraged you to work hard and do well too. If they valued fitness then their resources may have been invested in exercise and keeping healthy. If they valued loyalty and family they may have invested their resources in looking after relatives – perhaps having one or more to live with you. If they valued pleasurable experiences and possessions then their resources may have been invested in nice holidays, meals out, a good-looking home and fashionable clothes. If they valued charity they may have given their resources to helping others. And if they were religious they may have invested their resources in living out their faith.

Some of their values you may have adopted as your own, others you may have adapted to suit your own views and in some cases you will have rejected their values and developed your own.

Authenticity will also have played a big part in how you perceived those values. If your parents spoke a great deal about a value but didn't actually live it out then that may have impacted you. For example, if a family is very religious but behind closed doors the dad is very critical, unkind and unforgiving then the child may get a negative impression of what it means to have a belief. If a family goes on about hospitality and fun but then behind closed doors the parents complain about having to have people around then the child may believe hospitality is a chore not a joy.

On the whole we are more likely to adopt values that we consider positive, either because we saw them modelled in our house or because we didn't but wish that we had. For example, from our survey we discovered that of those whose families:

had lots of visitors – 79% enjoy entertaining themselves
didn't have many visitors – 66% enjoy entertaining themselves

planned things – 70% enjoy planning things
were spontaneous – 52% enjoy planning things

valued people for who they are – 96% do the same
valued people for what they do – 85% prefer to value people for who
  they are

were very open – 79% described themselves as open too
were closed and secretive – 57% are open themselves

enjoyed doing things with others – 80% prefer doing things with others
enjoy being on their own – 74% actually prefer doing things with others.

you and your family values

What was valued in your home?

How well were those values modelled in your home?

What did your family spend their money, time and effort on?

Which values have you adopted, adapted or rejected?

The following list may help you to think through some other ways
in which your family did things and some of the values they held.
Indicate on the line where your family came on the spectrum using an
'F' for 'family'. Then mark on the line where you would put yourself

now using an 'M' for 'me'. If you want to put other people on the line use an initial for them. Think through how your different positions impact on how you relate together now.

Example: If my family were not good at expressing their feelings but I now find it easier. I would put:

Feelings expressed ....M ....F ......Feelings hidden

Feelings expressed ....Feelings hidden
Opinions heard ....Opinions squashed
Take risks ....Cautious
Repair things ....Replace things
Spender ....Saver
Competitive ....Collaborative
Extravagant ....Frugal
Strong belief in God ....No belief in God
Hospitable ....Never entertain
Time on own ....Time together
People important ....Process important
Fit and healthy ....Not fit and healthy
Driven ....Lazy
Control ....Freedom
Prefer noise ....Prefer quiet
Take us as you find us ....Keep up appearances
Liberal attitude towards sex ....Conservative view of sex
Open ....Closed
Serious ....Fun
Disciplined ....Undisciplined

Adapted from a similar exercise from Session One, The Marriage Preparation Course

8. what is pressing your buttons?

We are never more discontented with others than when we are discontented with ourselves.

HENRI FREDERIC AMIEL, 19TH-CENTURY SWISS PHILOSOPHER

Anyone can become angry – that is easy. But to be angry with the right person, to the right degree, at the right time, for the right purpose, and in the right way – this is not easy.

ARISTOTLE, *THE NICOMACHEAN ETHICS*

Mark Twain used to say that it was possible to learn too much from experience. A cat, he said, that had squatted once on a hot stove lid would never sit down on a hot stove lid again. The trouble was that it would never sit down on a cold one either.

ISAAC ASIMOV

sensitive buttons

What presses your buttons? Who or what makes you feel angry, fearful, upset, hopeless, worried, annoyed, anxious, depressed, guilty, critical, defensive, exhausted or controlling? I don't mean normal or rational things like getting scared if you see a 15-foot shark in front of you in the sea, feeling a little guilty if you eat someone's last chocolate without asking or feeling tired because you just worked a double shift. Those are all quite normal responses. What I mean are the irrational ones, the reactions that are not in direct proportion to the event or stimulus that has supposedly just caused them.

For example:

- John goes silent and moody every time his girlfriend wants to talk about 'us'
- Anna gets anxious when the boss asks to see her, even though she doesn't know why he has called the meeting
- Wayne snaps at his brother when he suggests that he might find it easier to use an electric drill, rather than a manual one, to fix the curtain pole
- Tamsin screams at her five-year-old child who is struggling to get ready in time for school.

We will all have sensitive buttons (some of us more than others) that, when pressed, set off a negative reaction in us. Some of those buttons we'll be aware of, others we won't. Some will create minor reactions, some major ones. We won't always know why we have those sensitive buttons but we can safely bet it has something to do with our past experiences and our emotional wiring.

For example, I know I often get angry when people argue or fall out with their siblings, I get nervous around irons and I am overly critical of attention-seekers. I have plenty of other buttons but those will do for starters. So what has caused those sensitive buttons to exist for me?

When I see people argue with their siblings it makes me want to shake them and say, 'You don't know how lucky you are. At least they are alive. Make the most of having them because you don't know how long they will be around.' Don't worry, I don't say anything that insensitive but I do feel the negative response rising in me. It isn't hard to understand why. Behind the reaction is the anger and frustration I feel with myself because I didn't make more of my relationship with my brother when he was alive and I don't want them to have the same regrets. Deep down there is probably also some jealousy that they still have siblings who are around even if they don't get on with them.

My response to irons is easy for me to work out. When I was three I was left with a babysitter for the afternoon. She was doing the ironing and had propped the board up against my toy cupboard. When she went out of the room I tried to get to the toys and managed to knock the iron off the board. I picked it up and put it back. And yes, I had a very sore hand and was quickly rushed off to hospital when my parents got back. Irons and pain became linked in my mind after that!

My reaction to attention-seekers is a little harder to admit. I remember once being on a residential course and finding myself feeling critical of a girl who seemed to be trying a bit too hard to get attention from people, especially the tutors. It took me a while to work out why I was finding her difficult. The ugly truth eventually dawned – she reminded me of me! I was reacting to her because of a trait in me that I didn't like to admit to. That can often be the case – we get angry or critical at people who remind us in some way of ourselves. (I've learnt to ask myself when I get like that – is this reaction about them or is it about me?)

Faulty wiring

As you can see, my sensitive buttons were wired in my past. You are very unlikely to have similar reactions to any of those things. They are due to my own unique and weird wiring. You will have your own.

We saw a little of why this happens in the last chapter. You picked up lessons from your parents, early carers and family about how others are likely to respond to you. You learnt among other things whether people could be trusted, whether you were wanted and whether you were loveable. The blueprint for your emotional wiring was formed. What came next either reinforced that wiring or altered it.

Positive wiring

If your early experiences with your family were healthy and positive then your wiring would have been in a pretty good state. Then, while growing up, if you had good times at school, healthy relationships, positive experiences at work and not too many negative setbacks then that positive wiring would have been reinforced. You will have formed buttons that work properly. So, for example, if you see an iron you may be reminded of the pile of shirts waiting for attention and feel mildly frustrated but you are unlikely to feel panicked.

Creating the faulty wiring

It is possible to have had a great start in life but difficult events or relationships that happened later may have since caused you to develop unhealthy responses. Your healthy wiring may have been damaged. That is what happened to Rob:

I grew up in a happy home with a 'normal' childhood; I was popular at school and good at games. When I was eight a good friend of the family started paying me more attention than the others and this quickly turned into a 'secret' relationship, which led to abuse for a number of years. During this time I lived a double life, on the one hand life at home was good and carried on more or less as normal, and on the other hand it was hell. I was trapped at a very young age, mortified at the thought of exposure and prepared to suffer the consequences rather than tell anyone about it.

This person continued to ruin my life for a number of years but even after the abuse stopped I could not talk about it, so it ate away at me. When I got older I found I could cope much easier with life through drinking and taking drugs. My family were at a loss to understand what was wrong with me; I was throwing my life away for no apparent reason. It was not until I was older, with the help of my future wife, a couple of good friends and some spiritual guidance that I began the process of facing up to the demons of my earlier years. I stopped drinking and taking drugs and I began to realise what damage I had done to myself and others over

135

the years. It took a long time but I did manage to deal with the negative impact of the original abuse and also the impact of my subsequent behaviour on me and my relationships.

If you had an inconsistent, difficult, painful, confusing or abusive childhood, if you grew up with few boundaries or without much warmth, then you may have developed some rather more faulty wiring from a young age. And if your inputs after the age of seven were negative as well then you may have developed even more sensitive buttons as time went on.

But if, as you grew older, you experienced positive inputs (for example, a happy time at school, a teacher who encouraged you, good friends, a loving grandmother, a supportive and loving spouse and a fulfilling job) then you may have managed to rewire some of the faulty connections and consequently may have developed more healthy ways of reacting.

Our wiring will affect how we relate to others and their wiring will affect how they react to us. Every day we'll be pushing people's buttons and they will be pushing ours. If we can learn to recognise sensitive buttons in others it will help us to understand them better. If we can recognise our own, we can also learn to be more honest about where our reactions come from, take responsibility for them and work at re-wiring them.

the three big questions

What did people and experiences in your past teach you about how to respond? Did they reinforce what you learnt in those first seven years or did they help alter your wiring?

When we look back it can help to ask what the major events and people in our lives taught us about three big questions:

- **Am I worthy of love? In other words, am I OK? Am I loved for who I am and not just for what I can do? Am I valued and accepted? Am I wanted?**

- Am I competent? In other words, am I needed? Do I have a role? Am I respected? Does my contribution matter? Am I significant?
- Am I safe? In other words, can others be trusted with all that I am? Can I trust myself? Can I rely on people? Am I secure? Do my needs matter?

A trip back in time

It may help to draw a timeline like the one shown below. Think about all the major people involved with you at the different stages of your life. What were the major events that happened to you? Include family members and events, friends, school, work, relationships, major traumas or illnesses or any spiritual experiences. If you decide to draw it out you may want to mark whether it was a positive or negative influence and how it helped you to answer the three questions.

Life Experiences Timeline

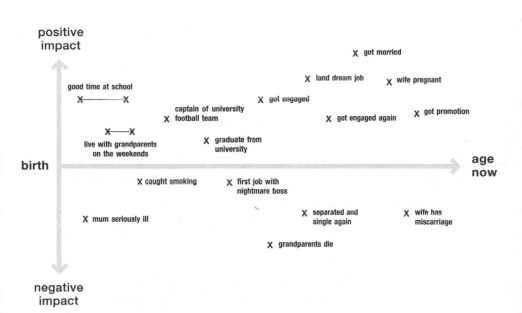

You may want to keep your drawing in front of you and add anything to it that springs to mind, as we go through the following categories:

Family
We looked a great deal at family in the last chapter. But what happened after the age of seven? If there was a divorce, illness, bankruptcy, redundancy, bereavement or relocation what impact did it have on you?

Connie's Dad and stepmother moved house a lot when she was a child:

> My step-mom often sold things while we were moving without
> telling us kids – so when we showed up at the new house, all
> that we found there was our clothes. All our favourite toys and
> stuff would have gone to the local charity. Now I don't like
> change and I am a serious packrat – my family will tell you that I
> refuse to throw things away. It drives them mad but they realise
> that my behaviour is overcompensation for my childhood.

What was it like growing up in your home? How were your teenage years? When did you leave home and what was that like? How did you and your parents and other family members relate after you no longer lived under one roof? What are those relationships like now?

In our survey we asked people who were brought up in the four family environment styles how they now got on with their mum and dad (or how they had done if they are no longer living).

Of those brought up in an authoritative home, 83 per cent have a good relationship with their mum and 74 per cent with their dad.

Of those brought up in a permissive home, 75 per cent have a good relationship with their mum and 61 per cent with their dad.

Of those brought up in an authoritarian home, 61 per cent have a good relationship with their mum and 51 per cent with their dad.

Of those brought up in a neglectful home, 45 per cent have a good relationship with their mum and 36 per cent with their dad.

The results would suggest that if our parents showed us warmth as a child we are more likely to get on with them as an adult and it also points to the fact that warmth is a greater indicator of a good relationship than strong boundaries. Predictably, if we didn't receive warmth or strong boundaries our relationship with our parents is more than likely to have been impacted negatively. That was true for Clive:

> For reasons known only to herself, my mother put me in a chil-
> dren's home when I was eleven, and signed papers to the effect
> that there was no one to look after me and I needed to stay there
> until I was eighteen. I suspect she was doing this to try and get
> at my father, but that she could use her own children as pawns in
> this complex game still haunts me today and my relationship
> with her today is not good. I find myself challenging anything
> she talks about, because fundamentally I don't believe a word she
> says to me.

Your own family

If you went on to have family of your own how did this impact on you? What does your marriage (or partnership) tell you about those three questions?

Annie struggles in her relationship with her partner because she feels that he let her down when their baby was born:

> He could not cope with the new responsibilities and left me to do
> most of it on my own. His behaviour made me feel abandoned
> and unsafe. I am now very self-reliant and I am unable to trust

him. I am now not prepared to have another child with him because I am unwilling to put myself in a vulnerable position again with him.

What about your children if you have them. And how well do you help them answer the questions? If you have been divorced what was the impact of that on your answers?

Peers

Our peers and friends can do a lot to alter our wiring. Did you have lots of friends, a few or none? Were they a positive influence or not? Were you a positive influence on them? What did you learn about belonging, trust, loyalty, acceptance etc? Did friends like you for who you were or for what you had or could do for them? What have your adult friendships been like? Can you spot a pattern in the types of friends you tend to make? Would you say your friendships are generally balanced? Or do you find you attract people who need you more than you need them? Or do you find you need your friends more than they need you?

Roz grew up in quite a serious home environment where laughter was discouraged and silliness was dismissed as immature:

My sister and I learnt to behave in a way that was acceptable to my parents, which meant being quiet, escaping into a world of books and seeing larking about as a waste of time and energy. I took this attitude into my adult life, being quite serious at heart and often finding it hard to relax or just have fun. I was also critical, and probably if I am honest, jealous, of others who were able to see the lighter side of life.

Then when I went to university I had the fortune of meeting a group of friends who taught me the benefits of humour. As they got to know me well, I relaxed around them and learnt how to laugh more. They taught me that an afternoon hanging out chatting wasn't necessarily a waste of time and that there is a funny side to most difficult or embarrassing situations. I went out in fancy dress for the first time and even managed to laugh at myself! Though I am still more serious than I would like to be, I am grateful to those friends for showing me that I don't have to live my adult life the way I did as a child.

School

Were your school years the best of your life or the worst? What did you learn about your strengths and weaknesses? What was your experience of authority? What did you learn about fairness, competition, failure and success? Were you bullied or involved in bullying? Did your experiences leave you feeling competent or incompetent?

Work

What about your experiences at work (if you've had any)? What have these told you about how competent you are? Were you valued for your contribution or did you feel overlooked? How did others respond to you and how did you respond to others? If you were ever made redundant, sacked or overlooked for promotion how did this affect you? If a project you worked on succeeded or failed how did it make you feel? If you've experienced conflict with a colleague or colleagues at work what impression did that leave on you? Can you identify any recurring patterns from your work life? Do you end up experiencing similar issues in different jobs? If you are retired, what was the impact of giving up work? How did this influence your feelings of significance?

Romantic relationships

And then there's your love life – from your first ever boyfriend or girlfriend to the present day. If you have never dated or have had no relationships was this a deliberate choice? If not, how has it left you feeling? If you have dated, what kind of people have you attracted? Were they similar to you or the opposite? Can you discern a pattern at all? How similar or different have they been to either of your parents? How did these relationships affect your self-worth?

141

How did you treat them? How have you responded to break-ups and how did these affect you?

Helen was divorced fifteen years ago and has been single ever since:

> I believe that because of my experience I have felt you have to give up too much of yourself and thereby lose your freedom in order to stay in relationship. For a while I felt that it wasn't worth it and I was better off on my own. More recently, however, I have had to face the fact that I have been feeling lonely, something which I denied for a long time. I have now got to the place where I have worked through issues that I had with my dad and my ex-husband and now I feel in a much more positive place to have a relationship. It has been a long journey.

Other people or events

We won't have covered all the significant people or events of your life in the above categories. There will probably be others. Perhaps you did some travelling or volunteered on a long project. You may have been involved in a group or a team that had a great influence on you. Perhaps you had an illness or an accident, experienced bereavement or some other major trauma, or you may have belonged or belong to a religious or spiritual group. Think about what impact these other people or things had or still have on you. What, if anything, do they teach you about the three questions? Do they make you feel loved, secure and significant or do they reinforce your belief that you aren't?

God

Are you able to believe that God loves you unconditionally or do you see him as distant and far removed? Or do you believe that there isn't a God? How has your background affected these views? If you do believe there is a God do you see him as someone who can be trusted and has a purpose for your life? Or do you struggle to trust him and wonder how you can ever please him? What has shaped your view of God? How does your faith help you to answer those three questions and how does it impact on your relationship with others?

Lydia believes that her faith has had a very gradual but revolutionary impact on her relationships:

I can safely say that before allowing faith to take a large role in my life, I lived strictly in dysfunction-ville. Most of my relationships, platonic and otherwise, hung underneath the shadows of a difficult childhood, so basic issues like trust and intimacy were very difficult for me. I was very isolated, very self-defensive and not easy to be around. My faith in God gradually brought me back to a place where, with the help of very good friends, I began to understand what it was to trust and love people. In learning how to trust, I began to learn how to be a friend without being afraid, how to speak positively to others and I learned how to forgive. I cannot overestimate how important this was and how impossible I think it would have been for me without a faith in God who forgives over and over again.

how do we protect ourselves?

Thinking back over the past can be a difficult journey for some of us. We may feel some of our sensitive buttons being pushed and it may feel painful or uncomfortable. It can be hard to realise that people or things weren't 100 per cent perfect and it can be even harder to realise that we weren't either.

How did you do with answering the three questions through each stage of your life? If you could truthfully answer with a big resounding 'yes' to all three then the chances are you feel secure in yourself and are secure in your relationships.

For the rest of us – whose answers were more a tentative 'yes' or some form of 'no' – we may find that we have a few or even a lot of sensitive buttons. We may have developed all kinds of complex strategies and defence mechanisms to cope with our perceived or actual lack of love, competency or safety.

Show me the love

For example, if we struggled to know that we were loved, we may have developed strategies to make ourselves more loveable or to protect ourselves from anyone else attempting to prove that we weren't. We may have tried to improve ourselves or to behave in ways that we hoped would make people like us. We may have found we had trouble with saying 'no' to other people's requests. We may have tried to hide the 'bad' bits of ourselves and to show only the bits we thought would get a better response.

We may have continued to be attracted to the types of people who didn't love us enough before – hoping that it would be different this time. We probably believed it was us and not them who needed to change. We may still do those things.

Our sensitive buttons may be linked to issues such as self-esteem, conflict or rejection.

Our worst fear (and perhaps our greatest expectation) may be that someone sees the real us and abandons us.

Who's the boss?

If we struggled to know that we were competent, we may have developed strategies to earn approval by doing well or developed ones to help us avoid failure. We may have tried to find significance through work and achievements or we only attempted things we knew we could succeed in – refusing to even try anything more risky. We may have found it hard to admit when we needed help or we may have struggled when other people needed ours. That may still be true for us.

We may have sensitive buttons over issues surrounding performance, respect, failure and criticism.

Our greatest fear (and perhaps our greatest expectation) may be that we will be found to be a failure, inadequate or not needed.

Don't mess!

Finally, if we struggled to know we were safe, we may have developed strategies to protect ourselves from getting hurt. We may have found ways to keep our distance from people or have tried to stay away from the types of people or events that have hurt us before. We may have developed ways of staying in control.

We probably became very good at spotting people who are loyal and can be trusted and staying away from others. If authority figures caused us problems in the past we will have been keen to avoid becoming dependent or answerable to anyone again (perhaps we found work where we could be our own boss). We probably wanted to belong and connect with people but our fear of getting hurt was often stronger. We may have allowed people to get so far but when people got too close we may have pulled back.

We may have sensitive buttons over issues of trust, loyalty, commitment and authority.

Our greatest fear (and often our greatest expectation) is that we will lose control and be hurt.

seeing yourself?

To some extent we may see a little of ourselves in all three categories. That may be hard for us to admit. I know I can sometimes engage in people-pleasing activities, I know I can sometimes catch myself striving to win approval and I know I can sometimes find myself withdrawing from relationships if they get tricky.

Don is all too aware of where his negative reactions and behaviour come from. His mum died when he was six and his dad, who had re-married, then died when Don was eight. His stepmother ill-treated him and then rejected him and he was adopted by his uncle at the age of nine. His only brother emigrated when he was thirteen (and he didn't see him again for twenty-eight years). By the age of ten he had already been to five schools and lived in nine homes.

I often have strong feelings of rejection even just from someone's look (it needn't be meant); it can happen right out of the blue and feel very strong, like I am falling down a lift shaft. I can understand why I have such a fear of rejection ... as a child I felt like I had been abandoned by four of the closest people in my life, my mother, stepmother, father and brother. My resulting behaviour was: do anything to avoid rejection, control the situation, always be right and achieve more and more.

Being a 'driven person' helps me to overcome the lack of affirmation that I received during my formative days. If I achieve I get a 'well done!', something I lacked as a child. If I am achieving then I am in control and I perceive getting something wrong as rejection.

This fear of rejection has coloured all my life. I have always hated conflict (in case I should lose) and therefore would never allow my three children to argue – I was as a parent a peace-keeper rather than a peace-maker. I have also found it hard to 'let go' and fool around ... probably related to a fear of being out of control.

I have been married now to Ann for forty-eight years. My relationship with her has been a wonderful support and healing experience. We are great friends but it hasn't always been easy. But my relationship with God (which started when I was seventeen) has been a great strength. It helped me to trust more and to understand what it means to be loved and to belong. The same has been true of my marriage.

My fear of rejection continued with Ann, and I can take any form of criticism or a comment over silly little things, like not leaving the bath tidy, as an attack which I need to defend. When we have had to sort out our conflicts, mainly around my defensiveness, she has been sensitive to how I must feel but she has not been willing to 'sweep anything under the carpet'. We endeavour to keep short accounts. She is much more secure than me and she has helped me to find the security that I was missing.

I think being authentic is critical and essential to building a deep relationship. The greater the vulnerability becomes in a secure relationship, the greater the openness and honesty which can be exercised. Pretence is not necessary, you can be yourself. This vulnerability depends on deepening communication, which entails spending quality time together and making choices. I have increasingly been able to show my feelings now with Ann because she understands what is going on inside me.

There are still, occasionally, times when I am in a heap, for example something on TV triggers a memory of the past and for a few minutes I am not in control! And that is OK – Ann understands and supports me in an appropriate way.

My behaviour can still, less and less but occasionally, appear quite irrational – however, if you know what is triggering this off, even if it is for 500th time, there is a way through.

what is under the bed?

What would you say is your greatest fear?

....

Is it to be unloved, unvalued or unsafe? Or is it something else?

....

How do your fears affect how you behave in your relationships?

....

What sensitive buttons are you aware that you have? What happens when these are pressed?

....

time for some rewiring?

During this chapter you may have identified some of the sensitive buttons you formed during your past. Remember that many of them would have developed initially for good and healthy reasons. They kept you safe. They helped warn you of danger. They were vital to help you survive.

However, we often keep them long past their sell-by date (for example, my fear of irons). We hang onto them because they are familiar, because they suit us in some way – it means that I don't have to do the ironing – or because we fear or don't know what it would be like without them.

But we do have a choice – we can keep them and carry on as we are. Or, if we want to improve our relationships and truly relate authentically from the inside out, we can take a deep breath and ask, 'How can I get over myself?'

looking in the mirror

What are you like now? Have a look at the list below and mark an 'M' (for me) on the line to indicate where you think you are. Consider why you are like that.

Then think about how you think others perceive you. Mark an 'M2'. If the two marks are different, then think about why that might be. You may want to check with someone else about how they do see you. Is this the same as you thought?

Then finally think about where you put yourself and where others see you. Would you want to change either of these? If so, how? Mark an 'M3' for where you would ideally like to be. What, if anything, is stopping you change?

Affectionate . . . . .Cold

Generous . . . . .Mean

Interesting . . . . .Boring

Sensitive . . . . Insensitive

Impatient . . . . .Patient

Loyal . . . . .Disloyal

Easy-going . . . . .Demanding

Caring . . . . .Selfish

Impolite . . . . Polite

Lazy . . . . .Hard-working

Compassionate . . . . Harsh

Dependable . . . . .Unreliable

Aloof . . . . Friendly

Modest . . . . Arrogant

Unattractive . . . . Attractive

Confident . . . . Shy

Submissive . . . . Assertive

Controlling . . . . Laid back

Cautious . . . . .Adventurous

Mature . . . . Immature

Predictable . . . . Unpredictable

Happy . . . . Sad

Insecure . . . . Secure

Humorous . . . . Serious

Competent . . . . Incompetent

Kind . . . . Hard

Tense . . . . Relaxed

Clever . . . . Thick

Creative . . . . Unimaginative

Fearful . . . . Bold

Open . . . . Secretive

Expressive . . . . Impassive

Critical . . . . Encouraging

Fit . . . . Unfit

Appreciative . . . . Ungrateful

9. how to get over yourself

The fool doth think he is wise, but the wise man knows himself to be a fool.
WILLIAM SHAKESPEARE, *AS YOU LIKE IT*

Almost every man wastes part of his life in attempts to display qualities which he does not posess, and to gain applause which he cannot keep.
SAMUEL JOHNSON, WRITING IN *THE RAMBLER*, 1752

What you are sounds so loudly in my ear that I can't hear what you say.
RALPH WALDO EMERSON, AMERICAN POET AND PHILOSOPHER

what is that horrible noise?

Have you ever watched the *X Factor* or *American Idol* auditions on TV? Thousands and thousands of people from all over the country queue up to sing in front of the judges in the hope of gaining a place on the programme and the chance to win a life-changing recording contract. The saddest and funniest bits are when people come on who can't sing a single note in tune. When the judges turn them down or make fun of their painful performance they can't believe it; they think they are brilliant – a star in the making! What I can never understand is how their friends and family can let them humiliate themselves in this way. Why didn't they point out that they couldn't sing before they went that far and made a fool of themselves on national TV? The even scarier thing is when you see the friends and family utterly amazed when their little darling is turned down. It seems they are completely deluded too!

Having faulty wiring and sensitive buttons is very similar to singing out of tune. If our wiring is OK we will be in tune and our relationships will be in harmony. But to the extent that our wiring is off, our buttons will produce a response that is off-key and likely to affect our relationships with others. Like the *X Factor* contestants we may not even realise we have a problem.

For example, Greg, Ann and Sam all give a presentation. Their boss takes them aside one by one and gives them all similar feedback. She tells each of them that it was generally a good talk but also points out a few things that could have been done better.

Greg is happy with the feedback. He shares his boss's thoughts on his talk. He knew he'd done OK but he also realised that there were things he could improve. He thanks his boss for her helpful pointers.

Ann is distraught about the feedback. Her shoulders slump and she slides further down into her chair. Her eyes are fixed to the floor. She focuses on the negative comments, which only reinforce what she already thinks about herself – that she's hopeless and much worse than the others at public speaking. The boss, sensing her dejection, repeats the positive comments. Ann doesn't hear them.

Sam thought his talk was brilliant. He laps up his boss's praise and smiles rather smugly. He knew he'd been the best. When she mentions the negative comments he becomes defensive (in a slightly aggressive way), making excuses for each one. The boss doesn't get the feeling he is taking any of the criticism on board. She'd be right.

In this scenario it is not difficult to spot the one with the normal wiring and harmonious buttons. Greg's reactions are appropriate and proportionate to the feedback he has been given. That isn't the case for Ann or Sam. The boss's feedback is clearly pressing sensitive buttons in them and their reactions are being influenced by some faulty wiring. But their reactions are different.

Ann's response is off-key and flat. If you think of someone singing or playing a flat note – a flat note is one that is played or sung lower than it should be. Ann's response is to withdraw, to feel hopeless, to feel inferior and to think less of herself than she should.

Sam's response is also off-key but it is sharp. A sharp note is one that is played or sung higher than it should be. Sam's response is to puff himself up, to feel pleased with himself, to refuse to accept any negative feedback and to think too much of himself.

The boss probably picked up on Ann's and Sam's rather different responses, although she is unlikely to know the complexity of the wiring that caused them. Ann and Sam themselves were probably less aware that there was anything odd in their reactions. For them, they were just being 'normal'.

time for a sound check?

In order to become more authentic we need to try and become more aware of all our buttons – both the ones that are harmonious and the ones that are off-key. That will mean being honest with ourselves as well as being open to receiving feedback from others.

We need to do that because as well as the buttons that we are aware of, there will be others that we aren't aware of but which are visible to others.

Diana's close friends often tell her that she has trust issues. She doesn't always see them herself but she does recognise where any fear may come from. 'My dad was physically abusive when I was young. I am afraid of people who have a temper and I have a lot of fear.'

It is a bit like when we look in a mirror and only see our reflection. We cannot see ourselves as other people do, nor can we know what it is like to be in our presence and the impact that we have on others. The only way we can discover these things about ourselves is if someone tells us.

If you got someone to do the last exercise with you in the last chapter you may have seen this at work. They probably saw you differently to the way you perceived yourself.

If we want to be authentic from the inside out, we need to work at becoming aware of our buttons and not hiding them. That will mean being open to feedback so that we can learn about our impact on others. And it will mean finding at least one person whom we can trust to reveal more of who we are on the inside.

playing in tune

Are you aware when you are off-key? Do you realise when you are out of harmony in your relationships (or do you always presume it is the other person)?

Are your sensitive buttons more flat or sharp?

The following lists may help you to spot if you have a tendency to be more flat or sharp. Tick any that apply to you. Some of us may have both flat and sharp buttons.

flat buttons

People with flat buttons may:
  often feel sad
  struggle with depression
  feel apathetic
  think they are a failure
  feel inadequate

feel passive
conform to wants of others
be prone to escapism
blame themselves
withdraw
avoid conflict
feel insecure
find it difficult to accept praise
dislike how they are
feel guilty (even if they haven't done anything wrong)

sharp buttons

People with sharp buttons may:
be competitive
be aggressive in words or action
feel hostile towards others
be openly or privately critical
be sarcastic
appear arrogant
think they are better than others
be stubborn and inflexible
struggle with authority
be manipulative
be possessive of things and people
find it difficult to take criticism
blame others
have a tendency to over-react
be controlling
be very unpredictable with their moods

you have to really, really want it

The good news is that we don't have to settle for how we are at the moment. We can do something about it. We can get over ourselves.

I mentioned at the start of the book that I realised that my relationships weren't up to much at the age of twenty-one. Since then, I have learnt to recognise some of my faulty wiring and have set about doing something about it. It has been (and still is) a long process, but I have made some definite improvements (with a lot of help from others). My relationships are a lot better now than they ever were. My wiring won't ever be perfect (no one's is) but I believe that we can all improve if we are prepared to be open to change.

To change we have to want to change. That means getting real with ourselves and admitting the things we don't like about how we and our relationships are at the moment. It means not being resigned to them staying like that. It means wanting to be more harmonious and authentic in our relationships. It means being proactive. It means taking responsibility for our own reactions and behaviour. It means being open and honest with ourselves and with others. It means becoming 'ourselves'.

Sabina remembers a time in her life when she felt desperately stuck and was going through a bad relationship:

Staying where I was looked awful, but leaving looked and felt terrifying. I remember receiving a quote at the bottom of an email someone sent me: *'And the day came when the risk to remain tight in the bud was more painful than the risk it took to blossom'*, Anais Nin. That really struck me. Moving from hopelessness to hope came by breaking down what seemed like an insurmountable problem into smaller more manageable steps and then just taking the first step. One step seems to then build momentum. I think the fear comes in the anticipation. Once you're moving and doing something about your problem it all becomes easier.

an interesting exercise to try

The other night I was watching a DVD of the film *The Kid* starring Bruce Willis. The character he plays is about to turn forty and is a rather unlovable, unsympathetic and controlling individual who has fallen out with his family, has no family of his own, is unscrupulous in his work and fails to notice that his PA rather likes him (although it is hard to see why). In the film his eight-year-old self comes to visit him and helps him to see where his wiring went wrong and to recognise how off-key he's become. At the end of the film, both the eight-year-old and the thirty-nine-year-old characters also encounter their seventy-year-old self, who is pleased with the changes they made.

If your eight-year-old self visited you today what would they think of how you are? What would excite them or disappoint them and what would they want to change about the way you relate to others?

Now what if your eighty-year-old self visited you today? (Or, if you are eighty go for your ninety-year-old self.) What would they say about how your life will be in the future if you keep doing what you are doing now? Would they be pleased with the way your life and relationships are turning out or would they wish you to do something differently today?

trying something different

Didn't someone once say that the definition of madness is doing the same thing over and over again expecting a different result? We will only be prepared to change when we realise that we won't get the result we want by carrying on doing the same things that we are doing today.

For example:

- Mike, who has had four failed engagements, is likely to have another unless he can change his pattern of relating.
- Leigh, who has been sacked or let go from ten jobs, is unlikely to be able to hold down a steady job until she accepts why she keeps getting into these situations and does something about it.
- Jay, who doesn't have any close friends, isn't going to until he realises that his aggressive and critical manner makes people feel threatened and does something to change it.
- Rachel, who is exhausted because she pours herself out helping other people but never accepts help herself, will continue to feel like that until she can see how she is contributing to her own problem and learns when and how to say 'no' and how to receive as well as give.

We can all work at becoming more harmonious. We can all change. To change we need to retune, retrain and refocus.

1. retune

Once we can see whether we are off-key and whether we are flat or sharp (or a bit of both), and the impact that is causing for us, we can then set about the business of retuning.

Retuning doesn't often happen overnight. It is normally a process. For some of us it may be a very long and difficult process and we may need professional and expert help (and that is OK). For many of us, however, it will be less complicated and we will be able to make the adjustments ourselves – perhaps with the support and help of others.

Look back with fresh eyes

We now know that we constructed our complex wiring system in the past because of how we perceived and understood what happened to us and the relationships we had. But that was our perception, and it may or may not have been right.

When looking back at a certain event, relationship or phase in our lives it can help to try and look back objectively. This may help us to change our feelings about it. Sometimes it can be like a jigsaw puzzle. Did I have all the pieces? Could I see the whole picture? Or did I make assumptions about myself or the other person that weren't totally true?

For example, Bella's parents got divorced when she was five. She remembers the day that her dad left. It was the day after her mum had yelled at her for breaking a vase and deep down Bella always thought that it was her fault that dad had gone. In her mind he left because she'd been naughty. Many years later, when she was thirty, she had a heart-to-heart with her mum who told her the real reasons about why the marriage broke up. It was nothing to do with Bella. Her mum and dad had been growing apart for years and her dad had been offered a job in Australia and her mum hadn't wanted to go. They decided it would be better to go their separate ways. Knowing the truth didn't take away the pain of her parents' break-up but it did help her to start letting go of the false assumptions she'd made about herself.

In Bella's example she was able to ask her mum about the facts. That may not be possible all the time. But we can think back and work out whether there was another way of looking at the past or another explanation for what happened. It may help to talk it through with a close friend – do they think your assumption sounds likely or would they have seen it another way?

Take responsibility

It can be tempting to lay the blame for all our problems on other people or external events. It absolves us of any responsibility. We are like this because of them. We are like this because of some event that happened to us.

I had a Science teacher at school and whenever he lost anything he would say, 'They've taken it …' I would picture this invisible army of people in white coats coming in the middle of the night and removing his test tubes and Bunsen burner.

It's easy to blame 'them', whoever 'they' may be. The truth is more complex. There will be things that happened to us that were beyond our control but there will also be things that happened to us where we did have a choice – a choice as to how to act or respond.

Mandy and Tracy were in the same class at school. They both loved playing soccer but they weren't the most talented pair on the field. One day, their coach agreed to let them play in a mini-league game. They were hopeless. Their team mates and their coach gave them a really hard time afterwards and blamed the loss of the match on them. Mandy got mad and refused to play ever again. Tracy went home and asked her older brother to help her improve. She practised with him every weekend and the next term she was back in the team and much better. Two girls in the same situation but they made different choices.

Leroy and Aidan were both seventeen when they got their respective girlfriends pregnant. Neither of them had any money and both were planning to go to university. Both girls were keen to keep the babies. Leroy decided to support his girlfriend and he gave up his place at college so that he could get a job and help her out. Aidan didn't feel ready for a baby and persuaded his girlfriend to have an abortion. He continued with his career plans as before. Two boys in the same circumstances but they made different choices.

We will have had a choice in our relationships too. Relationships are never one sided. There is always a dynamic that we will have played our part in.

One of my old bosses often left things to the last minute (sometimes well after the last minute). I could have told him I wasn't going to help because he was too late, it was past the time to go home or that I had to work on another project that also needed finishing. But I wouldn't do any of those things – instead, I would help him. Why? Because I am good in a crisis and I enjoyed the affirmation I got from helping rescue the situation. And also because I often left things to the last minute too. If I forced him to change I was going to have to change too.

A sign of maturity is recognising our own choices and taking responsibility for them. It is also about recognising our impact on others.

Laurence realises that his behaviour has led to breakdowns of relationships from the casual to the significant:

> I am an extremely impatient person and I am far too aware that this stems from my innate insecurity – a need to be constantly 'recognised', 'applauded' and 're-affirmed'. This has had a devastating effect on my ability to give of myself to others. For example, I wasn't good at listening patiently or allowing others to interrupt 'my' order or routine for the day. It's a hard journey to learn to 'lay yourself down' for others in a healthy sense and not be the victim. But I am learning to change and to take responsibility for my behaviour.

In our survey, only 50 per cent of people said that they were very aware of their impact on others. It is hard to take responsibility for our actions if we don't know the impact that we are having. Part of retuning is to recognise how we come across to others and where we are causing hurt, difficulties and problems for them.

I realised that when I didn't share my feelings with people I came across as aloof and arrogant. My reactions were sharp. It made others feel rejected and closed off from me. When I realised the impact I was having on others I wanted to change.

Letting it go

In order to change I had to let go of my old way of relating. I had to forgive myself for allowing myself to become like that and then I had to find a way of becoming more harmonious.

Whether others caused our faulty wiring or we helped cause it ourselves we have a choice. We can keep living with the regrets, the pain or the guilt or we can seek to let them go. Letting go of pain isn't easy – 49 per cent in the survey said they found it difficult.

Letting go doesn't mean forgetting or denying that painful things happened or that we did things wrong. It means forgiving 'them' and ourselves. It means bringing the cycle of blame to an end. It means drawing a line in the sand and saying, 'that was then and this is now'. It means saying we will no longer live under the shadow of the pains of the past. It means not letting our past hurt define us and it means not being bitter, revengeful or resentful.

Forgiveness is something we can offer ourselves. We can forgive ourselves for poor or bad choices we have made. Where we know we have caused hurt ourselves we can ask the other person for forgiveness (if they are still around and it is appropriate). If we are believers we can ask God for his forgiveness.

Forgiveness is also something that we can offer to others. That may not be easy. We may not feel like it but if we can bring ourselves to make the choice to forgive we will have taken a major step in the retuning process. (We will talk more about how we forgive in Chapter 13.)

Being able to show gratitude and appreciation can also help the healing process. As we focus on the good stuff – as we thank and appreciate others for being in our lives, for helping us and for loving us – we build stronger wires. As we look back we may even find things in the bad stuff to be thankful for too.

I can now look back on my time at boarding school and be grateful for all the different activities I was able to try, for some of the friendships I made and for the confidence that I gained during my time there. It is said that 'every cloud has a silver lining' and we just need to try and find it if we can.

Louisa managed to discover an up-side when she went through a hard patch a couple of years ago:

Months into being bed-bound with severe flu-like symptoms, no energy, and cracking, hangover-like headache I was diagnosed with ME. I am a real people person and an extrovert and day after day I was home alone on my sofa with no one to talk to and most days not well enough to get down the stairs of my flat. Soon enough I was struggling with the grey cloud of depression which I'd never had and didn't understand. I shut people out, would cry for most of the day and didn't want to eat or speak very much – it was quite a dark and miserable time.

The depression didn't last very long – and eventually the ME went also. But I am actually thankful that I had that experience as I know a few people close to me who suffer from depression and like many people I never understood it. Having had a brief glimpse into it I have a real empathy for those who suffer with it and no longer feel frustrated at their behaviour.

mining for silver

Look back at the timeline you drew of your life. What can you be grateful for in the good things and in the bad?

You may find it helpful to write and thank someone in your life and express gratitude for all that they've given you. Or you may want to list the things you are grateful for in a journal.

2. retrain

If retuning is recognising and letting go of the faulty wiring causing us to go off-key then retraining is the process of building new and healthier connections.

Retraining takes time and effort. It means finding new ways of behaving and responding that may not feel 'normal' to us. If we have a tendency to be 'sharp' it may be about reaching out to others, doing more to consider their needs and desires, accepting constructive criticism and understanding how our behaviour makes others feel. If we have a tendency to be 'flat' it may be about learning to hear the truth from others, taking risks to be known and stepping into our full potential.

Change rarely feels comfortable. A new way of doing something can feel odd at first. It's a bit like replacing an old pair of comfortable shoes with some new ones that don't feel quite right. They say it takes at least eight weeks to change a pattern of behaviour. That's why we need to keep our focus on the goal and to picture how things will be different if we do step out of our comfort zone and try a new way.

We can only make those changes through relationship with other people. We learn and grow as we relate with others. Hopefully, they learn and grow too. In fact, as we change others will have to change. Any change in us changes the dynamic in a relationship.

For example, if I'd said 'no' to the boss who left everything to the last minute he would have had to do it himself or find a different way of working. Changing my behaviour would have changed the status quo.

Learning from others

Learning from others can be difficult if we are used to being independent and relying on ourselves. It involves us building the bridge, taking off the prickly coat and showing our humanity to another. It involves risk but it is in that risk that we find growth.

There are many ways in which we can learn from others: we can seek expert help, read books or attend courses; we can seek feedback from a boss, a friend, a mentor or a spouse; and we can watch how others model harmonious living.

Ask the expert. Some of us may need expert or specific help to overcome some of our faulty wiring. If you have suffered or still do suffer from abuse, if you suffer from depression, severe anxiety, addictions, eating disorders or suicidal thoughts, or if you have severe problems with anger then it is vital that you seek expert support if you haven't done so already. Your GP should be able to help refer you to someone who can help you. I have also listed some relevant organisations and their websites at the end of the book.

You may also benefit from help if you are having difficulty moving forward with some particular issue. If you are finding it especially hard to deal with a bereavement; are struggling to say 'no' and finding it impossible to impose boundaries; fear commitment; suffer from stress, low self-esteem or anger issues; find it hard to cope with a particular relationship or situation; or want to improve your marriage or parenting but don't know how, then you may benefit from finding a counsellor, a cognitive behavioural therapist, a support group, a course or a book that deals with that specific issue.

There can be a certain stigma attached to asking for help. But seeking help does not mean that you are a failure. Quite the opposite – it means that you are taking a positive and courageous step towards helping yourself and improving your relationships. I can promise you that if you do seek help you won't be the first and you won't be the last. The year after my brother died I was struggling with chronic fatigue and my GP put me on anti-depressants. I remember being amazed but also reassured when other people I knew admitted that they had taken or were taking them.

Feedback. In many cases we'll be able to make progress and get support from within our existing network of family, friends and others. People often give us feedback anyway without us even realising it. When others criticise us, praise us, compliment us or react to us they are giving us feedback. If we tune into these reactions we can learn from them. We can ask ourselves, 'Is there truth in what they are saying?' and if there is we can learn from it.

We can also deliberately ask for feedback. We can ask someone we trust what in our behaviour pushes them away or draws them closer? We can tell a friend or a spouse that we are trying to improve in a certain area, seek their help and support and ask them to let us know how we are doing. If we have children we can give them permission to feed back to us too. Or we can ask our boss to give us constructive criticism or advice at work.

At one time Darren was working really hard – too hard – trying to get promoted and recognised at work:

I kept putting in the hours and the effort but found I wasn't getting anywhere. This had a negative impact on my relationships, which I started neglecting. I really respected my boss at the time and so I started watching his approach to work to see what I could learn. I also asked his advice. He suggested that I make more time for sport and my relationships and reassured me that finding a good work balance would not hinder my chances of promotion. In fact it would probably help. His encouragement enabled me to make the changes I needed and I am a much calmer person now and all my frustration has gone.

We may want to seek out a mentor to help us. Someone we can confide in, someone who is further along in the journey than we are and someone we will allow to ask us the difficult questions.

Seven years ago I started seeing a couple who agreed to act as mentors to me (they were a little older than me and a lot wiser). I would see them for a meal once every six weeks or so and they would ask me about work, life and relationships. As I grew to know and trust them I would discuss issues that I was struggling with and ask their advice. They would listen, encourage and challenge me. They would also share from their own experiences. When David and I got married, we started to see them together and we still do. They are good friends and we have learnt and benefited so much from that relationship.

Watch and learn. When an orchestra tunes up the musicians all listen and tune to the oboe. It is the same with us. We can learn to be more harmonious by being around harmonious people.

For the last seven years I have worked with a couple called Nicky and Sila Lee. They co-authored *The Marriage Book* and *The Parenting Book* and have created some excellent courses on marriage and parenting, which are now run world-wide. Over the years we built a very close working relationship and friendship and I learnt a great deal from them. I learnt from their teaching but more than that I learnt from watching them. I would watch how they treated each other, how they dealt with difficulties and how they related to people. Through their example and also through their friendship, support and encouragement I was able to become more in tune with myself and with others.

looking for your oboe

Who are the people in your life who help you to become more 'in tune'?

What is it about them that is different? What could you learn from them?

If you don't know any, why might this be?

How are your relationships affected by the company you keep at the moment?

How could you develop some more harmonious relationships?

Positive inputs

As well as learning from others, we also need to build healthy connections. We don't enter those relationships demanding or seeking to be loved. We enter them seeking to love and to be loving. Relationships are a two-way street. Some of us need to learn to give more but equally there are some of us who need to learn to receive.

The paradox of relationships is that as we stop focusing on ourselves – as we learn to give and to love, as we care for another – we often experience love and friendship in return. And as we build those healthy connections we will often find we grow and learn to love better.

My friendship with Amanda, my mentor couple and my working relationship with Nicky and Sila were all examples of healthy connections that helped me to grow. So too was my marriage to David. With David I felt I could be truly myself. For years I had struggled with feelings of 'not belonging' but with David it was different. His love helped me to feel more secure. He seemed to love me for myself and I didn't have to pretend to be anything else. And loving him back helped me to become less selfish and self-absorbed. For many people a close friendship or a healthy marriage can bring great healing.

Dr Sue Johnson, in *Hold Me Tight*, writes:

> When we learn to foster safe, loving interactions with our partners and can integrate new experiences into models that affirm our connections with others, we step into a new world. Old hurts and negative perceptions from past relationships can then be put away and not allowed to orchestrate our way of responding to our lovers.

As we trust others, as we reach out in love, as we open ourselves up to learn, and as we take responsibility for our actions we will grow, and become more in tune.

Learn from yourself

We can also learn from ourselves. We can challenge the way we think and behave. We don't have to hold onto the faulty wiring we formed, we can override our old beliefs with new ones.

When we react a certain way, or feel a certain way, we can stop and ask ourselves why. What is it that I am telling myself about this event? Is what I'm thinking realistic or is it irrational and off-key – based on my faulty wiring?

In the 1950s Albert Ellis came up with his ABC theory (part of the foundation of Cognitive Behavioural Therapy) to help explain how changing our thinking can help change our emotions:

- **A – is the action or event that causes us to start feeling or thinking something, for example, a friend walks past me in the street without saying hello.**
- **B – is the belief that causes us to interpret that event in a certain way, for example, he doesn't like me. I'm unlovable.**
- **C – is the consequence of our belief – how we feel and react; for example, I feel depressed and angry and from now on I intend to avoid that friend.**

What if we could challenge B – our belief about the event? What if, rather than telling ourselves that he is deliberately avoiding us, we consider the fact that he hasn't noticed us because he is too busy thinking or worrying about something else? Maybe he is under a lot of stress. Maybe he needs a friend right now.

Having changed our belief, C may now be different. Perhaps instead of feeling cross we now feel concerned and decide that we'll call our friend tonight to check that he is OK.

It is worth challenging ourselves when we are feeling anxious, angry or sad. What has caused it? What am I telling myself about that event? Am I telling myself the truth or am I just listening to the old tapes that play in my head? Is there another way to think about this? What would X think if it happened to them (where X is someone whose opinion you would trust)? Why am I behaving or reacting like this? What feelings or fears am I experiencing? Am I feeling unloved, rejected or insignificant? Are my responses to do with what has just happened or are they do with the past? Who does this person remind me of? Was my behaviour off-key and if so how can I make amends?

As an adult Lucy would often over-react to criticism or to comments that weren't even meant as criticism:

I cannot remember my mum having one single positive response to something that I bought or chose from the age of about thirteen. She was always critical. This was not always expressed openly, but more subtly, so the true meaning had to be interpreted. If I bought a new skirt she would say, 'Hmmm, did you try it in a bigger size?' (Meaning: I think it's too tight.) If I came home with a new top I'd hear, 'Did they have it in any other colours?' (Meaning: that colour doesn't suit you.) 'What are you going to use that for?', 'Did you choose that on purpose?', 'Do you have the receipt? Can you still take it back?'

Consequently, I learned to be very good at interpreting implied criticism and to expect it from her at all times. As an adult I developed an aggressive response to mask the hurt that I felt and I would become wound up by her within minutes of first contact, even when she was no longer intending to criticise or question. I would also do this with other people. I admit I wasn't the easiest person to be with at times and have had to learn to challenge my thoughts and ask 'what are they really saying?'

To learn from ourselves takes time and practice. We need to give ourselves that time. It means being still and having time for reflection.

For a while I used to ask myself the same question every night when I went to bed: 'How did I do in my relationships today?' I would run over the day in my head and reflect on whether I'd upset anyone, interrupted them, ignored them, been rude or done something else that I wasn't proud of. I'd then think about how I could make it up to them or do better next time.

But sometimes we need to try and turn off the tapes in our head and be still and be silent. It is in that quiet and reflective place that we can hear the still, small voice that knows us more than we know ourselves.

challenging our thoughts

Try finishing these statements to try and locate some of your internal beliefs. Write without thinking about it too much.

I am

People are

The world is

Life is

To be loved I need to be

To be accepted I need to be

To have significance I need to be

If you hurt me I will

Look at your responses. What are you telling yourself?
Are your responses rational? If you are not sure, try thinking what you would think if someone said to you what you've just written down. Would you think that sounded normal? If not, how could you challenge what you have written?

an ABC example

Think of the last time you were sad, anxious or angry.
What was A – the event that caused it?

What was B – the belief that you told yourself about it?

What was C – the consequence in terms of your feelings and behaviour?

Look at what you wrote for B. Is there another way to think about this? Brainstorm some ideas. How could these new beliefs alter C – your reaction?

----

3. refocus

As we retune and retrain we can then turn our attention to refocusing. We refocus when we focus on the present instead of living in the past. When we refuse to give airtime to any thoughts that begin with 'I wish I had …' or 'If only …' we learn to accept the past and realise that we can't change it. We learn to accept the good and the bad of the past and to see that both will have shaped how we are today.

We refocus when we take the focus off ourselves and place it on others: when we learn to care about them, their needs, desires, hopes and fears; and when we give up our right to be loved and instead concentrate on loving. We refocus when we reach out to others and help them to retune, retrain and refocus too. We refocus when we use our experiences to help and encourage others. So, as well as being mentored, we can mentor others. If we have been through a tough time or had bad experiences we can help others going through a similar experience. In the giving we will continue to grow and to learn.

We refocus when we are authentic – when who we are on the outside is a true reflection of who we are on the inside; when we allow people to see us, to know us and to love us; and when we feel safe enough to drop our defences and cut the faulty wires.

When we can do that we are free to be ourselves. Free to love, laugh and live.

tips: how to thrive (not just survive) with your family (for those who struggle)

Make contact. Don't leave it to them to initiate – keep in regular touch. Remember to celebrate big occasions and be there for them during the difficult times.

Show interest. Be interested in their lives, whether it is your teenage nephew or your great-granny. Ask them about things that they care about and don't assume you know everything there is to know about them. They may just surprise you.

Visits. If you are staying with a relative or they are staying with you, plan the length of stay so it isn't too long for either of you. You want to be able to leave each other while you're both still smiling.

Accept the things that won't change. Acknowledge the things that annoy you about your relatives and make a choice to either ignore them or confront them – don't stew on them.

Discuss expectations. Family misunderstandings often happen when we have different expectations. Talk about things such as how often you expect to see each other, to speak to each other or to be involved in each other's lives. Discuss things like Christmas, holidays, old age and funerals. Don't just assume that you know what the other person wants or is planning.

Don't judge, criticise or offer unsolicited advice. Just because you're related doesn't mean you can say anything you like. Be kind – even if they aren't kind back (they may eventually catch on!). And if you can't be kind, be civil, especially at family occasions.

Say the nice things now. Don't wait until someone is no longer around to patch up an old wound or misunderstanding – do it now. And remember to mention the good stuff too – don't just think it.

dealing with tricky issues

10. the challenge of differences

"Tigger is all right, really," said Pooh lazily.

"Of course he is," said Christopher Robin.

"Everybody is really," said Pooh. "That's what I think," said Pooh. "But I don't suppose I'm right," he said.

"Of course you are," said Christopher Robin.

A. A. MILNE, *THE HOUSE AT POOH CORNER*

You can do what I cannot do
I can do what you cannot do
But together we can do great things.

MOTHER TERESA

a world without clones

Thankfully, for the moment at least, there are no human clones in the world. Each one of us is unique. There may be times when we look at our child, sibling, work colleague, friend, partner or neighbour and think that it would be a lot easier if they were just like us. But if they were life would be very dull, wouldn't it?

Bill Hybels, in *Fit to Be Tied*, writes this about his wife: 'Many times I was tempted to take out a hammer and chisel and reshape Lynne into a replica of me. I even tried a little now and then. Thank God I didn't succeed. I realise that one of me is plenty in our home.'

In the last few chapters we've looked at how we have different families, backgrounds, rules, values and life experiences and how we will have developed our sensitive buttons differently. But there are plenty of other ways in which we are different. We look different. We may be different ages. We may have had different educations, training and work experiences. We will have different opinions, personality traits, abilities, skills, resources, prejudices, beliefs, expectations, habits, interests, hobbies, tastes and preferences. We may have different communication styles or ways of dealing with conflict. Our gender or sexual orientation may be different. We may have different faiths, come from different cultures, interpret events differently and look at things in different ways.

Those differences can bring spice, colour and variety to our lives and relationships. But they can also bring challenges, difficulties and conflict. The closer we get to someone the more potential there is for these differences to cause tensions and problems.

If I open a magazine and read about a man who is obsessively tidy, enjoys early mornings, internalises his thoughts and feelings, and is logical and inflexible I may be mildly interested in the fact that he is the complete opposite of me but his differences won't matter to me personally. But what if that same man becomes my new flat mate or work colleague? Now, all of a sudden, those differences are going to affect me. That's why, when we experience differences within a team, a couple or a family, there is so much potential for conflict. This is particularly true when we do something with each other, such as an activity or a project, or when we have to make a decision together. Then we have to find a way of bringing our two worlds together (without causing a collision).

What if my new work colleague and I have to work on an assignment together? We will each bring our different personality traits, approaches, beliefs and attitudes to the project. He may want to hold meetings first thing in the morning, come with data and charts for me to look at, tell me his conclusions and demand that everything is kept in very tidy files. I, on the other hand, would rather meet in the afternoon when I'm more awake and brainstorm ideas rather than study data. I would be keen to discuss lots of options and I would find it easier to be creative with a bit of mess and disorder around me. In other words, I may well be his idea of a nightmare!

What happens next will depend on our attitudes to differences and conflict. Will one of us go along with the other person's way of doing things? Will one of us sulk or throw our toys out of the pram? Or will we find a way of making our differences work for us? Will we find a time to meet and a working approach that suits us both? Will we manage to harness his logical approach with my intuitive one to create something much better than either of us would have come up with on our own?

That's the thing with differences. We can allow them to alienate us and cause tensions between us or we can embrace them and learn to appreciate them.

In our survey 17 per cent of people said they don't find it easy to understand or appreciate people who are different from them and 24 per cent said they find it hard to share their space with others.

But unless we are hermits we are constantly going to come into contact with people who are different from us. The challenge is to be able to see that as a positive rather than as a negative.

recognising differences

The world wouldn't just be a duller place if we were all the same, it would also be a far less efficient one. My fictitious work colleague and I are able to get more done if and when we combine our strengths. A football team wouldn't be much use if it was only made up of defensive players; a choir wouldn't have much range or depth if it only had sopranos in it; and a work team wouldn't get much completed if it didn't have anyone interested or good at working with the detail. We need each other. None of us can do or be everything and none of us have all the answers, even if we think we do sometimes.

To be authentic from the inside out we need to be aware of our own strengths and weaknesses and the impact these have on others. We need to play to our strengths where we can and encourage others to play to theirs. We need to understand our weaknesses, accept the ones that we cannot change and try and improve the ones we can.

We also need to learn to read the moment. There will be times when we need to step up and use our strengths but there will also be times when we will have to step out of our comfort zones and do things we don't like doing or aren't necessarily any good at.

For example, Jim is good with accounts but his two flatmates aren't. Jim isn't much use in the kitchen. It would make a great deal of sense if Jim looked after the flat finances and the others concentrated on something they enjoy doing. Perhaps they could do more of the cooking. But what if the guy who does most of the cooking is ill one day? Jim would need to step in and do it. He may even find he is better at it than he thinks. But even if he isn't he'll need to give it a try.

Clare never likes to raise her voice. She is very chilled and laid back and hates having to be assertive. But Clare is a single mum and sometimes she has to move out of her comfort zone and do things she doesn't like doing. If her toddler does something dangerous she needs to speak loudly and firmly to get him to stop. If he misbehaves she is the one who has to discipline him. In these instances Clare has to operate out of her comfort zone. Over a period of time she'll probably get better at it and more used to doing it.

Simon is the boss of a company. He doesn't like the limelight much. He is naturally shy and would rather take a back seat. But his company is going through some difficulties. Staff morale is low and there are problems with the suppliers. If Simon wants to turn the situation around he may need to jump into the front seat for a while and become more visible. He may need to take time to talk to the staff and re-envision them. He will need to address the issues with the suppliers and take a firm stand where needed. He will have to do things that he doesn't normally like doing.

knowing me, knowing you

Have a look at the following list of preferences. There are no right or wrong answers. Mark on the line with an 'M' for 'me' where you would naturally put yourself. You may want to think of someone else you know well and guess where they might be on the line – use another initial for them. (You may then want to check with them whether you were right.)

As you go through the list, think about the strengths and weaknesses of your preferences and of the other person's.

How are you different?

What tensions if any do your differences cause between you?

When and how do your differences help you both?

ISSUES

Money

Spend, spend, spend .... Save for a rainy day

Risk

Seek adventure .... Seek safety

People

Loves own company .... Needs people

Best time of day

Early bird .... Night owl

Tidiness

A place for everything .... Everything in its mess

Disagreements

Throw the toys out of the pram .... Keep the peace

Focus

Attention to detail .... Sees the big picture

Relaxation

Go out .... Be at home

Punctuality

Always early .... Always in a rush

Planning

Always stick to plans . . . . .Plans, what plans?

Organisation

Organised . . . . .Disorganised

Decisions

Spontaneous . . . . .Cautious

Family

See often . . . . .See rarely

Friends

A million and one . . . . .One in a million

TV

On all the time . . . . .Don't have one

Talking

Chatterbox . . . . .Quiet

Change

Enjoy change . . . . .Resist change

Initiative

Like to initiate . . . . .Like to respond

Adapted from a similar exercise in The Marriage Book, *page 126*

some other key areas of difference

If you have ever done a personality or psychometric test or a work style profile you will already have an idea of the strengths and weaknesses of your particular preferences. If you haven't, they can be fun to do. There are lots of free ones online that you can access.

The thing to remember with these tests is that they don't define you. The danger can be that we do one, read the results and then think, 'That is who I am – I can't change.' Or worse, 'That is how I am so don't expect me to be any different.' (Remember Jim, Clare and Simon – there were times when they had to change, even if it was only for a season.)

Our preferences show us how we prefer to behave and act. These are the ways that make us feel most comfortable and safe. But they are not rigid boxes that you have to stay in. Don't let them constrain you.

Listed below are some other behaviour preferences, described in their extremes. As I mention each one you may want to work out which one *most* represents you and think of the impact that your behaviour may have on people who are different to you. And think about how their behaviour affects you.

Expansion vs consolidation

If you prefer expansion you like to experience new things. You are always pushing the boundaries. You like taking on new projects or learning new skills and you tend to grasp ideas more quickly than others. You get bored easily. You prefer starting projects to finishing them.

If you prefer consolidation you like to do things competently. You like to develop structures. You are conscientious. You are slower at picking things up or grasping new ideas and are more reluctant to try new things. But once you have got going you like to master skills well and do things to a high standard.

Practical vs imaginative

If you prefer being practical you are likely to think things through. You use your common sense. You like being systematic. You say what you mean. Your feet are firmly on the ground. You see the trees not the forest.

If you prefer being imaginative you are likely to prefer concepts and creativity. You think around things. You dream and imagine. Your speech is more indirect. Your head is in the clouds. You see the forest not the trees.

Optimism vs pessimism

If you are an optimist you see the best in everyone and everything. You downplay difficulties and trouble and emphasise the silver lining in every cloud. You want to cheer people up and make everyone feel better. You may find it hard to empathise with people who are struggling.

If you are a pessimist you spot the pitfalls and problems in every situation. You see the risks and know why something won't work. You value realism and believe that people should embrace the negative, not deny it. You are a great person to have a moan with but you may not be first choice as a party companion.

Control vs spontaneity

If you prefer control you like to know what is going on. You like to plan things, to have diaries, 'to do' lists, and agendas to keep on track. You like rules and you like to make decisions. You want to get things done. You are structured, traditional and hate surprises. You prefer to work first and play later.

If you prefer to be spontaneous you like to go with the flow. You prefer to wait and see. You like to be flexible and open to new possibilities. You aren't a great one for rules and you don't like anything that is set in stone. You can be a bit disorganised, unpredictable and carefree. You prefer to play first and work later.

When we understand our preferences and those of the people around us it helps us to see how we can complement and work with each other.

The following quiz will help to illustrate that further. It focuses in on two categories we haven't looked at yet. It will help you to work out whether your preference is to be more outgoing or introspective and whether you prefer to operate more from your heart or from your head.

the colour quiz

At the end of the quiz you'll be able to work out what 'colour' profile most represents you – red, blue, yellow or green – and you'll find out what that may mean for the way you relate to others who are different to you.

Look at the questions in Part I and Part II. Choose the answer that *most* represents you. Don't think too hard, just go for the one that resonates the most. There are no right or wrong answers. In Part I count up the number of As and Bs you score. In Part II count up the number of 1s and 2s you score.

Part I

1. Do you find it easy to talk to people you don't know?
   Yes – A
   Not really – B

2. You find it easier to work:
   In a quiet place with no or few people – B
   With the radio on and loads of people around – A

3. When in a group you would naturally want to:
   Speak more – A
   Listen more – B

4. When someone asks your opinion you:
   Tend to answer straight away – A
   Prefer time to think about the answer – B

5. You would prefer to spend your birthday:
   With a handful of close friends – B
   At a huge surprise party – A

6. After a discussion which of the following might you say to yourself:
   'Why did I say that?' – A
   'Why didn't I say something?' – B

7. You think up better ideas:
   On your own – B
   In a group – A

Did you score more As or Bs in Part I?

Part II

1. You enjoy helping someone:
   Think through a problem – 1
   Work through their feelings – 2

2. You tend to write:
   Expressive explanatory emails – 2
   Short, snappy ones – 1

3. When you are in a stressful situation you are:
   Calmer than most – 1
   More stressed than most – 2

4. You make decisions mainly:
   With your head – 1
   With your heart – 2

5. You like to deal with people:
   Compassionately – 2
   Fairly – 1

6. You tend to be:
   More tactful than truthful – 2
   More truthful than tactful – 1

7. It is more important that we:
   Get things done – 1
   Get on – 2

Did you get more 1s or 2s in Part II?

What colour are you?

If you had more As and more 2s you are yellow.
If you had more Bs and more 2s you are green.
If you had more As and more 1s you are red.
If you had more Bs and more 1s you are blue.

Remember, these show your preference. They don't mean you have to or do behave like this all the time, they just show what you prefer to do. Don't worry if you have done something like this before and think you should be another colour. You may have changed if you were on the borderline last time and it also depends on how you are feeling on the day. However, if you are totally convinced the colour doesn't sit right look at the explanations at the end and work out the one that suits you best.

welcome to Hotel Colour-fornia!

Before we look at what it means to be each colour why not have a go at this exercise. This is a great one to try as a group. Split into teams of the same colour and then work through the following questions together. Give yourselves ten minutes and time it. Or, if you are on your own you can still do it and could compare your answers with friends who have also answered the questions.

Take a blank piece of paper. Your job is to design a brand new hotel. Money is no object. Think about:

a) what it would look like
b) what activities would take place
c) what facilities it would have
d) how it would be structured

Write down your thoughts on the piece of paper. (This exercise works equally well if you replace 'hotel' with business, school, community hall or church. Pick something that would be relevant to you or your group.)

When you've done that, carry on reading.

Let me guess

David and I used to do this exercise on a relationships course that we ran for five years. Before we got each of the different coloured teams to feed back we would try and pre-empt what they were going to say, and 80 per cent of the time we were pretty close.

See if it works with you.

The Red hotel

The reds normally have big plans. Huge plans. The bigger the better. It would be great if the hotel could be replicated to become a massive global chain or could attract amazing clients from all over the world. They want lots of guests and lots of profit. And they want to be in charge. They want a strong leadership team running their place, headed up by themselves. In fact, they may even want to name the hotel after themselves as well. They want an award-winning architect to design the building. There would be managers to look after all the different areas of hotel life and all the staff would have excellent training. The facilities would be world-class and there would be lots of them.

When we did this exercise on the course we would also guess how the exercise had been for the team and what they'd put on their bit of paper. The red team will often have struggled to listen to each other. Too many chiefs and not enough indians in this group! The piece of paper may well have the name of the hotel written on it and would include numbers to do with size: the size of staff, number of guests, number of swimming pools, projected profit etc.

The Yellow hotel

The yellows are less interested in figures and competitiveness. They want to make sure their hotel is FUN! They want to make sure that their hotel has great entertainment and social activities. There will be round-the-clock activities for people to sign up for. They will have welcome parties and lots of opportunities for guests to meet each other. No one would ever have to be lonely in this resort. Staff will be on hand to help entertain people and keep the party going. There will be bars, clubs, restaurants and activity centres where people can congregate. Staff will be trained to remember everyone's names and to make sure that they are having an enjoyable time. A key priority will be making sure that this is a great place to work as well as to stay.

The yellow team are likely to have had great fun planning their hotel. They are likely to have drawn pictures on their paper (possibly some smiley faces).

The Green hotel

The greens' hotel is likely to be a smaller affair, where a great deal of attention is paid to individual desires and preferences. Perhaps it is not even a hotel in the conventional sense – it may be more of a spa or a retreat – a place where people can be still and relax. The greens often want to make sure that everyone is included and looked after. There may be therapists, beauticians, fitness trainers and spiritual directors around to help people feel better about themselves. There will be quiet places with no mobile phones or talking. They will make sure that children have their own area and facilities and that there is good access for wheelchair users. The staff will also be well cared for and looked after. The building will also be very environmentally friendly – they want to look after the planet as well as everyone else.

The green team probably achieved less in the time allotted than the other groups. Sometimes they struggled to get anything written down at all. They were too busy listening to each other and making sure that everyone's opinion was heard and included.

The Blue hotel

And finally, the blue hotel. This often won't be as large as the yellow or red hotels but it will be very efficient. The blue team normally like to focus on the nuts and bolts. How does the hotel operate?

What makes it run efficiently? They care about the details. Will there be enough toilets? Is the car park big enough? Can each room have a sea view? Can the hotel be designed so that the guests don't have to see the staff going about their daily duties? What would it cost per head to provide meals? They will be thinking about margins and efficiencies. They care about the details and how things can work most effectively.

No one on the blue team would have been particularly keen to take charge. Their piece of paper is likely to include:

- Very neat, small writing
- Bullet points
- Lists
- Graphs
- Plans or a map
- Anything that indicates how things go together.

The interesting thing

The thing that interests us when we do this exercise is how each team looks at the others with a mixture of puzzlement and amusement. Is that really what you would want a hotel to be like?

Their first answer is 'yes it is'. But then when they look at the other teams and their hotels they realise that theirs isn't so perfect after all. What they would really like is the Hotel Colour-fornia – a hotel that encompasses the best of each of the teams' ideas.

The colours explained

You probably got an idea of how the different colours operate from reading about their different approaches to the hotel design. But here's a summary so that you can see them more clearly:

Reds – love action. They want to achieve and meet personal challenges. They are drivers who like to see things happen. They are determined, focused and competitive. On a bad day others may find them demanding, controlling and impatient.

Yellows – love fun interaction. They like to be noticed. They are sociable, enthusiastic, persuasive and expressive. On a bad day others may find them disorganised, indiscreet and over-excitable.

Greens – love supporting people. They want harmony. They are caring, encouraging, patient and relaxed. On a bad day others may find them slow, dull and worthy.

Blues – love accuracy. They really want to understand things. They are analytical, precise, questioning and deliberate. On bad days others may find them cautious, arrogant and aloof.

I'm probably red with a touch of yellow. David is blue with a touch of green. When I read about reds, particularly on their bad days, I think they sound awful and the others sound great. I've discovered that most people think that about their own colour! We can often become critical with ourselves or with people who remind us of ourselves.

That simple colour quiz looked at just two scales of personality: whether you prefer acting more from your heart or your head and whether you prefer being outgoing or introspective. But hopefully it helped you to see part of the impact that these attitudes may have on others – both for good and for bad. And hopefully it helped you to see the value of other people's preferences and why we all need each other.

Being aware of our natural default or comfort zone also helps us to be more informed about our choices. We can chose to do what we normally do or we can deliberately decide to do something different. For instance, when I write emails my tendency is to write short, snappy ones which are to the point. But I realise that if I send those to someone who is more expressive or sensitive (i.e. a typical yellow or green) they may think that I am upset or that I am being rude. So I have learnt in some instances to rewrite my emails to make them friendlier.

A typical email from me might read: 'Yes the 15th works for me

– see you then.' When I've rewritten it it becomes: 'Thanks so much for your email. I do hope your flu has cleared up and that you are feeling better. It would be lovely to meet you for lunch on the 15th and to hear all about your plans. I look forward to seeing you then. With kind regards, Sarah'

you and your colour

What did you learn from the quiz?

How easy or difficult do you find it to appreciate people who are different from you?

Do you get most irritated by people who are different from you or actually by people who remind you of yourself in some way?

How do you react to people who are different from you at work, in your family or in other groups?

Can you think of any examples of where you have (or could) moderate your preferred approach to accommodate the needs of others?

challenge or celebration

When it comes to differences we can't force people to be like us and it rarely helps if we refuse to change ourselves. If we take the stance that of 'this is how I am and I won't change' we miss the opportunity to learn, to understand and to connect with others.

Charlotte discovered this when she moved into a flat with Zara:

> Zara is a real home maker and loves putting up pictures and would spend time making our flat feel like a home. She was upset by the fact that I did not seem to care where the sofa was or what picture was on the wall. I had never had my own place before and growing up I moved around a lot so never really had a permanent home as such, so it was not that I did not care, it was more that I did not know how to make a home and it was not as important to me. We talked about our different approaches and our honest conversation helped me see my behaviour from her point of view and she was able to understand my behaviour too. I also learnt stuff. Yes ... thanks to Zara I have now come to appreciate the benefits of IKEA storage solutions, scatter cushions and have learnt to hang pictures in straight lines.

If we learn to recognise differences, if we seek to understand, if we are prepared to change where we need to, if we are flexible, if we open our minds and our hearts to others – then differences are more likely to be a source of celebration rather than challenge. And if we learn to appreciate differences then we are less likely to want everyone to be like us.

But if we ignore differences, if we fear them, if we believe we are always right or always wrong or if we are inflexible, and if we refuse to negotiate – then they are likely to lead to conflict (as we'll look at in the next chapter).

11. what is the problem?

When I am angry and want to hit someone – Mum says to take ten deep breaths.
ALEX, AGED SIX

In the middle of every difficulty lies opportunity.
ALBERT EINSTEIN

The aim of argument, or of discussion, should not be victory, but progress!
JOSEPH JOUBERT, FRENCH MORALIST

dealing with the tricky stuff

What happens when the rubber hits the road, when our different views or opinions seem insurmountable, when we disagree, when we argue, when we lock horns, when we get hurt, annoyed, frustrated or upset and when we fall out with people or they fall out with us?

The chances are that there is someone in your life who is causing you a little grief every now and again, or maybe even a lot of grief most of the time. Like it or not, conflict is an inevitable part of relating. Any relationship, whether it's between a husband and wife, parent and child, lovers, ex-lovers, friends, family, work colleagues or team mates will eventually manifest some degree of conflict.

Why is that? Truthfully?

There are three main reasons. First, because most of us are selfish: we want our own way and we struggle when we don't get it. Second, because we misunderstand each other and make wrong assumptions about what the other person has said or done or not said or done. And finally because we are different (as we looked at in the last chapter) and those different experiences, opinions, ways of doing things and expectations can easily become a source of tension between us.

1. We want our own way

Think about it – which do you think about most: your feelings, your wants and your desires or the feelings, wants and desires of others? However loving, compassionate or caring we are the chances are that we still think about ourselves more. It is our natural default. It is like when we look at a photo and the first person we notice is ourselves!

Most of us will feel frustrated, angry or upset if someone or something blocks any goal in life that we might have, no matter what it is. It is like:

- The child who can't have the sweet or toy they've spotted in the supermarket
- The woman who is overlooked for promotion
- The man who is in a hurry when the car in front slows him down
- The ex-husband who feels his wife is being too lenient with the children.

It can be tempting to see the other person as the enemy, even if they are our friend or lover. We want them to change their mind, to make things better, to see the error of their ways or to back down. We can see all the things they are doing wrong and we want them, and perhaps everyone else, to know it. We may find it harder to see where we are failing or not fulfilling our part. Our pride can play a large part in blinding us to the truth.

We probably don't like it if others criticise, challenge, attack or disagree with us. Our instinctive reaction is to protect ourselves and to do all we can to avoid being hurt, exposed or found guilty. It may be that our sensitive buttons are being pushed and we don't like it. That is likely to mean defending ourselves and blaming the other person (where we can). We may even lash out and attack them. Maybe we want them to know what it feels like or perhaps we just want to take the heat off ourselves.

When we know we've done wrong we can be slow to admit it. Our pride is at play again. We don't want others to think badly of us, or think we are a failure. We may fear that they'll withdraw their love or respect and we don't want that.

And even when we are in the clear – when it is the other person that is being unreasonable, unjust and unkind – we cannot be completely absolved. Our reaction can become part of the problem. We may think that our failure to confront them is selfless and kind, but is it? Isn't it more to do with our fear of conflict? And doesn't our failure to act just mean that the problem remains unresolved, our feelings are pushed down and the other person misses the opportunity to grow and to change? And if we over-react and retaliate we are also no longer in the clear. We have joined the other person in escalating the conflict.

The truth is that most of us just want life to be easy and life would definitely be easier if everyone was like us and just did things our way! But all you need is two people thinking like that and you have conflict.

2. We misunderstand each other

The second reason why we have conflict is because we get our wires crossed and don't communicate clearly. We judge the other person's actions. We think we know their motives and what they are thinking or feeling. We can be too quick to jump to conclusions without the facts. For example:

- The sister who thinks her brother is being selfish because he hasn't visited their mother for two months when the truth is that his wife has just had a difficult miscarriage.
- The guy who thinks the girl doesn't like him because she ignored him at the party when actually she does really like him but felt too embarrassed to go up and say 'how are you doing?'

Sometimes it can be like two separate worlds: the imaginary one in our heads where we believe people are thinking and feeling one thing and the real world, where the truth is actually quite different.

Selina tended to avoid confrontation and when people hurt her she always used to think they had done it on purpose:

> But then two months ago I confronted someone for the first time and found out that my imaginings about their opinion of me were totally wrong. It was a very small thing but it really upset me. This woman kept questioning my involvement in helping out with snacks for a children's playgroup and I thought that she did not want me to be involved at all, which made me feel rejected, lonely and sent me into withdrawal. But then one day I picked up the phone and asked her whether she had a problem with me doing the snacks, to which she answered, 'No, of course not!' She just thought that perhaps I was overburdened with a young baby and a toddler and that I felt obliged to do it. It felt great to be able to clear up the misunderstanding and to realise that I had got it wrong. Next time I won't feel so reluctant about confronting someone if I feel hurt.

Conflict has a tendency to escalate and so, if we don't deal with issues, hurt feelings, misunderstandings and different expectations early on – they will grow.

What's this all about? Sometimes we find the conflict we're experiencing today isn't just about what has just happened now. It is also about all the hurts and misunderstandings we had in the past that we didn't express to each other or, perhaps, if we did express them, we didn't resolve them or forgive each other for them.

It may also be that it isn't really about us and the other person at all. We may just be feeling tired, hungry or unwell or have had difficulties with someone else today and our response is more to do with that than anything else. David and I often get snappy with each other if we haven't eaten. We normally find the problem doesn't seem so bad after some food.

Ghosts from the past. Confusion comes too when those ghosts from the past come back to haunt the conflict we're having today (as we saw in the last section). You and I may think we are arguing about one thing but it could be that the feelings I am experiencing as we argue are less to do with you and more to do with someone in the past who upset me, hurt me or let me down. Something in what you are saying or doing now is reminding me of those times and the feelings I felt then are coming flooding back.

Dwayne struggled when he was younger when his parents didn't listen to him. It would make him feel angry and ignored. Sometimes now if he thinks his children aren't listening to him he'll react badly. Yes, he's annoyed with them, but he's also re-feeling those strong feelings that he knows only too well from the past.

Dwayne's problem with his children isn't just about them and him. It is them, him *and* the ghosts of his past.

3. We are different

The third reason we have conflict is because we are all different, as we looked at in the last chapter. We have had different experiences and we have different views, beliefs, personalities, preferences, expectations and fears.

Those differences can confuse us, threaten us and cause tensions between us. The closer we get the more likely we are to become aware of those differences and the more likely they are to cause conflict.

Think about a couple when they're dating. They love their differences – he admires her zest for life, her spontaneity and her extravagance. She thinks he's wonderfully solid and secure. She loves the way he plans and gives such thought to everything he does. Then they get married. Two years later they are arguing. Why? Because he's annoyed that she spends all their money, keeps inviting people round to their flat at the last minute and never seems to relax. She feels suffocated by his constant need to plan and thinks he is really tight with money.

We will often admire people who are different from us. We may sometimes wish we were more like them. But up close and personal those differences can become more difficult to handle.

looking back in anger

Think about the last argument you had or conflict you experienced. Who was it with?

What was it about?

What other underlying reasons may there have been for the conflict you were experiencing?

our attitude to conflict

If conflict is inevitable the question is how do we respond to it? We won't all react the same way.

Let's imagine three scenarios:

197

- Someone at work keeps putting you down, takes credit for some of your ideas and tries to take over some of your projects.
- Your close friends don't invite you to their child's first birthday but you see pictures of the party on Facebook and notice other friends of yours went along.
- Your relative comes to lunch and spends the whole time criticising you, your family and your home.

How do you think you'd react in those imaginary situations? Have a look at the following seven typically unhealthy responses to conflict and see if any of them resonate. You may identify with more than one or you may not see yourself in any of them. Perhaps you have your own unique response system or you're already pretty good at dealing with conflict effectively.

1. Conflict – what conflict?
This is when we experience the situations but we don't like to admit there's a problem and if we do we deny it or downplay it. We push down any negative feelings and keep on smiling and being nice. Perhaps we make excuses for the other person. 'That's just how they are. I'm used to it.' But behind the smile and the denials we do actually care and if we are being honest we'd have to admit that we are hurt and/or annoyed by what they did.

2. Skirting around the problem
This is when we know there's a problem but we don't want to confront the other person directly. Perhaps we are afraid of what they would do or say if we made a fuss. But the thing is, we can't totally let it go so we hint at the problem without being specific. Maybe we secretly hope that they'll realise there's something wrong and that they'll make things better. So with the work colleague we might say something like, 'Oh I thought I was giving that talk.' With the friend we might say, 'Did you do something nice last Sunday?' And with the relative, 'We thought you *liked* stew. We cooked it specially. Now, who would like pudding?'

3. Let them win

If we really hate conflict we may just decide to give in and to let the other person win. It seems the easiest option. Perhaps we say something about how we are feeling but if they are defensive or make a point we don't take it any further.

Perhaps deep down we think we don't deserve any better or that our feelings don't matter. Whatever the reason, we would rather just leave it be. With the colleague we might therefore say, 'I think you would do the talk much better than me. I'm really happy for you to do it.' With the friend, 'I saw some great photos of Jenna's party from Sunday. It was a shame that I couldn't have gone but I imagine you had lots of relatives there.' And with the relative, 'Yes, I'm sorry it's stew again. I wanted to do chicken but the butcher didn't have any … Yes, Johnny can be a bit of a handful … The new carpet colour? Yes, I'm afraid that was my idea. I didn't really know what I was choosing – the man in the shop was very persuasive.'

4. The two-faced approach

This is when we don't tell the person what we're feeling. But we certainly tell everyone else! That way we get to vent our frustrations, receive sympathy but still don't have to confront the person involved. It temporarily makes us feel better but it probably doesn't get us anywhere!

About the colleague: 'John is driving me mad. Did you hear how he spoke to me in that meeting? And I can't believe he took credit for my idea. He is impossible! What is his problem? And you'll never believe what he tried on this afternoon? He suggested he did my talk at the conference. I may as well just give him my job and my life. He doesn't seem to want me to have anything of my own. He makes me so angry!'

About the friend: 'I'm really upset. I thought Pete and Wendy were great friends but they didn't invite me to Jenna's birthday. I saw the photos on Facebook and it looked as if everyone else was there. I couldn't believe it when I found out. I can't work out why I've upset them or why they didn't want me there.'

About the relative: 'Oh I wish I never had to have Anna to lunch ever again. She is so critical of everything. If it isn't the food, it's the family or the state of the house. Why can't she just be appreciative for once?'

5. I'm off!

This is when we refuse to engage with the issue. We don't want to be in difficult situations or around tricky people so we leave or opt out. Our disappearing may be the first time the person knows there was a problem. Or they may never know – you may cut off contact without saying anything.

So we say to the boss: 'I'm handing in my resignation. I am starting another job next month.' To the friend: 'Hello. I'm not here at the moment. But if you want to leave a message please do so after the beep ...' And with the relative: 'I'm not listening to any more of your moaning and complaining. I've had enough! I'm going off for a walk and I hope you'll be gone when I come back.'

6. Attack!

OK, the other person chose the wrong person to mess with. This is when we give as good as we get. Well they did ask for it!

To the colleague we say, 'Stop being such a b******! I've had enough of your put-downs. And just because you couldn't come up with a bright idea if you tried there's no need to steal mine. And there's no way I'm letting you near my talk. My five-year-old nephew could give a better presentation than you.'

To the friend: 'Call yourself a friend. I heard that everyone came to Jenna's birthday party on Sunday. Did you think I wouldn't find out or did you just want to be mean? Well, I've had enough of all this pretence. I don't need friends like you.'

And to the relative: 'Will you just stop with that complaining? You should hear yourself sometime. Moan, moan, moan. It's not surprising you haven't got any friends and if we weren't your family we wouldn't put up with you either. You're lucky we bother!'

7. There's only one winner and it's me!

The final response is when our competitive (or revengeful) juices start flowing at the first sign of conflict. We don't mind how we do it but we're going to win this battle! We want revenge.

So, to the colleague we say, 'I've spoken to the boss and she says there's no way you're doing the presentation and I was relieved to find out that she knows that you keep pinching my ideas. It seems she thinks you are a bit of a nightmare as well.'

To the friend: 'Here's a present for Jenna. I'm so looking forward to her party. When are you going to have one?'

And to the relative: 'Oh look, our new carpet is featured in the latest copy of *Fab House Monthly* (or some such magazine) – how cool is that?'

confession time

Have you ever responded to conflict in any of those seven ways?

If so, what was the response you got? How well did it help you resolve the issue?

Which of the seven have you been on the receiving end of? What was the impact of that?

hide or attack?

I've never been very good at handling conflict (having read this far, you could probably have guessed that). At the first sign of an argument I would hide, run, pacify – anything to try and make it go away. David, on the other hand (being a hot-blooded Spaniard), was rather good at fiery disagreements.

If you look at those seven unhealthy responses again you'll notice that some involve hiding or ignoring the problem and the others involve attacking or over-reacting. When it comes to handling conflict we are all likely to have a natural tendency to avoid or attack.

On the marriage and parenting courses that they teach, Nicky and Sila Lee use a great analogy to describe how many of us can fail to express our anger constructively. They say that some people react to anger like 'hedgehogs'. When they are upset, hurt or angry, they curl up in a little ball, hide their feelings and stick out their spikes (that would be me). Others are like 'rhinos'. They let you know it when they are angry, hurt or annoyed. They put down their head and charge (that would be David then).

In our survey we asked people whether, when they are angry, they tend to make their feelings clear and go on the attack or brood on their feelings and retreat. Forty-one per cent confessed to being more like the rhino and 59 per cent more like the hedgehog.

hedgehog or rhino

Would you describe yourself more as a hedgehog or a rhino when it comes to expressing anger?

What are you like when you have conflict with someone who has a tendency to react in the same way as you?

And with someone different from you?

there must be another way

Thankfully there is. We can learn to deal with conflict effectively. That means neither burying our head in the sand and hoping the issue will magically sort itself out nor going on the attack. We need to recognise the problem and then sort it out constructively. And if we learn to do that we'll find that our relationships will become stronger, healthier and, yes, more authentic.

dealing with the right problem with the right person at the right time in the right way

I've had to learn that having a disagreement, experiencing conflict or feeling angry isn't necessarily a bad thing. In fact, research shows that it is unhealthy not to feel this way at all.

When we get angry, annoyed or upset with someone it is like an alarm system that tells us that something is wrong. If you hear a fire alarm go off it could be because it is warning you of the danger of a fire, or it could be going off because it has an internal fault that needs looking at. Either way it's indicating that something is wrong and that you need to act. When we are angry or upset something is wrong with us, with the other person or with the relationship. Whichever it is, we need to sort it out.

Dealing with the right problem

The real cause of the issue won't always be obvious.

'An argument', says Susan Quilliam in *Stop Arguing, Start Talking*, 'is a bit like a Russian doll, a Chinese puzzle or an onion. It has lots of layers, each tightly wrapped around each other. You may seem to be fighting about one thing, but the real issue may be several layers down. What you think you're arguing about is often not what you're really arguing about at all.'

If you are angry or upset with someone then before you approach them it can help to ask yourself some questions to try and work out what is really going on. Why am I so upset? Is it what they did? Is it what they said? Or something they failed to do? How has their behaviour affected me? Is this a one-off incident or am I annoyed with them for other things too? What is this really about?

Try and think about what triggered the problem. Be specific. The clearer you can be with yourself the easier it will be to explain the issue to the other person. Try and define the impact you experienced. What was the result for you and how did it make you feel? What was the worst thing about it? You may need to go down a few layers to get to the real answer. So, for example, with the troublesome relative in the earlier example the worst thing might be that she is selfish and critical. But then if I dig a little deeper I may think the worst thing is that she doesn't care about me or my feelings. And if I dig a little deeper still I may conclude that the worst thing is that I feel she doesn't approve of me and somehow I am not good enough. Keep digging until you uncover the root cause of your grievance.

Think about whether this is a one-off episode with the person or if similar things have happened before. Is your reaction to do with a recurring dynamic between you or just about this one thing? With the example of the relative the problem is one that keeps happening and because the issue hasn't been dealt with it keeps popping up again and again.

What are we telling ourselves about this issue? It helps to examine our beliefs and assumptions. What conclusion have we drawn about them and about ourselves from this problem? With the example here we may conclude that our relative is a critical and selfish person who can't ever be pleased. We might also conclude about ourselves, that we'll never be good enough.

Having thought through all those questions we should now be able to finish the following sentences:

The trigger was ...
The impact on me was ...
It made me feel ...
The worst thing about it was ...
It happened before when ...
It reinforced my belief that the other person is ...
It reinforced my belief that I am ...

Dealing with the right person

Sometimes, when we stop to reflect, we discover that we are over-reacting. It could be that this incident has reminded us of something or someone else and our anger is misplaced. It could be that our frustration has more to do with ourselves: perhaps the other person's behaviour has reminded us of something in ourselves that we don't like. They may have pushed one of our sensitive buttons.

It is worth asking whether we have been in situations like this before. If we regularly find ourselves in the same kind of conflicts (but with different people) then we may need to take a look at our contribution. What is it about *me* that keeps causing this sort of thing to happen?

Or it could be that we have misunderstood the issue. Perhaps we don't have the full story or we have made assumptions that are wrong. It can help to ask ourselves: have I got the wrong end of the stick? Could there be another explanation for their behaviour that I don't know about? Am I to blame in some way that I haven't realised?

As we reflect we may realise that the problem is not really about them at all or that it isn't such a big deal. We may conclude that we don't need to tell them about it or that it would be inappropriate to do so. If that is the case it is important that we look at our own reaction and learn from it. We will also need to make sure that we let go of any hard feelings towards the other person and don't hold onto them, otherwise those negative feelings will remain and fester and may come back to cause problems later on in our relationship.

However, if we decide our hurt or anger is targeted at the right person and we do want to sort the issue through with them then there are some other things we may want to work through.

First of all, it can help to get perspective. How bad was it? Think of a scale of one to ten where one is a minor irritation and ten is the most serious offence. How would this rate? Try not to make a molehill into a mountain.

It also helps to think of the issue like a jigsaw puzzle. Which pieces have we got in place? The bits we know are: how we felt about the incident, the impact it had on us and the assumptions we made about the other person's intentions; but what we don't know is their side of the story. We don't know what their intentions really were, we don't know how they felt about the incident and we don't know what our impact was on them. We only have half the picture at the moment.

We can try and think about what pieces they may have. It helps to try and put ourselves in their shoes. Just by pretending to be them we may find that there are other ways of looking at the situation that we hadn't seen at first. We may see ways in which we have contributed to the issue. And finally, we may realise we are missing information that we need in order to get the full picture.

Hopefully now we can also complete these statements:

On a scale of one to ten this incident was a ... (give number)

I assume the other person's intentions were to ...

The information I don't have is ...

I believe that my impact on them was ...

The way I contributed to the problem was ...

I know that when I get upset with someone, I can be very good at telling other people about it but not so good at telling the person involved. If we are going to deal with conflict constructively we need to resolve the issue with the person we have the problem with and not with everyone else. Telling other people only causes more problems, especially if they know the person. They are only hearing our side of the story.

Where possible the person who caused the problem should be the first to know. And ideally not with other people present. Put yourself in their shoes and think about it – if you were them, how would you like to hear about it?

There will be exceptions to this, especially if the person is abusive in which case it would not be a good idea to go alone. Also, if it is a work situation your HR department may have a set complaints procedure that you need to follow so it is worth checking that out before you do anything.

If we are unable to resolve the issue with the person or they refuse to address the issues then we may need to involve others and we'll look at how we might do that in the next chapter.

Dealing with it at the right time

I've realised that a lot of the conflict I experience could have been avoided if I had only dealt with an issue when it first happened. Sometimes the problem is caused because I didn't listen to my instinct and I got involved in a situation that I didn't want to be in. Or perhaps I didn't say what I had really meant about something when I should have and, the more I think about it, the more I resent the situation and the more the conflict grows in my head. For example, if my flat mate slams the door when they leave, it is easier to mention it the first time. The fortieth time is harder. By then they are wondering why I never said anything before and I am feeling the annoyance of the other thirty nine times so my response is stronger than it should be. If we mention the small things we can prevent them from becoming big things.

If a problem needs dealing with we need to tackle it as near to the time it happened as possible, while both of us can remember what went on. But before doing anything it is worth checking that we've calmed down. Screaming or shouting at the person may make us feel better in the short term but it won't improve our discussion.

Someone once said, 'Speak when you are angry and you will make the best speech you will ever regret.' If you're feeling mad, take a walk, count to ten (or some may need to keep going to 100), hit the punch bag at the gym, or whatever it takes to let off steam before you go to see the other person.

Dealing with it in the right way

Depending whether we are more like the hedgehog or the rhino we may be tempted to hide from the issue or go on the attack. We need to keep reminding ourselves that neither are good ways of solving issues and both approaches are in fact likely to make the situation worse.

It helps to examine our motives when we want to approach someone about an issue. Are we trying to get revenge, prove ourselves right, make them feel bad or force an apology? If so, we may find the conflict just escalates.

We will have more chance of resolving the problem if we can approach the person with an open mind and an open heart, with the intention of improving and restoring the relationship instead of being set on winning.

Are we able to finish these statements?

The reason I want to discuss it with them is ...
The outcome I am hoping for is ...
The worst thing that could happen is ...

ready to go?

Should we go and approach the other person if we think we are the injured party? Yes. Should we go if we hurt the other person? Yes. How does that work? Well it may be that the other person is a hider. Or they may not realise there is a problem. If either is true we'll be waiting a long time for them to approach us. And if they do realise that there's a problem and they want to sort it out too then they'll be relieved we brought it up. Either way we can't lose.

So now there's no way round it. We've worked out the issue and we know we need to discuss it with the other person. This is normally when many of us want to chicken out. We don't know what to say or how to say it and we worry that we'll make the situation worse. That is very normal – I don't think I've ever met someone who relishes having to have a difficult conversation.

In the next chapter we'll look at how we might handle difficult conversations in a way that will hopefully help, and not harm our relationships.

12. how to handle difficult conversations

Do not believe what you want to believe, until you know what you need to know.

REGINALD V. JONES, INTELLIGENCE EXPERT DURING WORLD WAR II

I love argument, I love debate. I don't expect anyone just to sit there and agree with me, that's not their job.

MARGARET THATCHER, FORMER UK PRIME MINISTER

Without head-on communication – you get head-on collision.

DR DAVID ABELL (MY HUSBAND!)

in search of restoration

Annabel, my goddaughter, was telling me the other day about a tricky situation she encountered at school. Two girls in her class were causing her grief. They were whispering behind her back and kept pointing towards her and giggling. She went up to them and asked them nicely if there was a problem. They wouldn't answer and walked away, but their behaviour continued. Annabel then told a teacher about it and the three of them were called behind during the break to talk it through. She told me what happened:

> I asked the girls whether they had been talking about me and they agreed that they had. I then gave them an 'I message' (that

is what I do if someone is nasty). I said, 'I don't like it when you are mean to me as it hurts my feelings,' and I asked them how they would have felt if they were me. I told them that it would be great if in future they could tell me to my face if they had a problem with me. The girls said they had done it for fun – their older sisters had done the same to them and they wanted to try doing it too. They could see that they hadn't been nice. They cried and said 'sorry'. It is all OK now and they haven't done it again.

Did I mention that Annabel was eight years old when this happened? I'm nearly five times her age and I don't think I have handled a difficult conversation with that level of maturity. Annabel didn't hide and pretend there wasn't a problem and she didn't go on the attack – she calmly and rationally tackled the issue and through doing so improved the situation and restored her relationship with the two girls.

Annabel took the authentic approach. She was genuine, she was real and she didn't shy away from saying how she felt or from addressing the problem. Wouldn't it be great if we could all react like that?

We looked in the last chapter at why we might have conflict with someone. We also looked at how to make sure that we are dealing with the right problem with the right person at the right time and in the right way. The next step is to approach them.

Making the approach

OK, deep breath. If we have decided that we need to deal with the issue then we will need to approach them in person (or, if that isn't possible, on the phone). Using an email, text or letter to explain our problem isn't normally a great idea as our tone and intentions can be misconstrued and we miss the opportunity to see and hear the other person's reaction and work through the issue together.

However, I do realise that, for most of us, approaching them will be as much fun as going to the dentist. In our survey 52 per cent admitted that they don't find it easy to tell someone when they've been hurt or upset. But, as with visiting the dentist, sometimes some short-term pain is worth it for the relief you gain in the long run. It is the same with conflict. If we don't resolve the problem it is likely to get worse and more painful and will be harder to deal with later on.

I always try to remind myself that resolving issues can actually help a relationship to grow, deepen and become more authentic. Just as in Annabel's case.

Picking the right moment

In the last chapter I mentioned the benefits of acting on a problem as soon as possible. If we weren't able to tell the other person about the issue at the time (perhaps because we or they were too emotional, there was not the time to talk it through, other people were present or we hadn't realised the impact yet) we will need to find a good moment when we can approach them.

This is where it is good to think about the other person. What would be a good time for them and how do we think they would like to be approached? It is probably best to delay the moment if they are in a bad mood, unless they are always in a bad mood, in which case you may just have to go for it. We may also need to put it off if they are very ill, busy, distracted, hungry or stressed (or if we are any of those things for that matter). Do we know whether they are better at dealing with things in the morning, the afternoon or the evening? Do we know if they prefer a direct approach or a more indirect one? If we know these things then we can take them into account.

We may want to book in a time to see them by arranging a meeting, or taking them for a coffee or for lunch (whatever is appropriate to the relationship and to the size of the problem). Sometimes being in a public place like a café can help make it feel less intense and the other person may also be less likely to lose their temper with other people in the vicinity.

If the issue is a minor one it may be worth just bringing it up as and when we are involved in an activity together or have just finished one. People can get very defensive if we wade in with the 'we need to talk' line. In fact, it is probably best to avoid that phrase at all costs. Many of us have an internal warning system that starts alarm bells ringing when we hear it. We presume it means we've messed up or failed or that the relationship is about to fall apart. Our emotions go into overdrive, as do our imaginations, and we will find it very hard to listen properly. So, instead of saying 'we need to talk' it can be better to just start talking.

So, with a work colleague for example, if we've just had a meeting or have been involved in an activity together we might want to say, 'Have you got a few minutes?'

If it is the person we live with (our flat mate or our lover) we may want to bring it up while we are involved in a task together, like chopping vegetables or doing the clearing up. (Although we may then need to stop the activity if it distracts us from listening to each other properly.)

If it is with a teenager we may want to discuss the issue in the car or when we are out shopping or walking (some people react better when they are not under any pressure to maintain direct eye contact).

If it is with a friend we may want to mention it after a nice lunch together or after we've just played a game of squash with them.

Check yourself

Whether it is a planned meeting or a more informal chat remember to try and stay calm. Try not to shout or to lose it. In my case, that is easier said than done. Because I find negative emotions difficult to handle I find that I often end up crying (which I hate). Thanks to the patience of a few of my friends, my husband, my parents and my last boss (who have all had to endure the water works) I am slowly getting better. If it happens with someone who has never experienced my strange idiosyncrasies before, I explain that I'm not great at situations like this. 'Bear with me,' I tell them, 'I'll be OK in a moment.'

It is all a bit embarrassing for a grown woman of my age but I try and remind myself that I am making progress. I tell myself that being able to have a difficult conversation and crying is one step further on than not having the conversation at all. I've recently managed a few without tears, so there is hope for me yet.

It can help to think about how you're likely to respond and to prepare yourself. Brian gets really nervous before a big chat with his boss so he finds it easier if he rehearses what he wants to say in front of his bathroom mirror. Taylor always feels more courageous before a difficult conversation if she is looking good. A new haircut and her favourite suit do wonders for her self-confidence.

know your response

How do you respond during difficult conversations? (Do you get angry, fearful, defensive, critical, tearful, moody or clam up? Or are you able to remain calm and composed?)

How does your response tend to affect the conversation and the other person?

If you don't like your typical response how would you like it to change? And what things will help you?

Invite the person into the conversation

When we start the conversation it helps to go in with a gentle opening (unless of course they prefer a very direct approach, in which case we may want to get to the point quickly).

Help them to see that you haven't come to attack but rather that you are keen to resolve the issue and to restore the relationship.

Remember, our main aim is to sort out the problem and be reconciled, not to win!

If we can keep our attitude warm and open they are less likely to feel threatened by us. We will make better progress if we can somehow get the other person to own the issue too. If both of us can admit there is a problem then the conversation can become more about how 'we' can fix it than the combative approach of, 'I have a problem with you and I want you to deal with it.'

Try and explain the issue as objectively as possibly. This means trying to think how they may see the problem. Remember the jigsaw – try and mention the whole picture (or as much as you think you have) rather than just the pieces in your hand (that is, try and talk about the dynamic at play between you rather than just how you see the problem).

For example, with the scenario we looked at in the last chapter, where a colleague, John, is causing problems at work, we might say something like this:

> John, I'm wondering if we could look at the way we work
> together? There seems to be a bit of tension between us. I know
> that I have found some things a bit tricky recently and it has
> been causing me to feel stressed and I imagine it probably hasn't
> been great for you either. It would be great if we could try and
> understand what is causing the issues between us and hopefully
> then we can work something out.

Start listening

During the conversation you're going to need to be good at listening to the other person. Remember they have bits of the jigsaw puzzle that you don't have and you need to discover them. This is where the reflective listening (we looked at this in Chapter 4) comes in handy. Keep feeding back their story to check that you have understood. Acknowledge what they are saying and how they are feeling. Acknowledging is *not* the same as agreeing. Keep checking their story until you feel it makes sense to you.

Hearing their story may help you feel differently about the situation. They may be able to help you see it in a way that you hadn't seen before. It may transpire that some of the assumptions you made about their intentions were wrong or you may have misread your impact on them. As you listen and show interest you will discover these things.

Help them understand you

When it is your turn to speak, explain the issue as you see it and how it impacted you. This is the hard bit! It is important to be as clear as possible and to remember to mention any feelings. If we've done the preparation we discussed in the last chapter this will have helped. Often, saying what we feel is the bit we want to leave out.

Stone, Patton and Heen, in *Difficult Conversations*, write:

> Difficult conversations do not just *involve* feelings, they are at their very core *about* feelings. Feelings are not noisy by-products of engaging in difficult talk, they are an integral part of the conflict. Engaging in a difficult conversation without talking about feelings is like staging an opera without the music. You'll get the plot but miss the point.

Avoid the blame game

Don't start blaming, accusing or labelling the other person. 'You did this … You always do that … You never do that … You … You … You …' Owning our feelings means saying how *we* felt. So, for example, 'When this happened I felt …', 'I felt upset when …', 'I felt confused when …'

Try to focus on the issue that you are discussing and don't keep widening the discussion to bring up everything they've ever done wrong. They will just feel cornered.

Avoiding the blame game also means taking responsibility for our own part in the problem. We will have contributed to the dynamic in some way and it will help if we can admit to it. So with John again, we might say:

> I find it really hard when you call me names or criticise my work, especially in front of other people. I'm probably not as robust as the other guys in the office. I feel put down by your comments. It makes me feel edgy around you because I am not sure what you are going to say next. I realise I should have probably said something earlier – that was wrong of me. But I am glad we are talking about it now as I don't want to feel like that with a work colleague. Can you understand that or do you see the situation differently?

Locate the missing pieces

We need to keep checking with the other person. Have they understood what we are saying? If they see it differently we need to keep hearing them out. What is their perspective? What was the impact on them? How do they feel about it?

We need to make sure that all the bits of the jigsaw are on the table – both their pieces and our pieces.

We may discover things we didn't know. Perhaps it turns out that John comes from a family of six boys and that teasing and being critical is a form of interest and endearment for him. He may say something like: 'Gosh I didn't realise you felt like that. You always seem to be so good humoured about it – I assumed you were OK with it. I feel awful that it had such a bad effect on you. It just didn't cross my mind that that was how you were feeling.'

Remember the last 10 per cent

We need to make sure that we have said everything that we want to say and checked that they have understood us properly and that we have understood them. If we haven't yet voiced the bit that really matters to us then we need to take a deep breath and go for it.

John Ortberg, in *Everybody's Normal Till You Get to Know Them*, talks about the last 10 per cent rule: 'Often, after going through all the hard work of setting up a difficult conversation, we shrink back from saying the hardest but most important truth. We fail to say the last 10 per cent. We get vague and fuzzy precisely when clarity is most needed by the other person.'

So, back to our example – with John we might be worried that he's after our job, so we could say 'When you criticise my ideas, it feels as if you are competing with me and that we're not on the same team. This makes me sometimes wonder whether you are after my job. It is probably my imagination but can you see why I might feel like that?'

Then let John reply. We may find he is horrified that we think that or it may even turn out to be true. If it is, at least we now know what we are dealing with!

Identify the dynamic

After a while it should be possible to identify the dynamic that has gone on between us. This will help to clarify the real issue and to bring joint ownership to the problem.

So with John we might say,

I think I can see now what was happening between us. If I've understood it right you are used to a competitive and combative environment and when you responded to my ideas in meetings you thought you were showing interest. I, on the other hand, am not used to being spoken to like that and I don't react very well when I feel people are criticising me. I interpreted your comments as put-downs and it made me want to clam up and not share my views and ideas. I can see that I didn't help the situation because I didn't speak up before and that didn't help you understand why there was tension between us.

Check whether they would agree with the summary of the dynamic. Try and get to a point where you can both see it together.

Using the 'S' word

During this discussion one or both of you may need to say 'sorry'. Some of us may find it hard to say 'sorry'. It is difficult to admit we were wrong or that we hurt someone. But we need to take responsibility for our part in the problem and choose to say 'sorry'. Sorry is the balm that helps restore and repair a relationship and I'll say more about it in the next chapter.

What do you want to be different?

Now you have understood the dynamic and owned your part it is possible to start working on a solution. This is the time to mention how you would like things to be different and to hear their view.

With John we might say,

> It has been a great help to talk this through and to understand where you are coming from. I will try not to take your comments so sensitively in future but maybe you could agree not to use quite so much bantering. And I will try to speak up more often if and when I think it has gone too far. Do you see that working or do you have some other thoughts on how we can move forward?

Find a solution together

It helps if you can see the issue as a joint problem to solve. Remember this is neither 'your' issue nor 'my' issue but 'our' issue. How can we sort this out? How can we make sure this doesn't happen again? How can we improve the situation?

If you can both take responsibility for finding the solution you are more likely to both 'own it' – rather than one person feeling dictated to or manipulated.

You'll need to think through possible solutions together until you find one that suits you both and one that you can both agree to.

Assess the solution and revisit if necessary

You may need to agree to revisit the solution after a set amount of time, to see how you are doing and whether the situation has resolved itself. If there are still problems you may need to look for alternative solutions.

> **Your turn**
>
> Think about the other two scenarios in the last chapter; the one with the friends who didn't invite you to the birthday party and the relative who keeps being critical. Would you approach them about the issues and if so, how could you do it in a way that will improve, not worsen, the relationship?

If we are the one who is approached

If we were the one who caused the problem (or most of it) then we need to be extra careful not to get defensive or go on the attack when the other person describes how we have hurt or upset them. And that can be really hard. We are listening to how we have made someone else feel. It takes guts to keep listening without defending or minimising our behaviour. And, even more, to keep asking questions about the impact we have had on them.

To push, or get the push

Sometimes we have to have difficult conversations when we need to end a relationship – perhaps if a professional or romantic relationship is not working out. In those cases we need to be clear but firm. Ideally there would have been other conversations before the *big* one. If someone is not doing well at work it is important that they get regular feedback and a chance to improve. The first time they hear of issues shouldn't be in their annual appraisal or when they are about to get fired!

Similarly, in a romantic relationship the other person will hopefully have had some signs of what was coming as you should have discussed issues and differences along the way. The most important thing is to be kind and authentic. (I say a little more about this in Chapter 17.)

However, it may be that you've just discovered that the other person has betrayed your trust or has done something horrific. In this case, you'll need to be clear and firm with them, explaining that their behaviour is unacceptable and that you feel unable to keep the relationship going.

Out of the box examples

Approaching a difficult conversation like this may seem like hard work or somewhat contrived to you. But in most cases an approach like this will help you to resolve the conflict in a constructive way. And if it is of any encouragement I have found that it does get easier the more you do it! You just have to persevere and keep your eye on the long-term goal of restoring and strengthening the relationship.

Several years ago, Isobel was very hurt by something that her mother had said about her boyfriend at that time. She decided that she would try dealing with the situation instead of brushing it under the carpet, which is what she tended to do.

I reflected on it and then gently told her that when she had given her opinion in the way that she did, it had really hurt and upset me and I would be really grateful if perhaps she could just think in future before she jumped in to give her thoughts. This was a real breakthrough, as I had never really confronted my mum, despite the fact that she is very judgemental and regularly jumps in with both feet before engaging her brain. I like to think that because I handled it very sensitively and used the 'I' word – i.e. I was upset when you spoke like that, 'my' feelings were hurt – she took it very well and apologised and said she would try to be more tactful in future. It really brought us closer and made me realise that it is healthier to gently confront a situation rather

than let it bottle up and let it fester and breed unhealthy feelings
of resentment.

However, there will be times when it doesn't seem as if we are
making any headway with someone who is causing us difficulties.
I just want to mention a little about that now.

dealing with difficult people

What happens if the other person doesn't want to be reasonable?
What if they aren't willing to change? What if they are just difficult?

Sometimes it will just be because we haven't listened enough. We
haven't understood them and they are still feeling defensive. We may
need to keep on until they feel heard and really understood.

Sometimes it will be because the other person is feeling disconnected from us and doesn't feel like talking. We may need to spend
time with them first and help rebuild the connection before we try
and address the issue.

Sometimes they may not be aware that they are sabotaging the
discussion. If we think that is the case then we can try to reflect
their behaviour back to them. 'Whenever I tell you how I feel you
don't let me finish and I feel as if you don't want to listen. How can
I tell you about this in a way that you would be able to hear it?'

But sometimes the other person just won't accept any criticism
or take responsibility for their actions. Perhaps they are in denial;
they may have lots of unresolved issues from the past and we are
just pushing heavily on their sensitive buttons, or maybe they are
difficult with everyone.

If we can't resolve it on our own then we will need help.

Involve others

Sometimes it can help to involve a third party. If it is a work dispute
this may be someone from HR, but if it is another kind of issue
we may need to bring in a mediator or a friend whom we can trust

(if the other person will accept them being there). If it is a romantic relationship we may want to go to couple's counselling or talk to a wise couple we both know and trust.

If you feel bullied by the other person or if you find it hard to put your view across the third person can help you to say what you want and can support you in the process. They can also act as a witness to the conversation and to any solutions that are discussed.

Support

If you are involved in having to negotiate a tricky relationship, it is important to have some supportive people in your life. Coping with a difficult dynamic can be draining and emotionally trying. It can make all the difference if you have a support network of people who can encourage you and can remind you how to laugh occasionally.

Heather discovered this when she recently went through a difficult patch at work:

> I'd always had a tendency to try to deal with problems by myself.
> I don't know if that was pride or a fear that others couldn't be
> relied on – perhaps a mixture of both. The problem with that
> approach was not so much that things didn't work out – some-
> how they usually did – but that going through problems alone is
> exhausting, and painful, and takes its toll. Happily, I have learnt
> to open up a bit more (a little bit anyway!). Recently I have been
> through a really difficult time at work, but have been supported
> enormously by friends in whom I have confided. What I am
> starting to see, also, is that letting other people help leads to far
> more real relationships and, in that way, problems can be turned
> into blessings.

Try boundaries

There may come a time in the relationship where you need to enforce a boundary. These can be helpful if someone is persisting in a behaviour which is causing you, your relationship or your loved ones harm and they will not take responsibility for their actions. (I have mentioned more about these in Chapter 13.)

If dialogue, mediation and boundaries simply fail to work then you may have to remove yourself from the relationship, at least until the other person is ready to own their part in the issue and is prepared to change. Let them know that they have a choice. If they are prepared to play their part and make amends then the relationship can be restored. This can be a very difficult boundary to have to make and to stick to but in some cases it may be the last resort that actually works.

Your tricky experiences

How well do you cope with difficult conversations?

....

....

Think of difficult conversations that went well and ones that didn't. What made the difference?

....

....

Are there difficult conversations you have been putting off that you think you need to have? If so, what steps could you take to make these happen?

....

....

tips: How to be a great team member (for those who want to fit in)

Take your turn. If there are ten of you, this means contributing to about a tenth of the discussion. Extroverts – you may need to button it a bit; introverts – speak up.

Be the first. If you notice that the water needs pouring, the football nets need putting up, the loo roll or printer paper needs replacing, be the first to do it even if you don't think it's your job. And try not to make too many selfish brews – include others in your tea round.

Encourage others. This one's simple. Everyone needs encouraging – even the leader.

Don't be divisive. Look at any good sporting team – they thrive on unity. Discuss problems in the open or with the person it concerned. Don't be the one to stir up trouble.

Respect the leader. If your team has a leader then respect their authority. If you don't agree with something, tell them (but don't keep telling them the same thing). Trust them to make the right decisions. If you don't like it, it may not be the right time, or the right team, for you.

Take notice. Look out for the others. Spot if someone needs help or support and remember birthdays and significant events. Be interested in who they are more than what they do.

Play to your strengths. Take responsibility for your role in the team and pull your weight. Operate in the area of your strengths and be prepared to learn and give new things a go without complaining.

Appreciate differences. Learn to think the best of others and enjoy the ways in which they differ from you. Focus on the good and face the bad (that may mean dealing with it or putting up with it). Don't take yourself too seriously and take responsibility when you need to.

Have fun. Look for opportunities to laugh, celebrate and socialise with the others.

having an impact

13. when feelings aren't enough

I have decided to stick with love. Hate is too great a burden to bear.
MARTIN LUTHER KING JR

The new easy-come, easy-go relationships give us more freedom – but less contentment.
THE DALAI LAMA

Everyone says that forgiveness is a lovely idea, until they have something to forgive.
C. S. LEWIS

love is a choice not a feeling

One school of thought (favoured it would seem by many advertising executives and Hollywood scriptwriters) is that if something feels right we should do it.

- If we fancy eating a tub (or two) of delicious chocolate ice cream in the bath – we should just enjoy it
- If we want new clothes – we should max out our credit cards and buy them
- If we don't feel like going to work – we should just throw a sickie

- If we feel the chemistry – we should have sex together (even if we, or they, are already in another relationship)
- If we feel angry – we should let it all out.

But what would happen if we acted on every impulse, every feeling and every emotion that we had? We would probably soon find ourselves feeling sick, overweight, broke, sacked, dumped and very unpopular!

Our consumer society wants to tell us it's OK to act on our feelings because often there's money to be made when we do. That's why we're encouraged to think that we can have it all and that we deserve the best. We learn that if a product or a service isn't working we can throw it away or switch to something else.

In a TV documentary on marriage, Bob Geldof said, 'We hop from product to product, channel to channel, station to station, and most damagingly, lover to lover, trading each one in for a new model as soon as passion fades.'

That's the problem when we start believing all this stuff. We apply our 'throw away' mentality to relationships and we find out that we, and others, are disposable: there to be used and then discarded. If we allow ourselves to get seduced by this way of thinking we soon find ourselves approaching others with a consumer mindset asking, 'What can I get from you? What is our relationship doing for me?' and before we know it we are giving up because things are tricky and we don't feel 'it' anymore.

By 'it' we often mean love. We don't feel 'in love' anymore, we don't feel our hearts lurch, our stomachs turn, our knees go weak, the butterflies flutter, our pulse races, the stirring in our loins (or anywhere else for that matter) and so 'it' (it now referring to the relationship) can't be right anymore. And then we do a runner.

Actually, 'it' doesn't have to be a loving relationship; 'it' can be any relationship. If it isn't working, if it is too much like hard work or if it takes effort, then forget it!

In our survey we asked people what worried them most about relationships in our society. Around half mentioned these very issues. Here are a few of their comments:

'People seem to view relationships as something which should be easy to get, right now, and not worth working on for the long-haul! Our life is so "disposable" that I think people are actually forgetting what being committed to something involves, and this also makes them more afraid of it.'

'What worries me the most is that people feel they can cash in and check out whenever it suits them – commitment is almost a dirty word. It's become politically correct to be selfish.'

'Nobody cares about anyone anymore – it's all about image – not people.'

'We constantly strive for more in this consumerist world and we never seem to be happy with what we have … nothing is ever good enough and we seek perfection. Nothing is perfect though, but some people don't realise that!'

'People like me don't believe in commitment – it is too easy to opt out of a relationship without really working at it.'

'People break up so easily when the fuzzy feelings go and they feel them with another.'

'Lack of commitment and the huge number of children growing up in broken homes where people don't work through relationships (I'm a teacher!).'

'People have forgotten how to work for the things they want out of life – both material and emotional. We have a society where people do not accept responsibility for their own failings and look too often to point the finger at others.'

'People want things to be instant, easy and always fun and life just isn't like that.'

relationships take work

Authentic relating is the antidote to this trend for consumer relationships. It is counter-cultural. When we relate authentically we don't approach other people for what we can get, and we don't give up at the first sign of trouble, or give in to every impulse and feeling.

Authentic relating involves sacrifice, commitment and empathy (as well as all the fun stuff). It is about love, but a love that chooses to love even when we don't feel like it. A love that is 'for' relationship not 'against' it. A love that takes the initiative and makes the choice to apologise, forgive, commit and extend oneself for the sake of maintaining and building our connections with others. Authentic loving is about treating others as well as or better than we would treat ourselves.

To love like that takes courage, self-discipline and perseverance. It means taking a long-term view and making decisions today that will benefit and not harm our relationships for the future. So, for example:

- When a wife doesn't accept a dinner invitation with a colleague she's attracted to – she benefits her marriage.
- When a dad decides not to spend the afternoon watching football so that he can play tennis on the Wii with his daughter – he demonstrates his love for her.
- When a friend stops what she's doing and goes to help a friend in trouble – she shows that she cares.
- When a boss encourages people not to keep working late – he shows that he values people's families and relationships.
- When a parent doesn't allow her child to have the toy he's just spotted (despite the tantrum) – she teaches him about delayed gratification.
- When an employee speaks out about the wrongdoing or corruption going on in his place of work – he stands up for truth and integrity.

Making the hard choices

Choosing to relate authentically won't be the easy option. Sometimes we'll have to make choices that we find difficult but it is to be hoped that the long-term benefits will compensate for the short-term discomfort or pain.

The paradox is that often when we chose to love the loving feel ings follow.

As C. S. Lewis wrote in *Mere Christianity*:

> The rule for all of us is perfectly simple. Do not waste time bothering whether you 'love' your neighbour; act as if you did. As soon as we do this we find one of the great secrets. When you are behaving as if you loved someone, you will presently come to love him. If you injure someone you dislike, you will find yourself disliking him more. If you do him a good turn, you will find yourself disliking him less.

When we change the way we think about someone or something and when we choose to act in a positive way our feelings will often follow. But the choosing comes first – we have to take that step even when we don't want too.

For several months Bill had a problematic relationship with Lee, the new caretaker of a building that he hired to run his seminars. Whenever Bill asked Lee for something – for the heating to be turned on, to borrow an extension lead or to get more toilet roll for the bathrooms – Lee would grumble, complain and make excuses, any excuse to not do whatever it was. Each week Bill would get more and more annoyed and frustrated with Lee's negative attitude. But then, one day, Bill and a few others from his organisation decided to try another tack – they started encouraging Lee, thinking the best of him and not complaining. As they did this they noticed an amazing thing happen. Not only did they feel better every time they encountered Lee but his behaviour also changed. He became much more positive and willing to help out. Now Bill and Lee have a much better relationship and are able to chat and laugh about things. Bill's choice – to think the best of Lee – had changed the whole dynamic between them and also had had a positive impact on Lee's behaviour too. In the next chapter we'll look in detail at how we can make a choice to reach out and love and care for others in practical ways. But for the moment I want to focus on four other difficult choices we will need to tackle if we are to build strong and authentic relationships: choosing to say sorry, choosing to forgive, choosing to say 'yes' and choosing to say 'no'.

choosing to say 'sorry'

In the survey, 30 per cent said they find it difficult to say sorry and ask for forgiveness. I admire the other 70 per cent. I don't think saying sorry is an easy thing to do. It is acknowledging that our words or actions, or lack of words or actions, have caused someone else to be put out or hurt.

The bottom line is that none of us is perfect and we all make mistakes (probably on a daily basis). Some of these mistakes will be small ones and some bigger ones. But when we fail to say sorry or make amends it is as if we are allowing toxins to form in our relationships. With each mistake or hurt the other person may pull back just a tiny bit and may respect and trust us a little less. The next time we do something wrong to them without apologising the toxin gets stronger and then, before we know it, the relationship has become poisoned and may eventually even die. The process of apologising and forgiving is like a good detox – it removes the poison and helps us to restore the health of the relationship. In chronic cases it can even revive a dying one.

To say sorry means that we're prepared to take a bite of humble pie. And that means understanding and taking responsibility for what we've done. To get to that point we may need to allow the person we have hurt or injured to tell us about the impact that we have had on them. That may not be easy to hear, and to listen to them without defending ourselves or making excuses will be harder still.

In our survey 77 per cent agreed that they get defensive if they feel they are being criticised. But if we can choose to overcome our defensiveness and allow the other person to tell us what happened and how they felt, we are letting them know that we care and that we want to make things better where we can.

When we say sorry we need to:

Admit that we messed up

This is when we come clean and say we know we did wrong. 'I am sorry ... I did a bad thing ... I messed up ... I shouldn't have said that ... I was wrong ... It was my fault.'

The more specific we can be with our apology the better; it helps the other person to know exactly what we are apologising for. So, instead of just saying, 'I am sorry I shouldn't have said that ...' we might say, 'I am sorry – I shouldn't have told everyone at my party that the necklace you gave me looked like a "string of rabbit droppings". It wasn't clever, nice or kind and I can completely understand why it hurt your feelings.'

We resist the temptation to:

- **Add a 'but' ... 'but you have to admit it is pretty ugly'**
- **Or an excuse ... 'I had had too many drinks'**
- **Or to blame the other ... 'Well if you'd given me something half decent I wouldn't have said anything bad'.**

In some cases it can help to explain why we did something (if we are aware of the reason). Explaining may help the other person to see what led to our wrong behaviour and will help them to see what caused our reactions. It may help both of us to see the dynamic that was at play. 'I was really disappointed with the necklace you gave me. I didn't feel as if you had thought about what I would really like when you bought it. That made me feel like you didn't care. I should have said something to you earlier but instead I blurted my feelings out at the party to everyone else. That was really wrong of me. I was behaving like a spoilt child and I can see I really hurt your feelings. I am sorry I said those things and that I didn't deal with the situation better.'

Really mean it

There's no point saying 'sorry' if we don't mean it. An insincere apology is worse than not apologising at all.

It can help to think about what it would be like to be on the other end of our behaviour. How would we have felt if we were them? If we are not sure then this is all the more reason to listen to the impact it had on them.

However, it could be that we don't accept that what we did was wrong. And that may be true if the other person misinterpreted something or has a different viewpoint to ours. But it is worth asking ourselves if we are partly at fault (even if not 100 per cent). That enables us to apologise for the bit we can take responsibility for.

For example, Roberto's mum is upset with him because he isn't spending Mother's Day with her this year and she thinks he doesn't care. Not only that, she only found out through his sister. Roberto apologises to his mum, 'I am sorry you are upset and I am sorry that I didn't tell you directly. That was inconsiderate of me.' However, he doesn't apologise for not being there because he has to be at an important conference that weekend for work. He does, though, give her a big hug and reassures her that he cares.

Seek to make things better

Is there some way in which we can make amends? If we've told a lie to someone else we can offer to tell the truth. If we've broken something we can offer to replace it. In the case of the necklace we can discuss how we might deal with a similar situation better next time. We can ask the other person what would help. We can make a decision to try not to do the same thing in the future.

sorry

How easy do you find it to say sorry?

What is your response when someone tells you that you have hurt them?

Is there anyone you feel that you need to say sorry to that you haven't? What could you do to make things right?

choosing to forgive

Twenty-six-year-old Anthony Fatayi-Williams was one of the victims of the Tavistock Square bus bombing on 7 July 2006. His Muslim father and Catholic mother forgave the bomber and set up a foundation for peace and conflict resolution in their son's memory. Mrs Fatayi-Williams, speaking at his funeral, said, 'I am distraught, but I am not angry. What would that do? Anger begets hatred, begets more violence, so let's forgive.'

You and I may not need to forgive such a big thing but we will need to forgive. Forgiveness is a powerful tool for dealing with hurts, however small or large. It also helps to let go of resentment, bitterness and revenge and it opens the way for healing.

As with love, forgiveness is not a feeling. If we waited until we *felt* like forgiving we would probably never do it. Forgiving is:

Not excusing or agreeing
We are not saying that it didn't matter or that what the other person did wasn't so bad. We are not even saying that we understand why they did it. We are saying we forgive despite the fact that it did

237

hurt, it was wrong, it was bad, and even if we can't understand why they did it.

Not forgetting
Forgiveness isn't saying I will erase the wrong or hurt from my memory (although forgiving can help us to let go of painful memories). Nor is it denying that it has had an impact or a consequence. It doesn't change the past but it may repair the future. For example, if a father apologises to his grown-up children for the times he neglected them or treated them badly that won't cause them to forget, nor will it bring back the years when they had a difficult relationship. But what it may do is open the door to the possibility of a better relationship in the future.

But equally, forgiving isn't holding on to the pain and bringing it up all the time. If we hold onto resentment we will never heal our hurts.

Philip Yancey, in his book *What's So Amazing About Grace*, writes, 'The word "resentment" expresses what happens if the cycle of blame goes uninterrupted. It means literally to "feel again". Resentment clings to the past, re-lives it over and over and picks each fresh scab so that the wound never heals.'

Not agreeing to reconcile
Forgiving doesn't necessarily mean that the relationship is restored. In many cases it may lead to reconciliation but in others this may not be possible or appropriate. The other person may no longer be alive. Or you may never have had a relationship with them in the first place (e.g. the thief who stole your bag). Perhaps it would be dangerous or unwise to be reconciled (e.g. with an abusive person, a serial adulterer or an addict who hasn't changed their behaviour).

It doesn't mean we trust them again either. Trust is something that we may need to rebuild over time as we see the other person change or keep their word. Trust will also be a choice on our part. It will involve risk – the risk of being hurt again. But if we don't open ourselves up to trust we will be preventing full restoration of the relationship.

Marcia and Phil had been married for eight years and had two children, when Marcia decided to confront Phil about the growing disappointment and resentment that she felt about their relationship. She had hoped that marriage would be about sharing life with a best friend but the reality was that while they had a nice lifestyle they had little emotional intimacy. Phil found it hard – almost impossible – to talk about his feelings. He had had a difficult childhood and had little idea of how to provide the emotional closeness that Marcia was craving. But she found it hard to believe that their marriage could survive without it and she told him that she wasn't sure that she even cared whether it did anymore. She had lost trust in Phil and their relationship.

Phil knew he had to do something to win her back. He asked for her forgiveness and told her that he was willing to do everything that he could to make this work. He resolved to make his wife his number one priority. He signed them up for a *Marriage Encounter* weekend, which taught him some valuable tools for communicating in a new way with Marcia. Over the next few years Phil worked on developing the skills he needed to be the friend that she wanted – a husband who would spend time with her, chat to her and encourage her with his words. As he did that their relationship improved and Marcia's trust started to grow again. But old habits die hard and from time to time Phil would slip back into his old ways – putting work first or not communicating his feelings to Marcia. When that happened, Phil would ask Marcia to let him know and he would make the effort to get back to his new improved self.

Marcia, meanwhile, had to make a choice to trust Phil and accept that any slip on his part was just a temporary hurdle and didn't mean he had reverted to his old self. As she trusted him and as he continued to work at keeping that trust they found their relationship improved and deepened. Twenty years on and four more children later they are in a much better place.

Not easy

It isn't easy to forgive, especially if the hurt was a big one. Some of us may never be able to forgive. We may find it too hard. Others may find they need to try and forgive for their own health and sanity.

Sandra was a young teenager when an older relative of hers sexually assaulted her:

> I never shared the information with anyone but I began to have flashbacks in my early twenties and needed to deal with it. Unfortunately, my relative had been killed in a tragic accident and was not around to confront. One weekend when I went away with some close friends I decided to tell them what had happened. By the Sunday night, after we had talked it through, I had forgiven him and felt a total healing and closure to this event.

Forgiveness may not always happen at once, it may take a long time, especially when the hurts run deep. It is often a process and we may have to keep forgiving the same person in our hearts again and again and again. Rob Parsons, in *The Sixty Minute Marriage*, writes, 'Forgiveness feels the pain but doesn't hoard it; it allows tomorrow to break free of yesterday. It is always hard, sometimes foolish, and at its heart Godlike. There is no hope for us without it.'

Not taking revenge

When we forgive we are giving up our right to hurt back or to make the other person pay. Part of us may want to get our own back or to see the other person squirm but when we forgive we are overriding those impulses.

That means putting a stop to our fantasies of getting one up on the other person or rehearsing scenarios in our head where we get revenge. For example, showing an ex we don't care by finding someone better and parading them in front of them, becoming more successful than a difficult boss and taking over his company or going back to a school reunion and showing them all how successful, rich, talented etc we are now.

Forgiving them

How do we go about forgiving someone?

If they have approached us, apologised and asked us to forgive them then it is our choice.

We can choose to say 'I forgive you' and to draw a line under it or we can choose not to. But it is worth remembering that when we don't forgive it often hurts us more than the other person. The toxic cocktail of hurt, bitterness and resentment can erode our insides, often impacting not just on this relationship, but all our relationships.

If the person hasn't come to us we may need to approach them. It may be that we need to tell them how we were hurt and to explain how their behaviour made us feel. If we do that they may or may not take responsibility for their actions. If they don't we can still chose to forgive and release them anyway.

In some cases it may not be appropriate to approach the person. We may no longer know them, they may not be alive or we may decide it isn't worth rocking the boat. If that is the case we can still go through the process of forgiveness.

Don, whom I mentioned in Chapter 8 – whose parents died and who was eventually adopted after his stepmother rejected him – was eventually able to forgive those involved in his difficult childhood:

> Not forgiving can only wreak havoc in the person who doesn't forgive and leaves you feeling angry, resentful and bitter.
> Forgiving for me has been quite a journey. First I forgave my mother for 'deserting' me. I know she didn't choose to die of cancer but as a six-year-old I didn't see it like that. I had to forgive my father and my brother too for leaving me.

I do have some regrets because I didn't forgive my step-mother until after she had died. In some ways she was the only one I had real reason to forgive and I didn't do it. Over recent years I have realised more and more what she went through just after the war. Married only one year and widowed with a six-week-old baby and two stepsons to look after. She didn't have support from her own or my dad's family. There was rationing at the time and I suspect she was also suffering from post-natal depression (not then recognised) – wow. Yes, I now have forgiven her perhaps through an understanding of why she did what she did.

If there is someone we want to forgive – but who isn't around – it can help to write a letter which we then don't send. We can write down all the ways that we felt hurt and let down, the impact these things had on us and then we can write 'I forgive you'. I've done that before and have found it helpful to then burn the letter. The burning is symbolic of the release of forgiveness.

It is never too late to forgive someone and it is never too late to ask for forgiveness. We can do it today.

Forgiving ourselves

We may know that we need to ask forgiveness from someone. Maybe we did something in the past that we deeply regret or that caused a breakdown in a relationship. Admitting our wrong and asking for forgiveness won't be easy but it will help to release ourselves from the guilt and may also help the other person to heal from the hurt.

Sometimes we may decide it is inappropriate to tell them of something we did wrong if they weren't aware of it. It may be best to leave it in the past. Telling them may not be a kind thing to do. If we are struggling to live with the guilt we can confess in confidence to a therapist, a support group or to a religious or spiritual leader or ask God for forgiveness ourselves.

We all need to forgive ourselves for stuff. Some of us are too hard on ourselves and give ourselves a harder time than we give others. Forgiving ourselves is admitting we are human and that we make mistakes. It is not beating ourselves over the head and making ourselves continually pay for our mistakes. It is letting go of our regrets and disappointments.

Forgiving ourselves involves accepting the past, acknowledging responsibility for our actions and choosing to do things differently from now on. Again it may help to write a letter – perhaps to ourselves or to God – outlining the things we need forgiveness for. Alternatively, we may find it easier to do it with someone else (for example, with a trusted friend, a therapist or a spiritual director).

When we seek forgiveness for ourselves we are freeing our future from the past.

forgiveness and you

What do you find it hardest to forgive?

How does it feel when you do forgive or are forgiven?

Is there anyone you need to forgive? How could you go about this?

Is there anyone you need to seek forgiveness from?

> What do you need to forgive yourself for? What impact did these behaviours have on you, the other person and your relationships?
>
> ---
>
> You may want to write them down in a letter to yourself or to God. Ask for forgiveness and then once you have received it you may want to burn the letter. Then think about how you want things to be different now.
>
> ---

choosing to say 'yes'

Authentic relating means sometimes saying 'yes' when we'd rather say 'no' (because deep down we know 'yes' is the right answer). When we are selfish or passive we can negatively affect our connections with others. For example, if we demand our own way or we opt out of taking responsibility. Saying 'yes' means extending ourselves, reaching out to others and taking an active role in our relationships.

'Yes' to commitment

Commitment is a choice. It is saying that we will stick with a relationship even when it gets tricky. It is saying we'll work through problems and we won't bail out. It means we are prepared to put the relationship before our own individual desires.

We can show commitment to our friends, our business partners, our boss, our children, our family or to our spouse. It is saying: I will help you, I will support you, I will be 'for you', and I will be there in the good and the bad times. It means I'll do something if I say I will.

Commitment is an active choice not a passive response. Researchers from Denver University have found that the strongest and most enduring couple relationships are the ones in which the two people see themselves as an 'us' rather than a 'you' and 'me'. They are the ones who make sacrifices and give priority to each other and to the relationship.

In other types of relationships, such as in business or friendships, we won't necessarily be committing for life, just for a season. But commitment means that during that season we will be trustworthy and we won't deliberately do anything to harm the relationship.

Commitment isn't a one-off decision, it is a constant one. Every day we have to choose to live out that commitment in our behaviour, our choices and our attitude.

'Yes' to working at this

In our survey 74 per cent agreed that relationships take work. The other 26 per cent are either very lucky or perhaps they have their heads stuck in the sand. Obviously some relationships will be easier than others, but most of them will need us to work through issues at some time.

With hindsight, Sheila wishes she had worked harder at her first marriage:

> I had an affair. I had been married for twenty-seven years and I
> didn't feel loved by my husband. I felt that he never listened to
> me and over the years we didn't have any intimacy left in our
> relationship. I met someone else who fulfilled all those unmet
> needs and believed it was the answer to everything. I finished my
> marriage and continued the affair. It wasn't long before every-
> thing went wrong and there I was, all alone. I then spent the next
> seven years trying to work through my feelings before meeting
> and marrying my second husband. Although I love him very
> much, I think back and wonder whether if my ex-husband and I
> could have worked harder at our first marriage, we could have
> avoided the break-up and the devastating consequences it had on
> me, him and our children.

Choosing to work at a marriage is a big thing but there will be small things too. There'll be moments when we have to choose to put ourselves out and do things we don't fancy doing or that are inconvenient. For example, cooking dinner when we're tired, doing something at work that we don't like doing, giving up our Saturday to help a friend move house or having a relative we don't like very much over for lunch.

'Yes' to taking responsibility

On the whole, relationships come with responsibility. When we say 'yes' to taking responsibility we offer to play our part in the relationship. We take the initiative in planning things, in doing things, in saying sorry, in looking after the other and in creating fun or happy memories. We don't just take, take, take but we give. (In the next chapter we'll look at this more.)

If we have children, elderly parents, employees or a spouse then taking responsibility means looking after and looking out for them. It means doing our best for them and by them.

saying yes

How good are you at saying 'yes' to your relationships?

Are there areas where you need to say 'yes' more?

If you are living with someone, or married to them, have you actively 'committed to them' in your heart? If not, what is holding you back?

choosing to say 'no'

As well as choosing to say 'yes' in relationships there will be times when we have to choose to say 'no', especially when it is the most loving and healthy response. But saying 'no' can be hard to do for many of us. In the survey 35 per cent said they don't have good boundaries and find it difficult to say 'no'.

'No' to doing everything

We may have to say 'no' to doing everything in a relationship. If we are doing everything then someone else is probably missing out on playing their part. At work, if we don't delegate or let people help we are not allowing others to grow and develop. If we clear up all the time after our children, we are not teaching them to take responsibility for their own mess and if we are the one always phoning or inviting our friend to things then we are not allowing them a chance to reciprocate.

We may find it hard to say 'no' if we think the other person won't want to hear it but if we don't learn to say 'no' (as I mentioned in Chapter 3) we will burn out.

'No' to rescuing you

We may need to say 'no' if we are being asked to do something that prevents someone else taking responsibility for themselves.

If a friend is habitually late or forgetful and always asks us to remind them, and we always say 'yes', then we are taking responsibility for them. We are not helping them to learn and to grow. What would happen if we didn't remind them? They might miss something important or something they really wanted to go to. But if that happens a few times they'll probably make efforts to change their behaviour.

If we cover up for someone with an alcohol or drug addiction or perhaps someone with uncontrolled anger, are we being loving?

There's a proverb that goes: 'The hot-tempered must pay the penalty; rescue them, and you will have to do it again.'

When we collude with or support people's bad habits we aren't loving them, we are just helping them to stay stuck.

'No' to unreasonable behaviour

We may have to learn to say 'no' if someone is treating us (or someone else) badly, using us or abusing us. Our 'no' may need to be in the form of a boundary. In other words, telling them that we won't put up with their behaviour anymore and that if they do it again we will do something about it (something being a realistic and enforceable consequence). The thing with boundaries is that they only work if we keep to our word and enforce them.

So, for example, a child bites her brother and her mum tells her that if she does it again she won't be able to go to her friend's birthday party. Being able to keep to her 'no' means that if and when the child does bite him again mum keeps to her word. That will probably be inconvenient for her. She'll have to phone up the parent of the birthday girl and explain why her child can't go. But if she caves in, if her 'no' suddenly turns into an 'oh well' or a 'just this time' or a 'well if I catch you doing it again', then her daughter knows that Mummy's 'no' doesn't really mean 'no' and this is likely to mean more trouble in the future.

Problems in a relationship often form and develop because we didn't say 'no' early on and stick to it. The other evening I heard about a couple going through a divorce. The man's wife was critical and controlling. If she gave him a list of ten jobs to do and he did nine she would focus on the one that he hadn't done. He had never said anything and now, after fifteen years, he had had enough. He said he realised that he should have said something in the first few years of marriage when the relationship patterns were forming. Now, sadly, he felt it was too late.

It doesn't have to be too late to start saying 'no'. We can start today by saying 'no' to anything that harms our relationships.

'No' to control

If we like to control everything we may need to say 'no' to ourselves. Control is damaging to relationships. We need to allow the other person to play their part, to make mistakes, to do things their way and to make choices. Often, the more we try and control people and their behaviour the more they are likely to want to rebel. It is a lesson I've had to learn. At work I would have a tendency to give someone a job and then keep checking up on them (David will tell you I sometimes do that with him too). It is counter-productive. I am sending the message that I don't trust them and they may think 'why bother?'. Also, if I am spending so much time fussing over them I could just as easily do it myself. And I am not letting them do it their way, which invariably turns out better than mine anyway.

If you are a controller learn to let go, to laugh at yourself and to focus on what is truly important. Ask the other person to tell you when you are doing it and then choose to stop it. Your relationships will be better off for it. Mine certainly are.

love is...

When we chose to say 'sorry', to forgive, to say 'yes' and to say 'no' we are choosing to love. We are choosing to do things we may not feel like doing for the sake of our relationships.

At our wedding we had the following reading from the Bible:

Love is patient, love is kind. It does not envy, it does not
boast, it is not proud. It is not rude, it is not self-seeking, it
is not easily angered, it keeps no record of wrongs. Love
does not delight in evil but rejoices with the truth. It always
protects, always trusts, always hopes, always perseveres.
Love never fails.

Every now and then I try an interesting exercise. I take out the word 'love' and I insert 'Sarah' instead. If those things are what love is, then how am I doing? 'Could do better' is normally my verdict.

you and love

What about you? Try inserting your name.

....

How true are those things of you?

....

In what ways could you improve and be more loving?

....

14. reaching out

I am of the opinion that my life belongs to the whole community and as long as I live it is my privilege to do for it whatever I can. I want to be thoroughly used up when I die.
GEORGE BERNARD SHAW

That best portion of a good man's life,
His little, nameless, unremembered acts of kindness and of love.
WILLIAM WORDSWORTH

The best way to cheer yourself up is to try to cheer somebody else up.
MARK TWAIN

making a difference

Someone once told me about the golden threads. Every day of our lives you and I have an opportunity to make a difference – maybe to just one person or to lots of people. It could be just a small thing, like smiling and saying hello to the person on the checkout at the supermarket or it may be something heroic like saving a life. Those opportunities are like golden threads that we have a choice to pick up or ignore. But all the ones we pick up are woven into an amazing tapestry. At the end of our life that tapestry represents all the investments we made in others – a precious treasure that will last long after we have gone.

When I was twenty I saved up to go travelling to Thailand for six weeks. I was a bit worried about going on my own so I found a male friend who was keen to go too. But once we got there it transpired that we had very different ideas about how we wanted to spend our time. I was looking forward to a bit of beach hopping and some gentle trekking but it turned out that he wanted to go freedom fighting on the Burmese border! My choice was to go with him or travel on my own – and I didn't fancy either option. Thankfully we had met two English girls, Sarah and George, in Bangkok and seeing my predicament they asked if I wanted to travel with them instead. I took them up on their offer and let my friend head off to the jungle. I am not sure what would have happened if Sarah and George hadn't rescued me. I am grateful that they picked up the golden thread that day and decided to help a stranger.

I remember once going out for the day with a friend, Andy. We were walking down a street when we passed a guy begging for money outside a supermarket. Andy stopped, chatted to him and then took him shopping to buy some food and other things that he needed. It probably took Andy about ten minutes in all and cost him five pounds or so but his kindness made a big difference to that man, who now had food to eat for a few days. Andy picked up that golden thread when others (myself included) would have walked straight by.

Another friend of mine, Marika, is a single mum. Once a month she hosts a Sunday lunch for other single parents and their children. She also does fostering respite care at weekends – providing a young teenage girl with a break from a difficult family situation. There are thousands of single parents and also children in care who could do with encouragement, support and love. Marika responded to the need and picked up that golden thread.

In these three cases my friends reached out to strangers and made a difference. But sadly most of us don't. A TV documentary in the 1990s did an experiment. They got an actress to pretend to collapse in a busy street. In a village it took ninety seconds for someone to stop and help. In the city nobody stopped for forty-five minutes! We tell ourselves we are in a hurry, that someone else will do it (or will do it better), we worry it will be dangerous or we convince ourselves that it may be a scam. We find an excuse, any excuse, to walk on by. But what if next time, instead of listening to our fear, we listen to the still small voice that says this is our turn to reach out and do something? I expect that the person's mum, dad, child or friend will be thankful we took the risk.

But reaching out to strangers doesn't have to be about the big things – we can make a difference in the small ones too, as when we give up a seat on the bus to someone who needs it, when we smile and say 'thanks' when someone serves us, when we include someone we've just met in our conversation at a party, when we introduce ourselves to the neighbours who have just moved in, when we stop and give someone directions, when we give our time or money to a good cause, when we let the car into the traffic queue in front of us or when we don't give the traffic warden a hard time when we get a ticket (and it was our fault!)

Someone once said, 'Most human problems stem from the fact that we treat people as things and things as people.' But when we reach out and pick up a golden thread (however small) we recognise the stranger as a person with feelings and needs and in the process we help make our society a more pleasant place to live.

strangers and you

How do you respond to strangers in need? If you find it hard to help, what are the things that hold you back?

How well do you connect with strangers on a daily basis? Are people likely to feel cheered or discouraged after an encounter with you?

In what other ways do you volunteer to help strangers? If you don't volunteer in any ways is there something you would like to do to reach out to people in your community? How could you start?

loving those we know

The golden threads don't just happen with strangers. Every day we have opportunities to reach out and make a difference to those we know. When we put the needs of a colleague, a family member, a friend, a date, a spouse, a child or a neighbour before ours, when we listen to their bids for connection, when we offer our help, time or our encouragement, we show that we care.

With people we know the temptation can often be to care for them, help or love them in a way that is convenient for us or in a way we think they may like or that we would like if it was us. But the secret to reaching out is to find out what they would like or really need and to do that. When we do that we uncover another golden thread.

When Mel's ex-husband abruptly stopped paying maintenance she was unable to find the money to support her four sons:

Good friends showed support by bringing food parcels around and offering 'once off' financial assistance in the form of gifts. But my brother and sister-in-law really topped it by taking me and my situation in hand. She was intuitive and rightly sensed that I was at a dead end and did not know what to do next. She stepped right in, encouraged me to put an ad in the paper to rent my house out and said I could stay in their 'four car garage' with the kids. They built an en suite bathroom for us. The arrangement was for a year. During that time she refused rent and helped me with a plan to get my debt down. The year passed and she indicated that the arranged time was up and we needed to move on. We did. We rented a place nearby and sub-let part of the house. They were an immense support in our lives and I will *never* forget that they were there for me when I was really in a tough spot. I am also grateful that they had enough faith in me to believe that I would not be their problem forever, a fear I think a lot of folk have when they think of doing something similar.

five lessons in love

One of the most helpful tools I've found for discovering what other people need comes from a book called *The Five Love Languages* by Gary Chapman.

He came up with the idea that there are five different ways that we give or receive love. He calls these ways love languages. They aren't just for romantic relationships: they can be applied to any type of close relationship and can help us make those close to us feel appreciated, known and loved.

The five love languages are:

- Words
- Presents
- Touch
- Time
- Actions.

Gary Chapman explains that for each one of us, one of those will be like our native language. It'll be the way that we naturally feel loved and appreciated. For example, for me it is when people say affirming words to me that I feel loved. But for David it is touch. He likes it when I hug him when we are out and about or if I lie on the sofa with him and watch DVDs. Those things make him feel loved.

255

Some of us will be bilingual: there can be two languages that really make us feel loved. As well as words, I also like presents. I love buying presents for my friends, and finding things that they would really like. For one of his birthdays I bought David a Star Wars light sabre because I knew that he'd really like that. (Well doesn't every boy in grown-up skin?)

The way in which we show love is often the way that we want to receive it. A great clue as to what someone's love language is is to see how they show love to others. If they are always buying great presents then the chances are that that is what they would like others to do for them. But if they are always doing nice things for others then actions may be what they would prefer. Another clue is to listen to what they complain about when they are feeling unloved or unappreciated. For example, do they complain that you don't help or that you don't spend time with them?

Hitting the target

It can be a great help to find out the love languages of those close to us. That way we won't be pouring all our efforts into showing them love in a way that has little impact for them.

For example, a husband may run around doing lots of jobs for his wife to show her that he cares but if her main love language is quality time then all the jobs he's doing might be nice but they won't be filling her love tank! She'll be more interested in him spending time with her.

And if a child's love language is words and his parents don't express their love for him that way but give him lots of presents then he may feel unloved and unappreciated.

If a friend's love language is presents and they always give you fantastic presents but you forget their birthday they may feel as if you don't care.

But just because we discover their main love language doesn't mean we should completely stop using the other four. It just means we can do more of the one or two that make the most impact.

President Obama has clearly learnt what is important to his wife. This is what he said in an interview for *Ebony* magazine:

> What I realise as I get older is that Michelle is less concerned about me giving her flowers, than she is that I'm doing things that are hard for me – carving out time. That to her is proof, evidence that I'm thinking about her. She appreciates the flowers, but to her romance is that I'm actually paying attention to things that she cares about, and time is always an important factor.

Learning to speak all five

We need to learn to speak love in all five ways, because the people around us may have different love languages to our own.

When we first got married David wasn't at all sure about buying presents and I got some pretty interesting things the first Christmas and birthday. And I struggled showing him affection in public. I felt self-conscious holding his hand in the street and if we bumped into anyone we knew I yanked my hand away.

We both had to learn how to speak each other's languages. But learning the love languages that aren't our natural ones can be hard. It is a bit like learning any foreign language: it takes time, discipline, effort and practice.

As you read about each love language it may help to ask yourself: 'Is this the main way that I show love to the people around me?'

1. Words. Words have great power. Mark Twain once said, 'I can live for two months on a good compliment.'

When we compliment people, it shows that we notice. It could be, 'You look great in that shirt, is it new?', 'What a fantastic haircut you've got', 'You did a brilliant presentation today' or 'You are so good at coming up with creative ideas.' Sometimes we think nice things but don't say them, but we need to try and vocalise them.

257

The same is true with appreciation. If we say thank you or we express our appreciation we show that we value what someone has done for us, or given to us, or that we are happy that they are in our lives.

We can speak our appreciation or write it in a text or an email but there is something special about receiving something hand-written. It is something you can treasure. Every Valentine's Day a friend of mine writes letters to each of his six children telling them how much he loves them and what he appreciates about them.

My last boss and his wife were brilliant at writing thank-you cards. If I worked hard on a project they would write expressing their appreciation for what I had done. Receiving those cards meant a lot. It helped me to know that they noticed, that they cared and that I wasn't taken for granted.

We can also use our words to encourage people. Encouragement literally means, 'inspiring courage', and as we encourage the people in our lives we're helping them to meet their full potential. This isn't false flattery, it is when we truly encourage someone to become all that they can be. Our encouragement can help them risk taking the next step.

For Zeta, encouraging words can mean the difference between feeling motivated or de-motivated:

I can't emphasise too strongly how great an effect words of affir-mation have upon me, or how utterly dismal I become in their absence. I don't possess fabulous self-esteem, but I am a reason-ably intelligent and capable woman nonetheless. Much of what I achieve depends on how other people perceive and approach me. If someone asks me, 'Can you do this, do you think?' I am never sure. If there is doubt in their voice then there is an even greater level of doubt in my head. But if someone asks me to do the same thing and expresses their confidence in my abilities, 'You're just the person; you'd do a great job!' why, I could take on the world, climb every mountain, ford every stream …!

For those whose love language is words, it won't be just what we say that will make them feel special but also how we say it, as Harry discovered with his wife Kate:

> We were going through one of those patches where we both felt a bit disconnected. Life, children and work had taken over. We'd spent too little time together, not enough time being friends. Often it's me who breaks the ice when this happens but this time it was Kate. I was so grateful to her. She came and sat down next to me. She said she knew I'd been chatting with her but we both knew my words hadn't really connected. I said I thought her love language was words. She said 'yes' but not just any words. It's the way I say them, the way I treat her.
>
> The key, she said, was that I occasionally came across as harsh, brusque or unkind. She knew that's not what I meant but it's what came across. What she needed was gentle, kind and caring. The ice is long gone now ... until I need reminding.

Examples of how to show loving words:

- **Encouraging a friend when they try something new, like giving a presentation or taking an exam**
- **Giving compliments**
- **Texting or sending a card to a friend or someone you love to say, 'I'm thinking of you'**
- **Sending a hand-written thank-you card when someone has done something for you**
- **Saying well done when someone does a good job (too often we only mention the bad things)**
- **Enquiring about personal issues like health, or a family incident, and remembering the details**
- **Leaving post-it notes on someone's computer at work or on the fridge at home to say thanks or well done**

- **Writing a letter to a parent, child or partner to tell them how much you love and appreciate them.**

2. Presents. Presents can be a visual symbol of love; they can have powerful emotional value for someone whose love language is thoughtful presents, as mine is!

They don't need to be expensive. It isn't about how much money you spend. Presents can be bought, found or made. We don't have to wait for special occasions, we can give presents to surprise people or when they're feeling down, or just to say I was thinking of you.

The important thing about giving presents is discovering things that the other person wants, or that they would like. It's not about what we'd like, but about what would suit them. It can help to make a mental note of things that they've talked about, or mentioned.

Some people like practical presents and some people really don't, so it is good to find out whether they are going to want saucepans or drill bits or whether they would rather something a little less utilitarian like a book, a plant or a picture you've painted. Some people like surprises and others would just like what they asked for (like David, who gives me a list of a few DVDs he would like before Christmas and then is very excited when he gets them. It beats me, but it does make shopping for him easier!)

And a final tip when it comes to presents: it helps to make them look nice. I heard about one man who would hand over a present still unwrapped in its plastic bag with the receipt still attached. But that isn't generally a winning formula! Going to some effort with the presentation (even if you aren't very good with awkward corners and sticky tape) shows you care and that you tried. And if you are worried about the environment (or the recipient is), you can wrap it in newspaper or cloth or paper that you can recycle and use again.

Examples of how to give loving presents:

- Buying a friend tickets to their favourite concert or sporting event
- Bringing back a small gift from holiday to say, 'I was thinking of you'
- Giving someone a DVD that you know they'd appreciate
- Picking or buying flowers for your mum
- Getting someone the thing that they admired of yours or something you know they've been looking for for ages
- Bringing in chocolate or cakes to the office
- Making something for someone like a painting, a piece of pottery, jewellery, carpentry or some biscuits
- Giving money or something anonymously to someone who needs it.

3. Touch. We were all created with the need for affection but, for some people, touch really speaks louder than any words.

Tender gestures can be really important in times of crisis for the person whose primary love language is touch. When they're really upset, they want that supportive arm, or that hug that says someone's close by.

We need to learn how to show one another affection through touch and that can be hard for some people, especially if love wasn't demonstrated in this way when they were growing up.

We also need to find appropriate ways to show this kind of love, with appropriate boundaries, and obviously that depends on the nature of our relationship with the person and the setting we find ourselves in. (It won't be appropriate to touch people at work *unless* you have an established friendship with them. If in doubt – *don't*.)

If we have friends who live on their own (perhaps they are single, divorced or widowed) and we know that they miss touch it can help to offer a hug. Elderly people particularly can go for days without human contact and that can be very hard if this is their primary love language. Without touch they can feel starved of love.

Examples of how to show physical affection:

- **Hugging**
- **Playing rough and tumble or tickling your children**
- **Walking with arms linked with good friends or family**
- **Giving a warm greeting: a hand shake, a hug, or a kiss where appropriate**
- **Giving your child a ride on your shoulders**
- **Holding hands**
- **Giving a neck or foot massage**
- **Placing an arm around someone when they're upset.**

4. Time. This is when we focus our attention on the person we're with, so that they really know we're there for them. We're not looking over their shoulder at something or someone else and we're not waiting to answer our mobile phone or text someone else.

Rick Warren, in *The Purpose Driven Life*, writes: 'Attention says, "I value you enough to give you my most precious asset – my time." Whenever you give your time, you are making a sacrifice, and sacrifice is the essence of love.'

I have already mentioned this at length in Chapter 3 so I won't repeat it all here. But spending time with people means hanging out together, talking, doing things together and eating together. Eating together is a wonderful way of building relationship. Too often today we eat in front of the TV, eat in a rush, and eat in separate rooms or at different times to our flatmates or family. But when we do that we miss the opportunity for connection that eating together brings.

On his journey across the world, Michael Palin commented: 'In almost every country I visited on *Pole to Pole*, the sharing of food was an important social activity, which is as it should be. A shared meal is the best forum for the airing of grievances and celebration of pleasures that has yet been devised.'

Friendships and relationships are built on shared experiences. As we have fun and spend quality time with our friends and family we create shared memories. We need to factor in time when we can hang out, do things together, share a coffee or a meal together; time when we can talk, laugh, cry and just be with each other.

I just want to mention something here on hospitality. Hospitality can fill some of us with dread; perhaps we feel that we don't have anything to offer, or that we wouldn't be any good at it, but we can all use what we've got. If we've got a spare bed we can offer it to a friend who is between places or is travelling through. We can ask people for a meal or a cup of tea. If we don't like cooking we can buy something ready-made. If we haven't got any money or we're feeling a bit tight, we can ask people to bring food along. If we're really shy we can organise something with another friend. If we haven't got a home where we can entertain we can plan a picnic or a trip to the cinema. We can ask people to join us on holiday or for a weekend away.

Tess is a single mum and it means so much to her when people offer her and her daughter hospitality:

One of the challenges of being a single parent is that you do everything on your own. Silly little things can seem overwhelming because there is no one to share them with and there's no one to make you laugh and show you the funny side when you are overtired. My friends are so important. I remember when my daughter was little I would love to be asked away for the weekend, it was such a treat to be part of a friend's life with their children. It took away the intensity of just always being my daughter and me. We also loved being asked for Sunday lunch. Weekends tended to be particularly lonely; going to the playground or park as a single mother was agony, there would be mothers and fathers holding hands and co-parenting their children; it would make me feel so lonely and such a failure. I also had another great girlfriend who was single parenting her daughter too so we would often meet up for walks in the park after school or go for outings at the weekend. This too really helped us both and our daughters had a wonderful time.

Most people love to be asked, so don't be put off if people say no because there will always be people out there who want to be included and do something. And if we are feeling excluded the best thing we can do is to take the initiative.

(Check the tips at the end of this section for ideas on how to be a great host and a star guest.)

Examples of how to spend quality time:

- Spending time chatting
- Just hanging out together
- Having long Sunday lunches with friends or family
- Playing games with your children
- Having lunch or coffee with a work colleague
- Visiting someone who's sick or elderly and spending time listening to them
- If someone has a problem, really stopping what you're doing and listening
- Having people over for dinner
- Having a family or date night
- Playing sport with a friend
- Going on holiday together.

5. Kind actions. Kind actions are expressing love through seeking to meet the desires and needs of others in practical and thoughtful ways. In *A Farewell to Arms*, Ernest Hemingway wrote, 'When you love you wish to do things for. You wish to sacrifice for. You wish to serve.'

Often, we're so busy, we run around thinking only about what other people are doing to help us. But actually we need to stop and say, what can I do to help support the people around me? It means thinking what would help them at the moment or what would make their life easier?

In his book, *The Road Less Travelled*, M. Scott Peck defines love like this: 'Real love is the work of extending oneself for the purpose of nurturing another. The more we do this, the more we love. True love is a choice which often transcends feelings of love.'

Showing love like this may mean doing things when we don't feel like it. It may mean sacrificing our own needs and desires to focus on someone else's. It means putting ourselves out for someone else.

My mum is particularly brilliant at showing love like this. She volunteers at the local coffee morning in her village, she visits people who are ill or stuck at home, she makes food for anyone she knows is struggling, she cooks David and me wonderful food when we go to visit and she'll even do my ironing (remembering my pathological hatred of irons!).

There may be particular people in our lives who could really do with our help and support at the moment, perhaps someone who is elderly, lonely or going through a hard time. Valerie can still remember the kindness of her friends from church when her husband was dying:

> My husband and I were truly blessed over the period of his
> illness. He remained at home and wanted me at his side almost
> constantly. Our friends helped with prepared meals, wrote letters
> or told Clive personally what impact he had had on their lives,
> kept him company if I had to go to college or to the annual book
> club lunch, sang Christmas carols to Clive from the patio below,
> listened to me, prayed with me, grieved with me, helped me with
> accounts and paperwork or banking so that Clive knew the 'house
> was in order' and I would be OK. When we knew that Clive's
> time to go was near, a dear friend of ours moved in with me and

took over all tasks so that I could remain by Clive's side. And then since he died the help and support has been ongoing, through the time of having to sort out the will, sell my house, move into another ... I have known and felt their love. And now I want to comfort others with the comfort I have received.

Examples of how to show kind actions:

- Helping someone move or do some DIY
- Doing someone's shopping for them
- Cooking a meal for someone
- Making the tea or coffee at work
- Babysitting for a couple or single parent who hasn't been able to get out for some time
- Offering a lift home to someone even though it's out of the way
- Helping with the washing-up
- Volunteering for a charity.

Things can change

Be warned – love languages can change over time. Children's love languages may change as they grow older. Mums with young children often find that kind actions and quality time become more important, even if they weren't their love languages before they had children! So it is worth checking that our actions are still having the desired effects.

Our survey results

We asked people in the survey which love language was most important to them.

- 31 per cent said loving words
- 2 per cent said thoughtful presents (this may well be a reduced figure as many people struggle to admit that this is really theirs!)
- 8 per cent said physical affection (again, this may not be one people want to admit to!)
- 37 per cent said quality time (this is probably a reflection on how little time people have for their relationships)
- 22 per cent said kind actions.

love languages

What is your love language? How does it make you feel?

....

What are the love languages of those people who are closest to you? (You may want to check with them.)

....

Think of ways in which you can show each of the five love languages to someone this week:

1. words ....

2. presents ....

3. touch ....

4. time ....

5. actions ....

267

15. living in colour

Friendship doubles our joy and divides our grief.
A SWEDISH PROVERB

*Character cannot be developed in ease and quiet. Only through experi-
ence of trial and suffering can the soul be strengthened, vision cleared,
ambition inspired, and success achieved.*
HELEN KELLER

*With hope and virtue, let us brave once more the icy currents, and
endure what storms may come. Let it be said by our children's children
that when we were tested we refused to let this journey end, that we did
not turn back nor did we falter; and with eyes fixed on the horizon and
God's grace upon us, we carried forth that great gift of freedom and
delivered it safely to future generations.*
PRESIDENT BARACK OBAMA, IN HIS INAUGURAL SPEECH

hopes and heartache

Three years ago David and I were trying to move home and to start
a family. We'd been trying for a couple of years and by this stage
I was 37 and aware of the ticking clock. We were living in my old
flat and we were looking for somewhere bigger with room to have
our parents to stay and to fit children, if and when we had them.
We were keen to stay in the same area as I'd lived there (on and

268

off) since I was fourteen and, unusually perhaps for London, we felt part of our community. We had lots of great friends living nearby and we liked and trusted our car mechanic, our doctor and our newsagent. But we weren't sure we would be able to find a property we could afford.

One day, I was looking out of my bedroom window when I saw a rainbow – in fact I saw two. One a little brighter than the other. I showed them to David. We'd never seen two rainbows together before. We saw them as a good sign. Maybe everything would work out with the baby and the house.

And then the following day a house came up in the one street where I had always wanted to live. It was two minutes from our flat, just the right size and was just within our budget. I made an appointment to see it right away. It was ideal and I loved it. By that evening David had seen it too and we made an offer which was accepted. We had two months to find a buyer for ours. With two days to go we had nobody interested and I had to go off to the States for work. While I was away two buyers came forward and with just a few hours to go we accepted an offer from one of them. I returned a few days later tired and thrilled and, a couple of days afterwards, it transpired that I was pregnant.

Sadly, the house purchase proved to be a nightmare and went on for months. I won't bore you with the details other than to say that we were in a tricky chain and the day before we were all meant to exchange contracts, the sale fell through. That same day I discovered I was bleeding. At the hospital we saw the eleven-week embryo on the scan: tiny, perfect but with no heartbeat. I miscarried. No baby and no house. We were distraught. Perhaps we'd got it all wrong about our rainbows. The next day we had a two-week holiday planned with my parents at their home in Devon. We needed that time to give my body and our emotions time to start the healing process.

When we returned to London the estate agent called with the news that the house sale was back on and a month later the removal van, with us following, made the 800 metre trip to our new home. We've been here nearly three years now but despite several rounds of fertility treatment there is, as yet, no baby. In the meantime, while we try and wait patiently, our two spare bedrooms are taken up by two very nice lodgers.

Those months were difficult times for us. They weren't the worst of times (we had both been through worse and we were aware of others who have to deal with things that are much worse) but they were definitely hard. However, while they were hard they weren't all bad. We were reminded that life doesn't always turn out as we hope or imagine and that is something all of us will have to grapple with at some time.

making rainbows

In fairy tales life seems so much simpler – the baddies normally get their come-uppance, the goodies fall in love and live happily ever after and everyone knows that at the end of every rainbow there is a pot of gold. But as much as we may want it to be so, real life is rarely that black and white. Real life is more, much more. It is a riot of colour. It is amazing, exciting, beautiful and fragile but it also includes suffering, pain, hardships and disappointments. And it is often unfair.

The rainbows that I saw out of my window that day only occurred after both the sun and the rain. And being human and authentic is about living in colour, experiencing both the good and the bad that life has to offer us. It is about knowing life's celebrations and pain, it is experiencing the joy of new birth and the grief of death, it is being able to laugh and to cry, and it is knowing when to reach out and when to receive. It is realising that even if life doesn't turn out as we had hoped we can still find the sunshine in the midst of the rain.

the search for happiness

It is very tempting to think that life has to be a certain way before we can be happy. We can easily get seduced by the great 'progression game' of life. We tell ourselves that when we get the great job, when we get married, when we buy the house, when we get the car, the promotion, the perfect figure/physique, the baby, the luxury holiday, when we pay off the mortgage, retire or ... (fill in the blank) then we will be happy.

But if we are not careful we can end up chasing pots of gold that are just illusions. I am not suggesting it is bad to have any of those things, but if life becomes about constantly trying to reach the next goal or stage then our emotional energy, our time, our hopes and our money will be focused on trying to get to it. And then, if it doesn't come or doesn't come quick enough, we are left feeling frustrated and depressed. When we see others get there before us – or we don't get what we want – we feel that life isn't fair. And if we do get there, after the initial burst of pleasure and satisfaction, we can soon find our attention turning to the next goal that we must achieve.

So how do we find joy, peace and hope in our outcome-focused, consumer society? How do we find contentment however apparently well or badly we are doing in the 'progression game'? How do we live authentically today in the light of what may or may not come tomorrow?

Let me share a few things that have helped me to embrace the sunshine and the rain and to hold on to hope whatever the circumstances.

Let go
Life can be extremely stressful if we believe that we have to control everything or everyone in it. It is easier to find peace if we can let go of control and of our demands and if we can lay down our preconceived ideas of how life *should* be. To do that we need to

271

accept the things in life that we cannot change, allow others to be free to be themselves and take responsibility for the things that are ours to take. If we can do these things then we have a better chance of letting go of the anxiety, striving and stress that so often surround us. We can stop thinking that we have to be master of our own domain or that life has to be or to turn out a certain way.

Tanya married when she was forty and gave birth to a son a year later:

When my child was born with Down's Syndrome, I was in a daze. Of course I felt sorry for and guilty about him. But I felt far more sorry for me – I hadn't done this right; I was flawed and not a real woman. I couldn't compete with other mums. I hated every boyfriend who'd let me down so that I was having children so late in life. And I felt desperately sorry for my husband who'd longed for a big happy family.

My lowness went on and on. I thought I had made it clear to God and the world at large that there were things I wanted from life, which could be viewed on List A; and things I emphatically did not want, which were on List B. You can guess which list a disabled child was on.

But, inexplicably, I got something off the wrong list. And I did not take well to the mix-up. But time and the need to survive help, and after eighteen months of howling with rage, distress and despair, I took a closer look at our delivery. We have a beautiful child (yes, really – he's on the books of a modelling agency). He has a fantastic sense of humour – perhaps overly focused on bodily functions, but you've got to start somewhere. Every morning he dances enthusiastically to his Abba tape. He hates the wind in his face and shouts indignantly at it. He adores his mum and dad, although he does have a soft spot for all blonde women. Someone stopped me on the bus the other day and said they thought he was an angel in disguise. Well, that's the kind of eccentricity you get in inner London, but even so, I felt they had a point.

The experience of my son has helped me acknowledge that perhaps I don't know exactly what will make me happy in life and that maybe List B isn't the list of horrors I thought. In turn, this has made me less worried and controlling, which can only be a good thing!

Live in the present

If we always have an eye on the next goal we can fail to see what is happening right in front of our eyes. When we live in the present we focus on what is important in the here and now. We concentrate on our relationships and we take the time to appreciate what is around us. We celebrate the good things – both small and large.

People who have faced death or have been through a serious illness often find it easier to live in the present. They know that a tomorrow is never guaranteed. Rita is in her late thirties and the mother of two young children. Six months ago she had a heart attack:

> My long-term goals are to enjoy my grandchildren, to suffocate in a bear hug from my grown-up son, to watch my daughter walk down the aisle ... but just in case none of these are realisable I'm focusing on the short term. Every day I inhale the scent of my son's downy fair hair, I marvel at the softness of his little hands and feet, I laugh with my daughter and squeeze her tight, I tell her that 'I love her, I love her, I love her and I always, always will.' I try to take time to play the things she wants to play; I try to create memories just in case that's all she has one day. I wish I could say I've become a better person but I haven't! I *have* learned to be grateful for now, for this moment. Life, as the saying goes, *is* precious.

The challenge for all of us is to make the most of the life we're living today. Not the life we may have one day, or we wish we had, but the life we have now. It means switching off the 'if onlys' and the 'but ifs' when they start in our head. It means not putting our life on hold but living it to the full now.

I remember when I was single I didn't buy any fluffy white bathroom towels because one day I hoped to get married and have some on my wedding list. I then heard someone say, 'Don't put your life on hold' and I thought how stupid I was being. When my mum next asked me what I wanted for a present I mentioned the towels. A male friend of mine in his twenties told me he loved eating porridge but never cooked it for himself because he imagined that was something married people do! When I told him my story he decided to cook himself porridge the next day.

Back in the sixteenth century the French poet Pierre de Ronsard reminded us: 'Live now, believe me. Wait not till tomorrow. Gather the roses of life today.'

Some of us might not be where we thought we'd be in life but there is nothing to stop us making the most of now and living life to the full. My friend Michelle is gorgeous, single and has just turned forty:

> Life has thrown me a number of surprises and I am certainly not where I thought I would be at this age but I am living a fulfilled life and this is without a significant other.
>
> Looking back to my twenties, I could not wait to have a wedding list where I could finally get a soda stream and a sandwich toaster for free! All my family were married in their early twenties and thought it was odd that I wasn't married by the time I was twenty-five. Even though I am still single now I am pleased that it did not happen when I wanted it to as I did have a lot to sort out in myself.
>
> I think the toughest time came in my early thirties, seeing a lot of my friends get married and having amazing marriages. There was a real temptation to think that there was something wrong with me or that I was somehow on the wrong track. But most of those thoughts were just lies I was telling myself.

About three years ago, after a period of time of being unsettled in my job and life generally, I decided to go abroad and work with a humanitarian aid organisation in Northern Uganda. It has been one of the most fulfilling times in my life and to be honest I would not want to be anywhere else right now. Sure, marriage is something I would still welcome but my eyes have been opened to a whole new world. Working with people whose struggles are so much bigger than mine has brought me healing and perspective. I have experienced a simplicity of life that has given me much more peace and the community of people I live with means that I am not lonely. I still wouldn't say 'no' to the free sandwich toaster but now it isn't the greatest focus of my life.

living your dream

How good are you at living in the present? Are you missing anything today because you are fixating on future goals? How could you change this?

Is there anything in life you are putting 'on hold'? Does it have to be on hold or is there a way you could start to make it happen now?

Are you living your dreams? If not, what are the things that fill you with purpose and passion? What do you want to do to make a difference in life? What one thing could you do today to start you on this journey?

Have a grateful heart

Being appreciative and thankful for all that we have is a great way to counter our restless hearts. It is better to focus on all that is good and beautiful in our lives rather than longing for all that we do not have or all that someone else has. To reach out and to be generous with our time, love, money and energy, particularly with those who have less than we do, can help us to take the focus off ourselves.

To celebrate with others, to laugh, to refuse to be too intense or serious, to be playful, to have fun and to be with the people we love, to just hang out with others, doing things with them just to be with them without a specific outcome in mind – these are all things we can do – things that cost us nothing but bring great benefits to ourselves and to those around us.

And when things are tough, if we can let go of a complaining and negative attitude we are more likely to find joy and meaning even in the midst of the worst circumstances.

Martin, a friend of mine, went through a horrific experience in his late twenties. He was the victim of an unprovoked knife attack and needed emergency surgery:

> My first memory coming round after the anaesthetic was the doctor saying it was a miracle that the knife missed all the major organs.
>
> I went through a number of phases during the recovery process. I struggled with the injustice of it, felt vengeful and very angry. I became quite self-absorbed and despondent and there was a danger of my reactions driving a wedge between me and Catherine [his wife]. Fortunately we had some very good friends around us at the time, who helped me to find a more positive perspective on things. They helped me to realise that I couldn't change what had happened and that I was actually quite fortunate that there was no permanent damage.
>
> Gradually, I was able to forgive my attacker, let go of the bitterness and rebuild my life. After that experience Catherine

and I now feel less panicked when bad things happen – we know we can work through things together. It helped us to focus on what is important and I think we are now much more sensitive and keen to help others when they are going through a tough time.

During the Second World War, Victor Frankl, an Austrian psychiatrist, spent nearly three years in three different concentration camps. In his book, *Man's Search for Meaning*, he wrote about his fellow prisoners:

We who lived in concentration camps can remember the men who walked through the huts comforting others, giving away their last piece of bread. They may have been few in number but they offered sufficient proof that everything can be taken away from a man but one thing, the last of the human freedoms, to choose one's attitude in any given set of circumstances, to choose one's way. The way in which a man accepts his fate and all the suffering it entails, the way in which he takes up his cross gives him ample opportunity, even in the most difficult circumstances, to add a deeper meaning to his life.

Give our soul a look-in

In our fast-paced materialistic society it is easy to forget that we have a soul or a spirit – the part of us that dreams, yearns, searches for what is beautiful and good, communes with all that is sacred and desires the eternal.

Many of us just block it out or pretend it isn't there. Of, if we do realise we have one, we are too busy to attend to it – there is just too much else going on.

For us to be truly authentic from the inside out we need to allow our body, mind and soul to be working in harmony. We are made up of all three and if we neglect one it will affect other areas of our lives. We can feed our body and mind with as much as we like but if we never feed our soul we will remain restless and hungry.

If we want to give our soul a look-in we have to slow down. If we want to appreciate the beauty of nature, enjoy a child's laugh, marvel at an amazing painting, breathe in a gorgeous smell, feel the warmth of a hug, listen to fantastic music and taste something delicious we have to take our time to savour them.

Our soul craves goodness. Not just to feel it, but to know it and to do it. It longs for us to reach out beyond ourselves, to pick up our golden threads and to create something beautiful with our lives. If we allow it our soul also wants to search for meaning. It wants to know what the point of life is. What is the meaning of all this? These are questions many of us avoid thinking about. We cover over our uncertainties with more busyness. If we are short of time we can't stop and reflect on our deep longings.

It is in our soul that we keep our real dreams and hopes alive. But if we don't listen to them or give them airtime they may slowly wither and die.

Our soul is where we hear the small quiet voice that will guide and direct us to all that is good, if we will allow it. It is where our intuition is located. But we need to be still enough and quiet enough to listen.

Faith (if we have it) allows us to trust in a higher power who is so much bigger, more loving and wiser than ourselves. It causes us to stand in awe of all that is majestic. It rejoices in all that is true, just, pure and holy and longs for communion with God. It finds contentment in today but longs for what is yet to come.

To connect with our soul we need to open our lives to give it space. We need to find a quiet place where we can stop and focus, preferably on a daily basis. Perhaps there is a quiet corner in your home, your garden or your neighbourhood where you could spend a few minutes each day sitting or walking, where you can pray or meditate or just 'be' in silence.

Going on retreat is becoming a more popular option these days and there are many places listed on the Internet that organise these.

A retreat is a great opportunity to press the pause button, to take stock and to give your soul a look-in. Ben started going on retreats three years ago. Now he goes several times a year – mostly for a weekend:

> If I haven't been for a few months, I start getting an itch to book one up. Although I often get the 'why am I doing this?' feeling as I drive up to the front door, I have never been on a retreat that wasn't a profound experience in some way (some more dramatic than others). There's something about just stopping and listening – to God or to that small voice inside – that helps put you back in right relationship with your *real* self and with others.

De-clutter our lives

Perhaps there is just too much going on. We may have somehow set up our lives so that there is no space to breathe or to stop. Is there another way of doing it? Could we make different choices?

Do our lives need to be this busy? Do we need to live where we are? Do we have to spend so many hours at work? Do we have to do this job? Do we have to say 'yes' to every invitation? Do our children (if we have them) have to be doing so much? Do we need all this stuff? Does our life have to be so complicated? Do we make enough time for our relationships? Does the way we live have a positive impact on our family, our society or the planet?

Perhaps the answer is 'yes' to all those questions. But have we stopped and asked? Or, let's think of it another way. If we lost our job or our money or our health or discovered that global warming was worse than we thought – how would we do things differently?

Several years ago, Miles, who is married to Deborah and has one daughter, decided he needed to review the way he was living his life:

At the time I was busy working as a banker, travelling abroad nearly every week and Debs was staying at home, feeling lonely and abandoned. We started asking, 'Is this worth it?' The salary, bonuses, perks – were they worth the cost of not seeing each other?

We started to ask ourselves, 'What is important in our lives?' We decided that the things we valued were community, our family, our marriage and me wanting to be around more for Debs and our daughter, but we could see that our life at that time was not designed around those things. So we decided to make some changes.

We moved house from an area where we knew few people, to a less expensive area, close to people we knew already. We found ourselves belonging to a close community centred around our daughter's school and our street. We stopped eating out at expensive restaurants and didn't miss it at all.

I left my banking job and began a consulting business, which took two years to establish. It was a far cry from my old salary but for me it became a vocation rather than a job. Something I was passionate about.

We were able to have time for each other. Walks, picnics, going to the cinema or just hanging out – things we never did before. I was able to take my daughter to school some mornings and was available to go to parents' events. I also became a school governor at a local school in a disadvantaged area. And because I was more available, Debs was able to start working part-time which meant she could pursue things that she was interested in doing.

It took time but little by little we began to live the life that fits with our values. We had less money but we were more content. We found that we did not need more of anything and in fact it was much easier to cope having less. We do not miss anything of our old life and feel that our new life is much more authentic. We don't regret making those changes at all.

Every January David and I batten down the hatches and refuse all invitations to go out with people (not that we seem to get many in January!). We use the month to step back and review our lives. We ask ourselves whether we are giving our money, effort, time and love to the things and people we want to? Or do we need to change something?

It may be that we decide to take just a small step. Even just de-cluttering our cupboards can be a start (I'm well overdue on this!). Have we got stuff in our house that we haven't used for a year? Could we throw or give it away? Can we ask ourselves, 'Do I really need this?' when we want to buy something new?

time to de-clutter?

How are your money, effort, time and love currently distributed?

Do you feel you allow enough time for your relationships?

Does how you live your life at present have a positive impact on friends, family, society and the planet?

Are you happy with your answers? If not, how could things change?

Where is your life too complicated or stressful? What could you do to change it or, if you can't change it, how can you improve it or change your attitude towards it?

Allowing others in

During times of rain – when we are struggling, grieving or suffering – we have an opportunity to allow someone else in to our lives. It can be a great help and a comfort to be able to tell a trusted friend about our fears, our sadness or our disappointments. To be human is to be vulnerable. We all need others with whom we can be vulnerable. People who are safe and whom we can trust. The ones who will allow us to be naked hedgehogs. We need them in our lives and they will also need us.

Steve is in his early forties and single and he has a few close friends he can go to when he's struggling:

> Being single can lead to a very self-centred life but my friend-
> ships are like a mirror, reflecting back to me who I really am,
> pulling me up on things when I am out of line and reassuring
> me when I am being too tough on myself. I know that if I did
> not have these friends beside me life would be so much tougher
> to deal with.

If someone we know is going through a tough time it is an opportunity to come alongside them and tell them that they are not alone and that we are there for them if they want someone to talk to. It may be that they would prefer practical help or someone to just be normal with. Find out what would be the most helpful thing for them.

When Eileen discovered she had breast cancer and she needed surgery, her sister (who'd been through something similar a few years before) offered to have her to stay and to look after her:

> It was such a comfort to have someone with me who knew
> exactly what I was going through and what would make me
> feel better. She took me to funny movies and ensured I didn't
> watch any sad ones! We went walking along the beach. We
> treated ourselves at the chocolate shop and went to scrap book-
> ing and beading lessons. Every moment was so filled up with

happy memories that it is hard to think of any time that was sad. As well as this, my friends from home would call and keep me up on the news. I spent most of the time on the phone laughing; sure there was crying too but they cried with me, not for me, and that is the difference. Real friends are the ones that see you through the toughest times. They are the friends that take hold of a corner of the blanket each and carry you to where you need to be – to hope, to positive thoughts and to the joy of living.

identifying our hard times

what has helped you the most to cope with difficult times in your life?

Who can you go to and be honest with when you are struggling? (If you can't think of anyone think of how you could nurture a friendship like this.)

How good are you at helping others who are struggling? If you aren't, what could you do to be better? If you know anyone struggling right now what could you do today to help them?

reflection

Difficult times can be an opportunity to reflect and ask ourselves questions. Is there anything I can learn from this? Is there anything I could do differently? Is there another way of looking at this problem? Is there something I need to change? How can I grow through this?

283

During the recent economic downturn the Bishop of London, Richard Chartres, while empathising with the 150,000 people in his diocese who might lose their jobs, said that some people may actually feel relief from being made redundant:

> It is difficult to know whether to sympathise more with those who have lost their jobs or those who are left carrying even greater loads with higher targets and fewer colleagues. Sometimes indeed people seem to be relieved to get off the treadmill and to be given an opportunity to reconsider what they really want out of life.
>
> One of the great implications of this turbulence for us is to re-boot our sense of what a truly flourishing human life consists of. The Crack-berry culture is dangerously addictive and coming off is notoriously difficult.[1]

It can be tempting to blow things out of proportion or to turn a problem into a crisis. To tell ourselves that this is the worst thing to ever happen (whether this is losing a job, having a miscarriage, not being married, falling out with someone or whatever). We can get angry, focus on how unfair life is and stew in our resentment. We can tell ourselves that we will never be happy and that things will never change. Or we can stop and reflect and ask ourselves whether there are any glimmers of sunshine in this situation that we haven't spotted?

In our survey 58 per cent of people agreed that they learn more about themselves and others during difficult times. We won't always see the growth when we are experiencing bad times, but I have noticed that when I look back on my struggles I can normally spot it.

However, let me say that if all you can see is rain – if your life is devoid of hope and is filled with a deep despair – then I would urge you to seek help (if you haven't already). Living with depression can easily stop us being able to see any sunshine in life but with the right help it is possible to find it again.

Dawn, who now works as a life coach, suffered from depression during a difficult time in a relationship:

It was situational depression – as in, caused by circumstances – rather then clinical depression. And I realise in the past I have felt depressed when I have felt as if I have no choices or options. I've seen that with friends and clients also.

Depression feels like a shroud. It feels like a tight smother-ing blanket that cuts off all stimuli. I also liken it to a giant vacuum cleaner, sucking all the colour and air out of life. I used to wake up in the morning and just didn't want to get out of bed, and felt no hope that anything good could possibly happen.

But what worked for me was just forcing myself to do things. I knew if I just got up, got out, and tried something different that would shake up my senses a bit and then I'd start to feel better. Fresh stimuli seemed to work just to reboot the old neurological pathways. I tried salsa dancing and exercising. But what worked and what helped me get out of that feeling was reading a lot of coaching books. I coached myself into seeing things from a different perspective, learning more about who I really am and what I really want and being able to create strate-gies and plans that get me from where I am now to where I want to be.

holding onto hope

Let me just return to the story that I mentioned at the beginning of this chapter and explain what I learnt from it. Having gone through so much to get our house I am now really appreciative of it – in a way that perhaps I wouldn't have been if the purchase had happened too easily. What I also learnt through that time was that I have some great people in my life whom I can talk to, and cry or pray with. I found a greater depth in my relationships. I

discovered that some of my friends had also been through miscar-
riages and through our discussions we were able to share at a deeper
level than we'd shared before.

I learnt that some days can be harder than others and that it is
OK to cry and that even when I think I am OK the silliest thing
may provoke a reaction. One day, I saw a photo in a newspaper of
a crocodile that had just had seventeen babies. I looked at David
and I caught myself saying, 'Why does she have so many and we
have none?' with tears pouring down my face.

I learnt that it is important not to dwell in self-pity but to focus
outwards – to look for others to help and support. I learnt to keep
looking for the sun and to put my trust in God. I was reminded
that just because I want something doesn't mean I have a right
to it. I can't control whether I have a baby or not but I can hold
onto hope – a hope that we will have a child one day, either our
own or through adoption. But there are no guarantees in life and
I don't know whether that will happen so I also hope that if we
don't we'll still be OK and that we'll have other people in our
lives whom we can love, nurture and support. And my hope is
that there will be lots more golden threads I can discover and
pick up.

I learnt to make the most of today because I don't know what
tomorrow has in store.

Three years ago, Jean's only child was killed in a car accident.
In the depths of her grief she found a way to keep living in colour:

Initially, talking was the only thing I could do to relieve the
pain. I could not talk enough, to anyone who would listen. Gratitude helped me through the very, very dark times – gratitude
for the nineteen years I had with my son, for the love I have for
him, for the experience of being a mother through hard times as
well as easy times. I would dance and sing my happiness at
having had nineteen years, not eighteen, or six or none. Acceptance of what is took longer and still needs work. I realised that
there are only two options – to live well and joyfully, or to live

long and painfully. My son would want the former, and in his honour, it is my duty to live my life as well as possible. If I fail, I have done him an injustice and his life and death are then meaningless.

authentic living for today

Authentic living is about being real, genuine, open and loving. It is about holding on to hope whatever the circumstances. It is about walking through life with others, allowing them to know the real us and getting to know the real them.

It is about embracing life. It is about following our dreams and allowing others to follow theirs. It means living our lives for today but in the light of what is to come. It means thinking of that golden tapestry and asking ourselves, 'How will my actions today affect my future? What will I think of how I lived my life when it comes to an end?'

When Peter Pan was fighting Captain Hook, the pirates declared that 'to die would be an awfully big adventure'. If we live it in colour – if we live it authentically – life too can be 'an awfully big adventure'.

tips: how to be a great host and a star guest (for those who aren't sure!)

Hosting

Be yourself. Relax and don't try and pretend to be anything or anybody else.

Entertain with love. Even if you can't cook, try making an effort in the way that you prepare and serve any food. Think about your guests and what they would like to eat, drink and do while they are with you. Introduce them to any other guests and make sure no one's left out.

Share your best. Give them the best helping and be generous (within your means). Don't hog the most interesting people, leaving your other guests to cope with the bore you don't want to talk to, and share your favourite box of chocolates!

Don't be precious. If you don't want something touched or broken then hide it! Guests won't relax if you keep watching over their shoulder saying 'be careful'. Only say 'make yourself at home' if you mean it.

Being a guest

Don't be fussy. Unless you have a medical condition, try and avoid being fussy about what you can or can't eat. Just politely ask for a small portion if you really don't like it.

Turn up. Preferably on time and with something for the host if you are staying or going for a meal.

Be helpful. Offer to lend a hand and don't out-stay your welcome. Better to leave when everyone still wants more.

Say thanks. Always thank your host and, if you have stayed with them or been for a meal, there's no better way than sending a hand-written thank-you note.

authentic in action

16. how to be a leader worth following

Becoming a leader is synonymous with becoming yourself. It is precisely that simple, and it is also that difficult.
WARREN BENNIS, BUSINESS CONSULTANT

Leadership is about who you are, not what you know or what skills you have.
SIMON WALKER, THE LEADERSHIP COMMUNITY

If a man's associates find him guilty of being phoney, if they find that he lacks forthright integrity, he will fail. His teachings and actions must square with each other.
DWIGHT D. EISENHOWER, 34TH US PRESIDENT

authentic leadership

Most of us, at some stage in our lives, will have been involved in some kind of leadership role, be it parenting, managing people at work or leading some kind of team, class or group. And even if we haven't we all know what it is like to be led. We can probably all think of a teacher, boss, leader or politician who has inspired us and for whom we have great respect and admiration. Equally, there will probably be those whose style we found difficult to stomach; perhaps they were cruel, bad, ineffectual, dishonest, arrogant or inconsistent.

In our survey, of those who currently work for someone, 20 per cent said they *always* respect their boss which means that 80 per cent don't always do so, which goes to show that not everyone is getting it right all of the time.

So what makes a leader worth following? Is it their intellect, skills, experience, talents, drive, vision, success or enthusiasm – or is it more than that? We asked those we surveyed what top three qualities they looked for in a leader and the answers that came up again and again were integrity and honesty. The next biggest hitters were fairness and vision, followed relatively closely by humility and trustworthiness.

That would seem to indicate that our character, perhaps more than anything else, dictates how others perceive our leadership.

Bill Hybels, in *Courageous Leadership*, writes: 'Followers will only trust leaders who exhibit the highest levels of integrity. People will not follow a leader with moral incongruities for long. Every time you compromise character you compromise leadership.'

a good leader

Think about a leader whom you have admired and respected. What made them a great leader? What qualities in them did you appreciate? How did their leadership make you feel and act? In what ways would you like to lead like them?

Then think about a leader you struggled with. What do you think the issues were with them? What qualities didn't you respect in them? How did their leadership make you feel and act? In what ways would you like to avoid leading like them?

Walking the walk

Wouldn't it be great if we could have leaders who aren't just great at what they do but who also have intrinsic values and are authentic to their very core? Leaders who don't just talk the talk but actually walk the walk. Leaders who can be trusted not to corrupt the power they are given and who care not about their own self-interests but are other-centred. Leaders who can relate to and connect with those they lead, who can serve as well as be served and who can read any situation and determine what kind of leadership style is needed for the here and now. Leaders who are not held back by their own fears, defences or personal ambitions, but are free in their leadership and can step down or away when the time is right.

Imagine if all our leaders were like that and imagine if *we* were leaders like that.

Where do we start? With ourselves. How we are on the inside – our character, our experiences, our relationship style, our values, our sensitive buttons – these things will all affect how our leadership is experienced on the outside.

For example, the leader who:

- ... seeks the approval of others to feel good about themselves, may find it hard to make unpopular or difficult decisions and may seek to avoid these at all costs.
- ... finds it hard to trust people, may struggle to delegate to others, relinquish control (when needed) or forgive someone who has made a mistake.
- ... measures their self-worth by their success, may be driven to work so hard that they neglect other parts of their life, such as their family, friends and health and may struggle to understand others who go home on time, take all their holiday entitlement or aren't prepared to work 24/7.
- ... fears failure may not be willing to take risks and may not encourage others to try risky strategies.

295

- ... has grown up in a family where they were always given praise (and little constructive criticism) may have an over-inflated opinion of their own abilities and may find it difficult to hear negative feedback.
- ... is very shy or introverted may come across to others as aloof, arrogant and uninterested.

All of us will lead out of who we are because it is impossible to separate who we are from how we act as leaders. What we exhibit on the outside is an expression of who we are on the inside and, whether we want it to or not, who we are will impact on those we are seeking to lead, for good or for bad. Gary can still remember the impact of one boss he worked for five years ago:

> I was being managed by a very detail-conscious woman boss, who never gave credit for anything I did, was a real gossip and always talked about people behind their back. I used to dread going home because she would always want to take the tube with me, so I would have to listen to her bitching about people for the thirty minutes or so it would take to get to my stop. It really interrupted my journey and meant I could never get on with any reading. It was such a relief when she got off. I endured it and looked for other jobs but in the end she got the sack for doing the same thing during a two-week visit to Head Office.

understanding your impact

In Chapter 8 we looked a little at the impact we have on others. I mentioned how many of us aren't very good at assessing the full effect we have on those close to us and how, if we have sharp or flat behaviour, we are sometimes the last to realise it.

If as leaders we have little or no awareness of how our behaviour affects those around us we may be tempted to think it is other people not ourselves who are out of tune. Bill Hybels tells the following story in his book, *Courageous Leadership*:

Some time ago one of my staff members was frustrated in his leadership role because certain people under his supervision seemed to be uncooperative. I started poking around his department to figure out what was wrong. Then the real picture emerged, one person said, 'He sets meetings and then he doesn't show up.' Another said, 'He rarely returns phone calls.' Someone else said, 'Often we don't know where he is.'

I scheduled a meeting with that leader and verified the assessments of his teammates. Then I looked him square in the eyes and said, 'Let's get something straight. When you tell your teammates that you'll be at a certain place at a certain time and you are late or don't show up, that's a character issue. When you promise to return a phone call and then neglect to do so, that makes people feel devalued. When your teammates don't know where you are during work hours, that erodes trust. You need to clean this stuff up or we'll have to move you out.'

He adds, 'Over the years I have seen that if character issues are compromised, it hurts the whole team.'

Like you, I have known quite a few leaders in my time and all of them had an impact on me of some kind – whether positive or negative. For example, there was the barber I worked with one summer holiday. He lied to his wife and sneaked his mistress and their child in to the staff room during lunch breaks. He lost my respect – I didn't think he was someone I could trust. Just after I left he was arrested for fiddling the books. Then there was the woman who gave me my first job on national radio, even though I didn't have enough experience. She gave me the confidence to believe that I had the potential to take on the role. But there was also the boss who didn't stand up for me when his bosses thought I had made a mistake (when in fact I hadn't), leaving me feeling betrayed and powerless. When the opportunity arose to leave his department, I jumped quickly.

But I am also aware of times when I have had a negative impact on those I've led. For example, when I have a tight deadline I tend to get more controlling and have a tendency to take the reins. I have no doubt that this leaves others feeling disempowered and frustrated. I have a tendency to lose enthusiasm and focus when a project goes on too long or is repeated. This can be dispiriting for those who are involved in the maintenance or completion of the project, because they don't have my full interest or support.

I thrive on deadlines and love the adrenaline that goes with trying to meet them. I will do everything I can to get the job done on time, even if it means working too hard or risking my health. Working like that can occasionally be productive but when it becomes the norm it isn't a healthy way of operating. Those I work with feel they have to work that hard too and they can feel they are being disloyal or letting the side down if they don't keep up the pace.

Dr Henry Cloud, in his book *Integrity*, describes our impact like the wake of a boat that we leave behind us at work. From our wake we can see how well we got the job done and how well we met our objectives, but we can also see how well we did with our relationships.

Are a lot of people out there water-skiing on the wake, smiling, having a great time for our having 'moved through their lives'? Or are they out there bobbing for air, bleeding, and left wounded as shark bait? In other words, would they say that their experience with us has left them better off for our having 'moved through their lives,' or would they say that it has left them worse off? Did they consider it a blessing that they were associated with you, or a curse? What is the nature of the wake? Are they smiling or reeling?

A friend of mine, Christy, was left reeling after working for her first boss after graduating:

One day, a florist arrived with a dozen red roses for my boss. It was Valentine's Day. Ah, sweet – flowers from the boyfriend. My boss wasn't in the office and wasn't due in until the next day, so I accepted them and put them in her office. The next day she came storming out of the office and threw all twelve red roses with sharp thorns at me (out of the vase, but dripping wet), screaming that she should have been told they arrived, that she'd got in a huge fight with her boyfriend because she didn't thank him for the flowers the night before because, of course, she didn't know they'd arrived. My fault, obviously!?!'

what's in your wake?

How does who you are affect those that you lead?

If people complain or give you negative feedback what is it normally about?

What 'wake' would you like to leave with the people around you? How well do you think you are doing with this at the moment?

What negative impacts would you like to change or work on?

Your impact on your team or organisation

However, our 'wake' may spread further than just the immediate people we work with. The more power and control we have, the more who we are will affect the whole culture of the team, group, family or organisation we are leading.

James had always had good relationships at work until one day a new boss, Melanie, arrived in the office.

She was inexperienced and had never been given such responsibility before. But instead of showing humility and learning from the rest of her team she pretended to know it all and was very aggressive towards anyone who questioned her decisions. I and the rest of the team stopped making suggestions and felt unwilling to help her or support her as we were constantly being reprimanded and undermined. Brilliant members of the team started to leave, which left Melanie even more exposed.

Meanwhile, uncharacteristically I found myself losing confidence in my abilities. The constant criticism was taking its toll. Eventually though, the company directors realised that the ship – under Melanie's leadership – was sinking and she was removed from her post. Under a new leader – who showed humility and a willingness to work with the rest of us – we all started to thrive once again and order was restored. But the process took three years and the company lost many key people as a result.

Many leaders, if they have the power to do so, will fashion their organisation or their team in their own image. Simon Walker, in *Leading out of Who You Are*, writes:

Being in leadership gives you the authority, the power and the resources to structure your environment. A leader has the positional power to make changes, to dictate timing and establish rhythms and determine what happens when and how. Unlike most people, who have to make the best of a world someone else has shaped, the leader can set her own rules within her particular domain. It should be no great surprise, therefore, how often you find that the personality of an organization reflects the personality of its leader.

This will be particularly true when the leader has had the opportunity to start up his or her own company, team, group, family etc.

For example, if they are a dynamic, charismatic leader they may create an organisation that is buzzy, exciting, competitive and expanding. The focus may be on winning, beating sales targets and being the best. People may be attracted to the company and the culture they have created because it is where the action is happening. However, they may also find it a difficult and tiring place to be if and when they fail to keep up with the fast pace or when they long for a more reflective or caring environment.

However, if they take a more behind the scenes approach to leadership they may enjoy creating a decentralised organisation that is non-hierarchical and collaborative. Think Wikipedia, eBay and Alcoholics Anonymous. These are all organisations created with minimal or no central command or control. The impact of a leadership style like this is to empower the members to take the initiative and get involved. Members are likely to feel a great sense of belonging and responsibility. Everyone has a part to play.

We can see that these two different leadership styles create two different cultures. That is why, as leaders, we need to be aware of the style we are exhibiting and the effect that this is having on those we lead and the culture we operate in.

finding the courage to change

It may be that as we look at our impact we realise there are areas of ourselves we need to work on or change. That will take courage and honesty.

Take the example of what happened to the CEO of Dell. Back in 2001, after he had successfully steered the company through a global crash in computer sales, Michael Dell undertook an internal review of his staff. He discovered that nearly half his employees would leave given the chance and that many viewed him as 'impersonal and detached.'

Dell decided to embrace their comments head on. He met with his senior staff and admitted that his shyness could make him appear aloof and unapproachable. He promised them he would make an effort to change and to build better links with his team. His talk was videoed and a copy shown to all his staff.

Notice Dell didn't say, 'That's just how I am – live with it!' He took steps to change himself and the way he led for the greater good of the company.

And his willingness to be vulnerable and to improve his leadership style paid off - morale at the company improved.

Jim Collins, in his business book *From Good to Great*, identifies the factors that help turn a good company into a great one. He and his team of researchers discovered that the critical turning point often coincides with the arrival of a CEO who combines 'extreme personal humility with intense professional will'. So it would seem that being an authentic leader isn't just good for you and those you work for, it is good for business and the bottom line too.

To be authentic leaders and ones that people will want to follow we need to:

- Be open to change
- Be willing to seek out honest feedback (not just from the people who will say nice things)
- Leave our comfort zones and step into unchartered waters
- Work on improving areas of our character that create a negative impact on those around us
- Be prepared to use different leadership styles when the situation calls for it (this may mean developing styles that we are not usually comfortable with, i.e. we may need to learn to be more confrontational and assertive or we may need to practise being more collaborative or vulnerable)
- Create a fun and encouraging environment in which others can grow, learn and take responsibility
- Listen and learn from the people we lead as well as from any that we serve (customers, fans, members etc.). Don't just assume we know what they want and how they feel

- Not allow ourselves to be dominated by fear
- Lay down our need to be great, acknowledged or liked
- Be fully available to serve those who serve us
- Sacrifice our own needs for the sake of the greater good
- Hold on to our position (and all its perks) lightly.

know your drivers

What things would you find hardest to lose – your job title, income, reputation, power, success, influence, control, respect, popularity or status?

Why do you think it matters so much to you? What would happen if you lost it?

How do you think your desire to keep hold of it influences the ways you behave in your role as a leader?

building your team

Perhaps the greatest challenge and the greatest privilege of being a leader is looking after the people for whom we have responsibility, be it our children, our team, a group or our staff. We have it in our power to make being involved with us a fun, rewarding, inspirational and growing experience.

How do we do that?

Be clear about the vision
Make sure everyone knows their responsibilities and understands and feels equipped to reach their goals. It helps if your staff, team

or followers can buy in to your vision and come to own it for themselves. This will mean explaining the vision in a way that is clear, compelling and passionate. Why do you believe this is the way forward and what will life or the business be like when you get there? What will it take for you all to make it happen?

Focus on people first not processes

Don't think of people as a commodity but recognise them as individuals. Learn about them. Know their names and what makes them tick. Help them fulfil their dreams (even if that means they may need to leave you). Celebrate their achievements and help them learn from their mistakes.

If people struggle help them to know it is OK to go through difficult patches. If you can share your vulnerability and perhaps let them know about a struggle you experienced in the past it will help them to grow.

And if, as a team or an organisation, you face a challenging time – lead from the front, be honest and think about the impact it is having on the individuals you are responsible for managing. Sam, who is the director of a busy media department, was recently faced with some difficult decisions:

When I was asked to implement extensive budget cuts and close posts across my team, I took a very tough line to protect the people I thought were vulnerable, and the jobs which I thought were vital to the business, even when it potentially jeopardised my own position. I was absolutely honest and straight about everything I knew the whole way through the process. I told my team what I had to do and how I was going to go about it so by the time it came, they knew what to expect. People thanked me afterwards for dealing with it so fairly and treating everyone with respect. I believe that if you don't have integrity, you can't expect respect and that is vital to being a good boss.

Think of yourself as a conductor

Your role is to bring out the best in others and to help them play their parts as well as they can by coaching them, encouraging them and providing critique for them where needed. You see the whole score and know how every part fits together. Take responsibility when things go wrong.

Recruit people who will thrive in your environment

But don't be tempted to just surround yourself with mini clones of yourself. Choose people for their character as much as (or even more than) for their skills.

Bill Hybels, in *Courageous Leadership*, writes: 'My selection process is based on "three Cs": first character, then competence, and finally chemistry with me and with the rest of the team. Character. Competence. Chemistry. After experimenting with different selection criteria through the years, I have landed on these three in the precise order in which they are mentioned.'

Model what you want to see in others

If you want people to look after themselves and their families, make sure that is what you do. If you are a captain of a team and you want them to play fair, make sure you do. If you are parent and want your children to grow up honest don't lie to them or in front of them. If you want people to help you, help them. My last boss was always the first to pour the coffee or get water during a meeting. I also remember him staying late to help us assemble folders that were needed for a conference the next day. His willingness to help us spoke volumes to the team and invariably meant his staff were happy to go the extra mile for him when needed.

Embody the values you want to see developed

Remember, the culture starts with you. Julian Richer, in *The Richer Way*, writes:

The Richer Sounds culture is built on integrity and loyalty to each other. I have tried to create an organisation that has a common bond, a kind of overgrown family unit. Other companies will have very different cultures. But every organisation should have a culture which is respected by its staff. It is important to employees that the bosses be seen to be responsible citizens. They are carrying the standard for the people at work and it does much to raise morale. If your business is involved in tax dodges, what message does that send staff about the standards of honesty they should apply at work?

passing it on

There comes a time in every leader's journey when it is time to move on and give up the reins to someone else. That will be very hard if we have invested our identity and significance in the role but if we hold onto our leadership lightly we will find it easier to let go when we need to.

Julian Richer writes: 'People like to feel indispensable and if they've built up an organisation, they can't bear to think it doesn't need them anymore. But it will be good for you, your staff and the entire business if the company is not resting solely on your back.'

a leader worth following?

In all areas of society we are crying out for leaders who are worth following. It won't be an easy calling but it will be rewarding. Are you willing to take that path?

17. how to date like you mean it

Never date a woman whose father calls her 'Princess.' Chances are she believes it.
ANONYMOUS

Men want the same thing from their underwear that they want from women: a little support, and a little freedom.
JERRY SEINFELD

When you really don't like a guy, they're all over you, and as soon as you act like you like them, they're no longer interested.
BEYONCE KNOWLES

keep reading

If you are married, or are single but not interested in dating, then you may be tempted to skip this chapter. I would love to suggest you read it anyway as you may have a friend, child, grandchild, godchild or work colleague who is single and may ask your advice on dating. And even if they wouldn't come to you for advice, reading this will help to remind you of some of the issues and challenges that they may be facing. The more you understand, the more you'll be able to support and encourage them. In just the same way, if you are single you may also want to read the next chapter, on marriage.

confessions of an inauthentic dater

It doesn't take a psychologist to work out that one of the reasons I am so passionate about talking (or writing in this case) about authentic dating is because I wasn't very good at it myself. To preserve some dignity, and that of some old boyfriends, I won't catalogue all the mistakes that I made in the twenty-one years I dated before marrying David at the age of thirty-five, but let's just say my dating days were far from perfect. I learnt many lessons the hard way but I hope that some of the advice, wisdom and tips that I picked up will be of some help to you on your journey.

There's so much I could write, but I will just mention eight things that I wish I had known a long time ago. Hopefully these eight things will enable you to date like you mean it.

1. date for the right reasons

Why do we want a boyfriend or girlfriend? Because everyone else has one? Because we're bored or lonely? Because it is fun? Because it helps us feel better about ourselves? Because we crave physical intimacy? Because we had one too many drinks and he or she seemed quite attractive and ...?

what is it all about?

Think about why you want to be in a relationship? (Or why you are, if you are already in one?)

Try finishing the sentence: I want to be in a relationship because ...
(or I'm in a relationship because ...)

Helping or hindering?

I think deep down – whether we'd admit it or not – most of us want a relationship because we do actually want a lifelong mate, someone we can build a home with, share life with, hopefully have children and enjoy growing old together with. And in terms of authenticity, someone we can be ourselves with.

But while many people aspire to get married the reality is that fewer people these days are actually choosing to tie the knot. According to a recent Government survey 39 per cent[2] of women under 50 in the UK have never been married, compared to 18 per cent thirty years ago.

One of the issues is that there are no social norms when it comes to dating and marriage anymore. Go back a century and it was a lot more straight forward. Most people expected to get married, and did, and everyone knew the rules and expectations of courtship (even if they chose to ignore them).

But today no such road map exists and as a consequence we are more likely to find ourselves doing things that hinder rather than help our chances of finding (and keeping) a life partner. For example:

We choose people who are unavailable or unsuitable. If the reason we want to date is to find someone to be with forever then choosing to get involved with people who are not suitable, are not interested in commitment or are already committed to someone else is only going to hinder our chances of happiness. The time to say 'no' is before things even get started, however flattered we might be that they are interested. In hindsight, Jade wishes she had never said 'yes' to that first drink:

> It started on a drunken night out with work colleagues. I fancied him, he fancied me, a colleague started matchmaking and then suddenly he was all I could think about. I knew that he was not married but he lived with the mother of his children and they were very much a family. We spent two years having an affair. I

never asked him to leave her; at the time I didn't think I wanted him to. I honestly believed I could be an independent woman and have him as a bit on the side. I now realise I kept it going because he wanted me and my self-esteem was so low that I was happy to accept being his second choice.

We don't engage our head early enough. Jade's story is an example of what can happen when we act on our impulses instead of thinking through the implications with our head. The desire to be needed, to be intimate with someone, to belong, to be sexually attracted and attractive to someone is natural. But problems are likely to arise when we allow our desires to drive us, whatever the cost. It is a bit like a thirsty traveller in the desert who will drink anything to try and quench his thirst, even though the liquid he finds could do him more harm than good.

It's easy to tell yourself that this is just a little bit of fun, it means nothing, it is just for now, but before you know it you are two years down a dead-end that was never going to lead anywhere. If your long-term goal is to have a committed marriage or relationship for life then it helps to ask yourself the question right at the beginning. Is dating this person a wise move? If you aren't sure of your own judgement, ask a friend you can trust. And if the answer is no, then get out quick. Don't dwell on your feelings for them, and avoid situations were you could be tempted to cave in.

And it isn't just ourselves we need to be thinking about. If we know that we could never commit to the other person is it fair to use them for our short-term fun if they want something more? That's why we need to be honest about our intentions.

I remember when it finally dawned on me that I kept picking boyfriends whom I was never likely to marry. I realised I was probably choosing them because deep down I was actually afraid of commitment. Through my behaviour I was not only jeopardising my own chances of happiness, I also wasn't helping theirs.

We have sex too soon. It is not unusual for people to have sex with someone first and then decide whether or not to have a relationship with them afterwards. But sex is a powerful bonder and if undertaken too early in a relationship it can easily 'blind' a couple to any fundamental problems between them. (We probably all know people who have had a passionate affair with someone only to 'wake up' two months later and realise that they don't even like the person and that they have nothing in common with them.)

If you want to increase your chances of finding that life partnership try reversing the trend. Hold off having sex until you are sober, until you know you like the person, until you know you can trust the person, until you are able to be emotionally vulnerable with each other and until you are both totally committed to the relationship. Then, when you do have sex it isn't just sex it is something so much more amazing and authentic. It is the joining of two people who love each other, who are bonded to each other and who are willing to be 'naked and unashamed' with each other. Mike Mason, in *The Mystery of Marriage*, writes:

> To be naked with another person is a sort of picture or symbolic
> demonstration of perfect honesty, perfect trust, perfect giving and
> commitment, and if the heart is not naked along with the body,
> then the whole action becomes a lie and a mockery. It becomes
> an involvement in an absurd and tragic contradiction: the giving
> of the body but the withholding of the self. Exposure of the body
> in a personal encounter is like the telling of one's deepest secret:
> afterwards there is no going back, no pretending that the secret is
> still one's own or that the other does not know. It is, in effect, the
> very last step in human relations, and therefore never one to be
> taken lightly. It is not a step that establishes deep intimacy, but
> one which presupposes it.

We attach before we commit. Another temptation is to set up home with someone before there's a commitment in the relationship or to never make a commitment. It may start with leaving a toothbrush in the bathroom or getting your own drawer and then, before you know it, you are sharing a flat, the bills and the chores. Many people believe that living together is a good trial or test to see if they want to marry. But researchers from Denver University[3] have discovered that actually the opposite is true. You are less likely to get divorced if you don't co-habit before you get engaged. Writing in Scott Stanley's book *The Power of Commitment*, his colleague Galena Kline says:

> Here's what we found: couples who lived together prior to being engaged were most likely to experience difficulties in their relationships both before marriage and about a year into marriage. They had lower satisfaction, poorer communication, more conflict, higher rates of physical violence, and less confidence in their relationships than people who waited until after they were engaged or married to move in together.

They also discovered an apparent gender difference when it comes to commitment. Women are more likely to commit at the point of moving in with a partner. But on the whole men who 'slide' into a relationship – moving in before they get engaged – will often remain less committed to the relationship (even if they do get married) than men who 'decide' first that they want to get married and then move in. In other words, if a man goes into a relationship thinking, 'I'll just see how it goes' it is less likely to work than if he goes into one saying, 'Yes, this is what I want – I commit to this.' Part of the problem is that inertia makes it harder to slide out of a relationship once a couple has set up home together.

Many couples thus end up trapped in a relationship from which they might otherwise have walked away had they not had the added complication of living together. It becomes harder to break up when you have a joint mortgage and shared possessions. The couple then slide on into marriage or parenthood, one of which eventually forces them to confront reality, and then if and when they do split up the consequences are often more painful on all those involved.

Some people don't see living together as a test – they see it as the final destination. Perhaps they believe marriage is irrelevant or are fearful of divorce (especially if their parents experienced one). But the truth is that *not* getting married is more likely to mean you'll experience a break-up and go through the very thing you were hoping to avoid (and without any legal protection). And it isn't just the couple's relationship that is at risk. Children, if you have them, are more likely to experience family breakdown if their parents are unmarried. Research that looked at data from a sample of children born in 2000-1 found that parents who cohabited were consistently 2 to 2.5 times more likely to have split up by the child's fifth birthday than parents who married.[4]

We are all likely to know exceptions – friends who have bucked the trend and have been happily living together unmarried for years. But if you do want a lifelong committed relationship it is worth thinking about those statistics. You are more likely to reach your goal if you marry instead of co-habit and if you delay moving in together until after committing to marriage.

We sit and wait for 'the one'. Blame Hollywood or the fairy tales we were fed as children, but many people believe that there is a specially prepared Mr or Mrs Right out there and if they can find them then a 'happily ever after' is guaranteed. It is in many ways an attractive thought. There is often something rather comforting in believing that our other half is out there – that our soul mate is just waiting to complete us and make us whole. But this belief in 'the one', who could magically appear in our lives any day, can actually hinder our hopes of finding a partner and of staying with them after marriage.

Why? Because the problem is that if we believe that fate, the universe or God has someone mapped out for us we may be more reluctant to take the initiative or make good choices ourselves. We don't ask people out or get to know them, because we are waiting for our prince or princess to come along. Or, if we do date people, we end the relationships when things get tricky because we don't think we should have any problems if this really was 'the one'. And even worse, we marry the person thinking we've found the fairy tale ending and then when the relationship runs into trouble or we meet someone else that we are strongly attracted to we think that we made a mistake and that our perfect partner is still out there.

Giles and Claudine had dated on and off for several years before they got engaged. Giles found it difficult to commit as he kept wondering if Claudine really was 'the one'. In his times of doubt he would end the relationship, try dating someone else for a bit and then a few months later he would be back. The man who married the two of them was very wise and he knew their story. During the ceremony he turned to Giles and said, 'Your time for choosing is over. Before today you had a choice but now that you have made your vows to each other – Claudine is 'the one' chosen for you and don't ever doubt that.'

While it is great to ask or to pray for guidance, the important thing is making sure we own the choice we make and take responsibility for it. That way, when we experience difficulties in our relationship (which all couples do) we can't just blame God or Lady Luck for getting us into this mess. It was our choice too and therefore it is our responsibility to work through the issues.

Being 'authentic' and intentional means being clear with ourselves as to why we are dating and also realising the impact that our behaviour has on ourselves and others. It is being honest about what we are doing and why.

why date?

Some questions worth asking (sometimes a friend who knows us well can help us with the answers!):

What do you think are good reasons to date?

Would you like to get married one day?

If yes, how has your dating history so far helped or hindered this aim?

If no, have you worked through the reasons you are opposed to, or fearful of, marriage?

And, if you are not interested in (or are scared of) lifelong commitment are you honest about this with the people you date?

2. have a realistic picture of marriage

Wanting to get married is a great desire but wanting it at *any* cost and because we think it will magically make our life better is not. If we put marriage up on a pedestal we may find ourselves rushing into an inappropriate relationship or wasting too much time fantasising about how our life will be transformed when we swap rings and vows with someone.

Judy's major focus and goal, for as far back as she can remember, was to get married:

I didn't really think beyond that and my greatest fear was that I wouldn't achieve that goal. I was desperate to go out with someone (ANYONE!) and the longer I remained single the more panicked I became. In retrospect, guys could probably pick up my needy vibes from a mile off! By university I had a firm belief that I would be permanently on the shelf and threw myself at any guy who showed even the slightest bit of interest in me, however fleeting. Convinced that 'men only want one thing' I fell into bed as soon as possible with quite a number of guys who had no real long term interest in me.

I was quite prepared to marry every one of them (perhaps not all at once!) and I happily fantasised about our wedding from the first kiss. I was willing to sacrifice anything and everything in order to secure my goal. But the longest any of those relationships lasted was seven weeks. I deeply regret my choices now and would love to undo the past.

Now I always tell my friends or anyone who will listen: 'Don't lose who you are or what is important to you in an attempt to win yourself a partner. And remember being needy is not attractive – it makes other people run a mile. You've got to like yourself before you can expect others to like you.'

While some people like Judy may struggle with an over-rosy view of marriage others who have been divorced or who witnessed their parents divorce may find that they experience the opposite issue: scepticism and a lack of belief that marriages *can* work. If that is true for you, you may need to ask yourself if your own painful experiences are distorting your view of marriage. If they are, it may be well worth you working through your thoughts and feelings with a close friend or a professional therapist. Don't let the past rob you of a fantastic future.

What we all need is a realistic picture of marriage. It can help to talk to friends – to people who have been married a short or a long time. Ask them about the joys, the challenges and the struggles and dare to share yours with them. Married and single people aren't different species living on separate sides of the fence. We are all individuals who have good and bad days and who have needs, hopes, fears and dreams.

3. be prepared

While it is important we live life today there are also things we can do now that will improve our chances of making good dating and marriage choices, if and when the time comes in the future. The first thing is to check there is nothing in us that is holding us back from having a great relationship, and that will mean being honest with ourselves.

Davina is nearly thirty and apart from a few six-month relationships she has spent most of her adult life single:

> I always expected that love would 'find me' and that I didn't need to do anything. I thought I was open to the idea of a relationship, but couldn't quite work out why my friends were meeting people and heading off into the sunset of mini-breaks and cohabitation, while I was still on my own. Then, about two years ago, a close guy friend pointed out some home truths. 'You think you're open to a relationship,' he said tentatively, 'but you give off a vibe that says "I'm not interested." You're friendly, but only to the point of politeness. Guys need a bit of encouragement.'
>
> After peeling myself off the wall, I realised he was right. I had been so concerned with not giving guys I *wasn't* interested in the wrong impression, that I wasn't giving *anyone* the right one! I read a few dating books, joined an Internet dating site, lightened up and tried to be more friendly in social situations. Since then I've been on lots of dates, mostly with people I would have written off a few years ago. I haven't met Mr Right yet, but I've had lots of fun, surprised myself at the people I've met, and grown up a lot in the process.

asking the tough questions

Try asking yourself these questions. If you are feeling brave you may want to ask a friend what they think. Sometimes they'll be able to see things you can't see about yourself.

Is there anything from the past that is holding you back from being totally available and open to having a relationship? If yes, how could you get over this? (It could be a fear, a bad experience or an old relationship you haven't truly let go of – anything that means you aren't really available.)

Is there anything in the way you behave or portray yourself that would suggest to potential dates that you are not interested in having a relationship? If yes, how could you work on changing this?

What have your past relationships been like (if you have had any) and why did they end?

What have you learnt about yourself and your choices from those relationships? What would you want to be different in the future?

What are you like at sharing your space with others? What do you think being married to you would be like? Are there any bad habits, selfish traits or character flaws that you could work on towards eradicating now?

Do you tend to be needy in a relationship and find yourself pushing the other person away? Or do you struggle to get close and back away when things get too intimate? Why do you think this is and what could you do differently?

If you have never had a relationship, why do you think that is? Is there anything in you that is consciously or subconsciously holding you back from wanting to get involved with someone? If yes, how could you overcome this?

Check your expectations

If you are looking for a job or a house you normally have some idea what you are looking for. Thinking about what you want in a life partner can also be a great help.

I don't mean you should have some unrealistic checklist, a detailed description of a woman who has the looks of Barbie and the character of Mother Teresa, or a man who is a cross between George Clooney and Superman. You might be waiting a long time to find them and, if you do, I'm afraid there is no guarantee they'll think *you* are *their* perfect match.

What I do mean is thinking about the things that are important to you. In the survey we asked people what were the qualities they thought were most important in a spouse. The ones that came up over and over again were: someone who is loving, honest, kind, trustworthy, has a good sense of humour, a similar outlook on life and who is a great friend. In other words, someone who is authentic from the inside out.

Deal breakers

Are there things you are not willing to compromise on? I heard one American author call these 'deal breakers'. It's good to know your deal breakers before you start dating.

For example, not dating someone who is already married or in a long-term relationship. It may be that you have strong spiritual beliefs and would want to date someone who shares them. It may be that you have a child or parent who is dependent on you, and it is important that whoever you marry gets on with them and is willing to help look after them too. Or perhaps your deal breaker is that you wouldn't marry someone who is an addict or is unkind or dishonest or has an uncontrollable temper.

your deal breakers

You will have your own deal breakers. What are they? What are the things you MUST have in a potential spouse?

1. ....

2. ....

3. ....

4. ....

5. ....

It may help to share these with a trusted friend who can then remind you of them if you even think of dating someone who doesn't have one of these. For example, what is the point of dating someone, however gorgeous, talented and fantastic, if they won't consider having children and you really want them (if that was a deal breaker)? Don't assume that people will change because there is no guarantee that they will and you are only setting yourself up for heartbreak further down the line.

Are you being too fussy?

It may be that as you and your friend look at your list you'll spot areas where you are just being too fussy. Perhaps you've said they have to be blonde, or a certain height, or in a certain job, or good at a certain sport. Don't limit yourself unnecessarily. Be willing to be surprised – many people end up having amazing marriages with people they didn't think were their type!

I nearly ditched my now husband on our second date as he was wearing a tight polyester football top (I'm not a great fan of man-made fibres). And on top of that, I also wasn't sure about him being seven and a half years younger than me. It was only when someone tried to set me up with someone twenty-seven years older that I thought David was probably a good bet! If we get too restrictive about what we are looking for we will miss out.

4. be intentional

Are you meeting people? That may seem a silly question but some people complain that they aren't dating anyone and then it transpires that either they don't have any time in their life to socialise and meet new people or they never go to places or have opportunities to meet anyone.

If you're not meeting people, think about why this is and what you could do to change it. You may decide to spend less time at work, take up a sport or a hobby, join a society, take part in a religious or political group or tell your friends that you are up for meeting new people. If you haven't already, you might consider joining an Internet dating site, as Roxy did after she got past her initial scepticism.

I always thought Internet dating was for losers – one up from the 'lonely hearts column' in the local paper. But as I got further into my thirties, the number of eligible single men I was meeting through friends decreased and I realised that Mr Right might not simply turn up on my doorstep. A couple of friends had sheepishly admitted to dallying with online dating (one had met her husband that way) and I thought I'd give it a go.

At first it felt like shopping and I would feel rejected when 'Dan from Twickenham' said he wasn't interested. But I persisted. I'm currently single, but the experience has been over-whelmingly positive. I've been on more dates than ever before, (largely) got over my 'first date nerves', learnt a lot about what I 'want' from a guy, and had one fun relationship. There have been a few awkward cups of coffee with people I didn't click with, but it's a numbers game and I'm confident a few 'good ones' are in the pipeline! Almost all my single friends are doing some kind of online dating, and I think it's done us all the world of good.

If you do meet someone you like, do something about it. Ask them for a coffee, a drink, or to an event – anything that will enable you to get to know them a little better. Asking someone out for a coffee does *not* mean you want to marry them or sleep with them. It just means you want to spend a little time with them.

In male–female relationships some people are quite traditional when it comes to who should ask who out or make the first move. If you are a woman who believes men should do the initiating but a man you like hasn't asked you then there are plenty of ways of inviting a man out without actually asking him on a 'date'. For example, you could ask him to lunch with a few other friends, to an event you're organising or to a group you are involved in. But if, after a couple of invitations, he doesn't reciprocate and ask you out the chances are that he isn't that into you. Most of my male friends tell me that they will do something about it if they like someone.

And a quick note to the guys. If you like a woman, just go for it. Ask her out. Most women I know love it when a man makes the first move.

Whoever you are, if someone asks you out, be kind. If there is no way you are interested, turn them down gently. If you aren't sure then why not just go once and see how you get on. You may be pleasantly surprised.

But I think the worst thing anyone, female or male, can do is to allow a relationship to grow in their head when there is no basis in reality. People – and often it is women – can waste months or years being 'in love' with someone who isn't the remotest bit interested in them. If you find yourself in this situation, or if a friend is, and it has been going on for a few months, I would encourage you (or them) to be honest with the object of your desires and tell them how you feel. That may be embarrassing or painful but if they like you (but just hadn't realised it) they can now do something about it and, if they don't and never will like you that way, then at least you know and can concentrate on moving on.

Becoming a couple

Whether it takes a few dates or a few months, there comes that time when you make the transition from just being two people going on a few dates into being a couple. Call it what you will, 'going out', 'going steady', 'dating', 'seeing each other', you are now in an exclusive relationship where you are no longer seeing other people. That transition can just happen seamlessly or you may need to chat about it and make it clear to each other that you are both on the same page. That can be a tricky conversation to have, especially if you are not sure that the other person feels the same, but it can be worth a little embarrassment to know where you stand with each other.

Now assuming you are both keen to commit to somebody for life, there are two ways your relationship can go. Either you will split up or you will make a lifetime commitment (marriage or a civil partnership). You are unlikely to know this early on which it might be, but if at any stage either one of you *is* aware that they couldn't see yourself spending your life with this person then the honest and authentic thing to do is to end the relationship, because it has no future.

5. enjoy the journey

Going out with someone should be fun. This is a time to get to know someone – what they like, what they hate, what makes them tick, and what their values, hopes, fears and dreams are. It is a time to see who they are with you but also how they are with their friends, their family and with strangers. If they are rude and impatient with the waiting staff in a restaurant or with a shop assistant then the chances are they may be like that with you one day. The same is true with families. What are they like with their mum or dad? How do they treat them?

That is why it is so important, when dating someone, to see them in lots of different contexts. The temptation can be to lock yourself in a little secluded bubble for two but the problem if you do that exclusively is that you miss experiencing each other in different situations and with different people. Hopefully you'll like what you see, but if you don't then it's better to learn that early on in the relationship than after you have made a lifelong commitment to this person.

This is a time to be yourself – to let the other person see the real you. It is not the time to try out being the person you'd like to be or the person you think they'd like you to be. After all, you don't want them falling in love with a false projection – you want someone who loves you for all you are, with your good bits, your not so good bits and your little quirky bits, all the things that make you you.

And this is a time to enjoy the journey, not to fixate on the destination. Enjoy getting to know each other and do all you can to encourage each other and build each other up through the relationship.

I have two American friends, Jack and Susan. When they first started dating Jack said something like this to Susan: 'I don't know if we'll get married in the future but I want to treat you so well that if we split up one day and you end up marrying someone else – I would be able to look the other guy in the eye, shake his hand and say: "Here is Susan, I looked after her for you."' They did end up marrying each other but I thought that was an amazing thing to say. Wouldn't it be fantastic if people were better off in life from having had a relationship with us, not worse off? That means being kind, considerate, loving, honest and gentle with each other and treating each other as we would like to be treated.

6. don't ignore any red lights

If at any time you discover a red light in your relationship you should end it as soon as possible. A red light is a 'deal breaker', whether it was on your list or not. Kate had been seeing her boyfriend for two years when she discovered one:

> Evil Brett (presumably not what his mum christened him) and I
> were quite serious – he gave me a key to his flat and even
> proposed to me (although I think he was probably drunk). One
> morning when I went round to meet him for breakfast I found
> him in bed with someone else. That really hurt and made me
> very angry – especially because he did it all on purpose.

Red lights are anything that indicate that the relationship with this person is not going to work. Other examples might be: consistent lying, uncontrollable anger, physical or emotional abuse, untreated addictions, a constantly critical attitude, or if you find you stop 'being yourself' when you are around them.

325

Mike discovered a red light he hadn't anticipated when he dated a girl who was extremely materialistic:

Most of the time I was happy to buy things for her and I enjoyed being able to make her happy but over time this wore me down. I was constantly under pressure to be able to afford her expectations, which over time became demands. This pressure carried over to my work life, my relationship with my family and I was generally just miserable all the time. When we did break up it was a relief.

It really helps to listen to your friends and family, who know you well. If they aren't sure about the relationship listen to their objections. Try to be open to hear their comments. It may be that they have spotted something you haven't. I remember being with one boyfriend and some friends said he didn't bring out the best in me. They felt he put me down and that this affected my self-esteem. Those were comments worth listening to. But they won't always be right – you may have to discern whether they are speaking out of their own prejudices or beliefs. So, for example, with another boyfriend some of my family didn't approve because he had long hair and an earring (that wasn't a red light – just their preference!).

7. work through the amber lights

At some stage in every relationship you will encounter problems. That is not a bad thing and does not mean a relationship should end. People can be too quick to finish relationships at the first sign of conflict or when they have to start working at it. But a sign of a good and healthy relationship is when you *can* both communicate and can work things through.

It is good to learn how you both react when you are angry, upset, fearful or worried or when one of you doesn't get your own way or is in the wrong. It is really helpful to find out how you react together when things are tough, when you don't agree, when one of you is being selfish or hurtful or when you misunderstand each other. And part of the discovery process is finding out how you are different from each other, what your families are like, what your attitudes are towards children and parenting, what your beliefs are, how you like to spend your time and what your goals in life are. It is only really through working through these things that you can know whether you want to commit to each other in the long term.

But if you find, after working at issues, that you can't see a future together then the authentic thing to do is to end it.

Splitting up

Ending a relationship is never easy. It helps to try and do it as soon as possible after you've made the decision – delaying the inevitable can make things worse, as Shaneen discovered:

> I had dated Nathan for three years, we were living together, he had moved cities to be with me and was very much a part of my family. We were very much in love but I had realised that I didn't want to marry him, so decided I had to end our relationship. It was a few weeks before Christmas and I confided in my mum who insisted I had to wait until after Christmas to break up with Nathan as he was joining us on our family Christmas holiday and he had no family where we lived and she thought it would be just 'too mean'.
>
> I did what Mum suggested but Nathan wasn't stupid and he realised that something was wrong during the holiday. He kept asking what it was, but I didn't want to upset my family or him and 'ruin Christmas' so I pretended it was all OK.
>
> As soon as we were back home I told him it was over and, yes, he was upset. But what hurt him most was knowing that I had felt that way for weeks but I had carried on as if nothing was wrong. He felt lied to. It was so awful and I decided to

never again let the convenience or feelings of family or friends dictate the timing of my relationships.

If you do have to end a relationship, do it kindly. Think about how *you* would like to be told. Make sure you do it face to face (where possible). I think texting is a definite 'no no', as is email or just changing your status on Facebook! If you can't physically be in the same place at least do it on the phone so you can have a two-way conversation.

Don't bottle it and get your best friend to give the bad news on your behalf, as happened to one friend of mine. And don't leave the person to guess that the relationship is over, as happened to Blake:

> I was in a long-distance relationship. My girlfriend came back home to England to visit just before Christmas and invited me to come with her to Sydney for New Year's Eve. It was a great idea although logistically it was going to be hard to organise a flight that close to the time ... a few options of how I could do this were racing through my head until she said ... 'It would be great, you can meet my new boyfriend' ... It wasn't the greatest way to find out and needless to say I didn't take her up on her offer.

When it comes to explaining why, be clear (and gentle) about your reasons. Clichéd lines like, 'It isn't you – it's me,' aren't helpful. Give them an opportunity to ask questions and fully take on board what you are saying. You may have been deciding this for weeks but they may not have seen this conversation coming so it may take them a little while to get their head around it. You may need to give them a little time to think about it and then chat again a couple of days later, when they have thought of all the things they want to ask.

It can help to discuss how the break-up is going to work. Will there be any contact? What will happen if you are both going to the same event, party, friend's house, meeting etc? Will there be a time when you can be friends? How will you let the other know if one of you starts to see someone else? These are difficult conversations to have but the clearer you can be the easier the break-up will be for both of you.

The worst thing we can do is to give false hope that you may get back together again one day if that is *not* true. The truth can hurt but lies can hurt even more. I have heard too many stories of people who have told their boyfriend or girlfriend that they just don't want to get married at the moment or aren't ready for a big commitment and then four months down the line they are engaged to someone else.

8. recognise a green light and 'get going'

If there are no red lights, and you have worked through any amber ones (areas you are not sure about or need to discuss) then the time will come eventually when you need to make a decision. Do you want to be with this person for the rest of your life?

Marriage isn't something you should just 'fall into'. It needs both of you to commit – to choose 'yes' and to say 'I will' and mean it – because there will be times in the future when your relationship will be tested and it is important that both of you committed and continue to commit to the relationship. By choosing to marry you are choosing to be an 'us' and to put that 'us' before anything else.

Some people find that a really scary decision and despite there being lots of green lights in a relationship they find it hard to take the next step. If that is you, I would recommend speaking to someone about your fears and where they come from. Is it really this person who is making you feel this way or would you feel this fear whoever you were with? Don't let that fear keep you trapped.

are you ready?

In *The Marriage Book* Nicky and Sila Lee suggest asking yourself these seven questions:

Do I want to share the rest of my life with this person?

Does our love give me energy and strength or does it drain me?

Do I respect this person?

Do I accept this person as they are? (And not how I would like them to be!)

Are we able to admit our mistakes, apologise and forgive one another?

Do we have interests in common as a foundation for friendship?

Have we weathered all seasons and a variety of situations together?

A few wobbles

Don't be surprised, though, if you do get engaged and still find you have a few wobbles or doubts. That can be very normal.

Nicky and Sila write: 'We have happily married friends who could have answered yes to all seven tests, but on their wedding day were still wrestling with hesitation and doubts. It takes courage to tie the knot and to say words that will affect the rest of our lives.'

And while it isn't pleasant, if at any time during the engagement you know that getting married isn't right then have the courage to break it off.

How to prepare for marriage

Engagement can be a very exciting time but for many people quite a tense time as well. If you are not careful all your time can be taken up with wedding preparations. That is why it is so important to make sure you take time to prepare for your marriage not just for your wedding.

I would highly recommend doing some form of marriage preparation together during the run-up to your wedding. Not only is this a rather nice break from all those decisions about flower colours, invitation lists and seating plans, more importantly it is time to go deeper and fully understand the commitment you are making to each other. David and I went on The Marriage Preparation Course run by the Lees and it was a real eye-opener. We talked about stuff that we hadn't talked about before and we picked up good tips on how to deal with problems when they surfaced. (The tips were very useful when we eventually did have our first argument.)

how to hold on to hope

If you are still reading this chapter but are not in a relationship and are worried it will never happen for you, I want to say: 'Hold on to hope.' Don't look for a magic formula that will help you find love. There isn't one. People find love in all sorts of different places and in all sorts of different ways. Some people marry their first sweetheart and some wait until their twilight years. Some date for years before they commit while others take the plunge in a matter of months. Some 'just know' it is right and others agonise over the decision to marry. And some people don't marry but still have fulfilled lives full of love and great relationships. Every person's story is different – each journey is unique.

The important things are to follow your passions, to be you, to be open and to be authentic. Love often comes when you least expect it.

18. how to make your marriage matter

the wonder of 'us'

If you stop and think about it marriage is an extraordinary thing. Two individuals with all their many similarities and differences (more often differences) make a choice to become an 'us', to form a new family unit together, to travel through life by each other's sides, to stick with each other through thick and thin, illness and health, good times and bad, promising to love, comfort, honour, protect and be faithful to each other until one of them dies.

On their wedding day they make their vows in front of friends and family. They publicly and legally become an 'us'. They symbolically leave the past behind and embrace a joint future together. Two become one. Independence gives way to interdependence.

A scary thought

I remember when we returned from our honeymoon, waking up and looking at David sleeping beside me and thinking how amazing (and slightly scary) marriage was. The large, handsome, hairy man breathing rather deeply, hogging at least half the duvet and taking over *my* side of the bed was here to stay! Here was someone who loved me and had chosen to share his life with me. From now on he would be part of me and me of him. We were now linked: 'Sarah and David', 'The Abells'. The bed was no longer mine but 'ours', our things were now sitting side by side together in one flat, our money was merged into one account and our futures were now inextricably linked – for better or for worse. If we both live healthy and long lives we could be together sixty or more years, much longer than we'd spent as single people. Lying in bed that morning I felt both excited and daunted by it all.

Two become one

But becoming an 'us' doesn't just happen overnight. It is a gradual and constant process. It doesn't mean we stop being who we are or morph into a clone of each other. But it does mean becoming a team. We each bring different strengths, weaknesses, abilities, ideas and experiences to the side. Hopefully, together we are more effective than we are on our own.

For a team to be strong it needs unity not division, and collaboration not competition. Therefore, becoming a team will involve us sometimes having to sacrifice our own needs and wants for the sake of 'us'. It will mean letting go of having to have our own way and that, as we all know, isn't always easy.

333

A living work of art

When you watch the elderly couple walking hand in hand along the pier, matching each other's strides, anticipating each other's needs, gently teasing each other, finishing each other's sentences and sharing their memories and private jokes you are seeing the result of years of growing together.

Their marriage is like a work of art, painstakingly created over the years, probably through much sacrifice, understanding, patience, love, tears, suffering, joy, laughter, forgiveness, time together, shared experiences, commitment and enduring love. Perhaps, if you asked them, you'd find out that there were times when they drove each other mad, times when they didn't 'feel in love', times when they hurt each other or acted selfishly, times when they faced hardship or trials and times when they were tempted to stray or to leave. But the fact that they are standing in front of you telling you these things now is because they made a choice – when things got tough they chose 'us' over and above all other things.

A work in progress

For most of us our work of art is still being formed. How we choose to act and react today will affect how it will turn out. Will we behave in a way that helps and strengthens 'us' or harms and hurts 'us'?

Our choice won't just affect us as a couple: it will also impact on others involved in our lives. That's because a marriage isn't just a private affair, a work of art hidden away in a cupboard. It has a public side: it is on display for others to observe and witness. Others will be touched by our marriage: our children, if and when we have them, our friends, our family, people whom we meet along the way and even our society. If our marriage suffers or fails they will feel and know the repercussions. But if it grows, flourishes and has a positive impact on all those who encounter it then we will have created something that is bigger than our individual selves.

Making an investment that counts

Strong and healthy marriages that last a lifetime take hard work and commitment. They don't just happen by chance. But it is never too late to start – you can decide today to make an investment that counts.

If we make a conscious choice to invest in 'us', to protect 'us' and to understand the impact of 'us' then we can make our marriage matter. We can create a unique and an enduring work of art that will not just bring joy to 'us' but also to all those we come across on our journey together.

Winston Churchill had many achievements to be proud of but he was reported as saying: 'My most brilliant achievement was my ability to persuade my wife to marry me.'

investing in 'us'

To invest in 'us' means being counter-cultural – it involves prioritising our relationship over everything else, putting 'us' before 'me' and refusing to give in and throw 'us' away when we hit trouble or difficult times.

Here are just a few ways in which we can make sure we are investing in our relationship, helping it to grow and be all that it can be:

1. Taking the time

In Chapter 3, I mentioned the importance of investing time in our most important relationships. This is especially true with our marriage. We need to be deliberate about spending time together – time when we can talk, plan, dream, connect, have fun, romance each other and have sex. Time when we aren't just co-parents or room-mates but when we are able to develop our friendship and our love for each other.

A regular date. One way of doing this is by having a regular date night together once a week.

This can be at home (food, candles and music all help) or it could be going out (perhaps a picnic in a park; a walk on a beach; climbing a mountain; a coffee, a drink or meal out; a trip to the cinema, a concert or an exhibition; a dance, surfing or cookery lesson). It could be rediscovering the things you enjoyed doing together when you first met or new activities you'd love to try. In *The Marriage Book*, Nicky and Sila Lee recommend that these times are fun and memorable.

> It is time to hold hands, time to laugh, time to enjoy doing things together and above all time to talk. This is the time to share our hopes and fears, excitements and worries, struggles and achievements. Such sharing builds intimacy. It's simple but very powerful.

The Lees call these date nights 'marriage time' and recommend that couples book them in their diaries and protect these commitments from anything else that may try and get in the way. David and I try to do that. We sit down and go through the diary several months in advance and book out an evening a week. To keep an element of spontaneity to these planned times, we take turns to organise them. Sometimes we'll know what the other has in store for the date and other times we'll keep it a surprise. One tip: it helps to think of things the *other* person would like to do.

Pack your bags. Going away together for a night or a weekend once or twice a year is another fantastic way of investing quality time in the relationship. If you have children this may mean calling in a big favour of the grandparents or someone else you would trust to look after them. Take the opportunity to do something you both love and make the most of having each other to yourselves. As well as injecting an extra burst of romance into your relationship this can be a great time to talk more deeply about important things: how you are both doing and your hopes, fears and dreams for the future. (If money is tight take time together at home but still make sure the children are taken care of so that you have the place to yourself.)

time for two

How much quality time do you spend together at the moment? Do you both feel this is enough?

If not, how could you increase the time and what will have to shift for you to do that?

When did you last have a date, weekend or holiday on your own together? If you did, how did they help your relationship grow and how can you make sure these continue to happen in the future?

If you haven't done one or any of those things recently, how could you introduce them into your life?

2. The fun factor

Date nights and time away are great times to have fun together. But fun certainly doesn't have to be kept just for those special times. We can make even the most mundane chores fun if we choose to. For example:

- Have a vegetable chopping race (just watch your fingers!).
- Learn Spanish together on a CD in the car on long journeys (or in David's case, listen while your wife tries to

learn Spanish in the car and resist the temptation to
correct her every time she mispronounces something!).
- Pretend you are on an edition of *Ready, Steady, Cook* and
take turns being the chef or the glamorous assistant. The
chef is allowed to give all the orders – the assistant just
obeys them and smiles!

What are you smiling at? Laughter is one of the greatest free gifts
in life and yet, when we allow our lives to get too serious or intense,
we can go for far too long without a good old belly laugh or giggle.

Laughing at ourselves and with each other are great ways to keep
the fun alive in our relationship and also to carry us through any
tricky times. Recently, when I had to have daily injections for my
fertility treatment David would do them for me (as I'm not all that
keen on needles). Every day he would make it fun (well, as fun as
it could be) by joking around and keeping the chat light. My job
was to try and lie still and make sure I wasn't giggling when the
needle went in! It certainly helped improve what could have been
quite a difficult process.

However, it is important not to abuse humour. Humour shouldn't
be a veiled way of being nasty or unkind to our partner or of
avoiding a tricky or difficult conversation.

Shared activities. We will need time apart when we do our own
things: when we each see friends, just spend time on our own or
pursue our own interests, sports or hobbies. But it is important we
also find things we enjoy doing together.

If you have very different interests it may mean thinking about
something that you would both enjoy or it may mean taking turns
in doing something the other would like.

David and I love cooking together, eating, entertaining, travelling,
seeing friends and family, walking, playing tennis, trying to play
golf, going to the cinema and watching DVDs. We don't always
have the same taste in films, but for date nights we'll take turns
in choosing a film that we know the other one wants to see.

having fun

What things did you enjoy doing together when you first met?

How many of those things are you still doing? Are there some you could re-introduce?

Can you think of a new activity you could start doing together?

Our own traditions. Every couple will form their own traditions and different ways they do things together: who sleeps on which side of the bed or sits on which chair; what happens on your birthdays, Christmas and special occasions; little rituals you do when you go to sleep, on weekends or on holidays, such as saying 'I love you' last thing at night, having Sunday breakfast in bed, or playing 'who can spot the sea first'; or perhaps your own names or language for different things. For example, if David and I go to a restaurant and we don't think we're going to like it, it's too expensive or we've changed our mind, one of us will turn to the other and say: 'You know what? I think I'd prefer egg and chips.' That's our code for, 'Let's get out of here' and we'll make our excuses and leave.

Our traditions will grow over the years. We will have inherited some from our parents, some we will have argued over and refined over time, some will have just developed and others we will have deliberately made up. These traditions help to give 'us' a shared sense of identity. And if and when we have children we'll share some of these together as a family.

339

A store of memories. Traditions also help us to build shared memories. When we have good, happy and fun times together we build up a store of positive memories. These are like a deep reservoir that we can draw on when times get hard. If one of us is ill or depressed, if we have no money for treats, or things just seem bleak we can reminisce over fun times we've had in the past (and also dream of things we'd like to do in the future). Just reliving the memories or reviewing the photos can bring a smile to our faces and remind us of all the good things we can be grateful for.

3. Heart to heart

We looked at effective communication earlier and it is vital in a marriage to be able to tune in to each other – to really hear and understand each other. Sometimes we can get lazy, complacent or think our partner should just know what we are thinking, and we don't take the time to communicate properly. Marriages often break down when the couple stops talking about what matters. So, if we are going to invest in 'us' we need to give our best listening and our best understanding to each other. We need to be able to reveal our deepest thoughts, feelings, fears and hopes to our husband or wife.

In safe hands. It is important that we can trust each other with what we reveal to each other. If we choose to be vulnerable, open and honest with each other we give each other power. We must do all we can not to use that power against each other.

It can be too easy in an argument or during a huge conflict to get out our biggest weapons. If we know our partner's greatest fears, their weak spots and vulnerabilities, we can kick where it hurts. The problem is that if we do that we will lose their trust and they will no longer see us as a safe pair of hands. So it is important we don't use our knowledge to cause hurt and damage.

Don't try these at home. If we want to protect our marriage there are a few things that we should definitely avoid doing. Here they are, so we remember *never* to try them at home:

1. Don't threaten divorce (if you don't really mean it).
2. Don't compare your spouse (negatively) with either of their parents.
3. Don't say, 'You never ...', 'You always ...' or 'I told you so ...'
4. Don't refuse to ever talk about a topic.
5. Don't sleep in separate rooms (unless it is temporarily because of illness or a screaming baby).
6. Don't be unkind or put each other down, especially in public (it is the marital equivalent of an own goal!).
7. Don't lose the mystery (you really don't need to be there when the other is going to the loo unless they are ill, frail and need your help!).
8. Don't keep score, i.e. 'I did this ... so you need to do that.'
9. Don't try to get your children or your parents on your side in an argument.
10. Don't forget your anniversary or your husband or wife's birthday.

The study of you. We also need to keep on learning about each other. We can't just assume we know all there is to know. People change and so it is important we keep on discovering new things about each other.

Mr and Mrs

See how many of these questions you could answer about your partner. Perhaps try to do them first and then get your partner to answer them.

What is their favourite film of all time?
What book would they take to a desert island?

Where would they want to go on holiday for two weeks (if money
   was no object)?

What is their biggest regret in life (so far)?

Who was their favourite teacher?

What was their first job?

What bit of your body do they find the most attractive?

What is the most embarrassing thing they ever did?

Where would you most like to go for a date night?

Name one thing that makes them really angry.

What was the thing they hated most about school?

Name the one person who has had the greatest positive influence
   on them.

What is their greatest anxiety at the moment?

What is their favourite meal?

What would they want to happen at their funeral?

How would they spend their ideal day?

What would they do if they won the lottery (at least £1 million)?

What is their earliest memory?

What would they like to do if they had no fear?

What is their favourite flower or plant?

Who is their favourite band, singer or group?

What job would they do if they could do anything?

If they could have any pet, what would it be?

Keep thinking up questions – there is no end of things to discover
about each other!

4. Giving it everything

It can be very tempting in a relationship to think you are the one
putting in most of the work, that you are doing more, giving more,
earning more, sacrificing more, investing more and putting up with
more. But the chances are that your husband or wife thinks the
same!

When we start thinking like that we are not investing in 'us', we are back thinking about ourselves. It becomes a competition between 'you' and 'me'. We are likely to become resentful, bitter, annoyed and frustrated as we compare each other's inputs and outputs in the relationship.

Instead of focusing on what your partner is or isn't doing it can help to take a different tack. Concentrate on being a great spouse to them, meeting their needs and trying to put your all into the relationship. The paradox is that if you do that and they feel loved and looked after they are far more likely to reciprocate and look for ways to meet your needs. If you are both giving everything you can you may find you no longer need to complain, nag or compete with each other again and both your 'love tanks' will be full to overflowing.

Tony and his wife Sally found this approach helped them:

Society often teaches and encourages us to look out for ourselves, for number one. But I have found that our marriage works at its best when we look out for each other. So for example, instead of focusing on what Sally isn't doing for me I try and think what can I do for Sally? How can I best support her today? I've learnt that if I put her needs before mine – like if I spend time with her, help with the clearing-up without being asked, listen to her when she wants to talk through a problem, and if she looks out for me and my needs – gives me a little space on my own when I need it, supports me if things are a bit tricky at work and suggests I go out for a game of squash with my mate when she notices I haven't done so for a while, we are so much happier and stronger as a couple.

5. 'Will you be my hero?'

The world can be a hostile place at times but our marriage can and should be a safe haven – a place where we can be ourselves and where we can receive love, support and understanding.

A great way to invest in 'us' is to build each other up – to be each other's number one fan. That means believing in each other, encouraging each other, supporting each other and cheering each other on. It means telling each other when we feel proud of our husband or wife, when we are grateful, when we feel loved or loving, it means speaking well of each other in private and in public and it means helping each other be all that we can be.

I couldn't have written this book without David. He encouraged me to give it a go, he agreed to me giving up my full-time job with the resulting drop in income (and the sacrifices that would entail), he helped me compile the questionnaire, he takes on more jobs around the house and, when I doubt myself, he tells me I can do it.

protecting 'us'

As well as investing in 'us' it is important to keep protecting 'us' too. It is a bit like with our home. We invest in it by giving it a lick of paint, redoing the old bathroom and cleaning the carpets. But we also protect it by making sure the burglar alarm is working, the locks on the window are secure and by having an annual gas check to make sure nothing is going to explode.

Our marriage is likely to come under pressure at some stage – either internally (by what we do to it) or externally (by what we allow to affect it). But there are ways in which we can protect our relationship mentally, emotionally, physically and spiritually. Just as with our home, we need to make sure our relationship is as protected and as secure as possible.

Mentally

What do we think about? We can strengthen or weaken our marriage through our thoughts. If we allow ourselves to dwell on all the negative aspects of our relationship, constantly rehearse our partner's faults in our minds and think the worst in every situation we are likely to feel rather depressed and pessimistic about 'us'.

But if we focus on the positive, look to work on our own faults and think the best in every situation our outlook on our marriage is likely to be much more optimistic and hopeful.

The mind is a powerful thing and we need to make sure ours is working for 'us' and not against 'us'. We can't necessarily stop the thoughts and ideas that come into our minds but we can choose not to dwell on the harmful ones when they do come. For example:

- We can stop ourselves fantasising about the good-looking person we have just met or the ex we 'let go' in the past. Instead, we can turn our thoughts to our spouse and fantasise about them.
- We can refuse to look at pornography or compare our spouse to someone else we know or wish we knew. Instead we can turn our appreciation to our spouse – reminding ourselves about all the things we find attractive about them.
- We can make sure we don't think the worst of our spouse in every situation. Don't assume that if they've bought you flowers or cooked your favourite meal it means they are feeling guilty. Don't presume they will always get something wrong and don't assume they will forget things that you tell them. Instead, think the best of them and their motives.
- We can stop thinking of everything as 'mine' and 'yours' and think about things as 'ours'. If we are competitive, possessive or selfish with our money or possessions then we only reinforce our independence. If instead we are generous, willing to share and consider everything to be 'ours' we reinforce our inter-dependence and our sense of 'us'. It helps to involve each other in our decisions.

Emotionally

What do we do with our feelings? Do we share our deepest emotions, fears, hopes and dreams with our husband or wife or do we bottle them up? Do we express our hurt, anger, frustrations and sadness or do we let our negative emotions fester, build and grow inside us?

Hidden emotions can cause a wall to grow up between 'us', a wall that will eventually erode intimacy and stop us from really seeing each other. If we want to protect 'us' we need to do all we can to take responsibility for our feelings and express them to each other. Not to attack each other with accusations, harsh words and criticisms but to come to each with openness and vulnerability and say, 'This is what I am feeling …'

The greatest danger to 'us' is when, instead of coming to each other with our emotions we take them elsewhere. We share our frustrations, our loneliness, our confusion and our disappointment with the under-standing work colleague, the friendly ex or the compassionate person on the Internet. Affairs often start as emotional ones (long before the first kiss) when we think we've discovered someone who really wants to know, who gets us and who understands and cares.

If we want to protect 'us' from emotional infidelity we need to make sure the person we are emotionally naked and vulnerable with is our spouse. And we need to make sure they feel able to be naked and vulnerable with us. We need to assure them that we won't judge them, criticise them or laugh at them when they reveal themselves to us.

Physically

How are we physically protecting our marriage? Do we make sure we are physically connecting on a daily basis? Do we hug, kiss and hold hands? Do we look into each other's eyes as we chat? Do we lie in each other's arms in bed? Do we romance each other? Do we keep our sex life going and growing? Do we dance with each other around the kitchen singing, 'Shall we dance?' from *The King and I*? (OK, maybe that is just us!)

We can endanger 'us' physically when we constantly say 'no' to the other's bids for affection or sex, when we stop showing each other tenderness, when we disrespect each other physically, when we allow ourselves to become physically intimate with someone else, when we make our partner do something they feel uncomfortable with or if we hit or lash out at them physically. (If a relationship is physically abusive it is vital that the abused person seeks help from someone they can trust. Helping 'us' in this instance means getting you and any children into a safe place and for your husband or wife to get the help they need with their issues. It does not mean suffering in silence or defending their behaviour.)

When we are protecting 'us' we are remembering that our bodies aren't just our own – they belong to the other. We look for ways to show our affection, to give reassurance, to say, 'I'm here with you', to give each other pleasure and to be 'naked and unashamed' in each other's presence.

Protecting 'us' also means looking after our bodies – making sure we have regular check-ups, keep fit and eat healthily. I'm not always very good at this but I try and remember I am not just doing it for me but for David's sake as well.

We particularly need to seek help if we are suffering from depression or an addiction, if we suspect we may have something physically wrong with us or if we are experiencing sexual problems. (Most couples will experience sexual problems of some kind during their marriage but the good news is that the majority of problems can be sorted out.) The important thing is to be able to talk about these things with each other and to seek outside help early on. Problems have a nasty habit of getting worse, not better, if they are ignored.

Spiritually

What are we doing to protect our marriage spiritually? If you are not a spiritual person then that will probably seem an odd or irrelevant question.

Perhaps a better one would be how much have you discussed and discovered your core beliefs? To what extent are you agreed on these and how do they affect how you live your lives together? Do you give space in your relationship to think about and contemplate some of the big questions of life, such as, Why are we here? Why is there suffering in the world? What happens when we die?

If you have different faiths, or only one of you has a faith, do you take time to find out and understand your partner's beliefs? Our beliefs are often at the core of who we are. If we don't show any interest in our partner's beliefs then there is a whole part of them that we don't know. We don't have to agree with each other or try and make the other person believe as we do, but it can help to take the time to understand what and why the other believes what they do. It is part of getting to know them. Try listening without judgement or criticism.

A joint faith can be amazingly bonding in a marriage. It can give you a shared sense of purpose and direction, as Zac and Toni have discovered in their own relationship:

> A shared faith means that we make decisions together from the same core beliefs. It also means that when we have an argument, when we are being selfish or mean to each other that we have a common foundation and understanding. That normally nudges us towards being able to say and to mean those difficult words, 'I am sorry, I was wrong.'

your different beliefs and values

How do your beliefs affect your outlook on life and the way in which you make decisions together?

If you share a faith, how do your beliefs determine how you live out your lives together?

Get help before and when you need it

The final thing I want to say about protecting 'us' is that you shouldn't be afraid of getting help. The best time to get help is before we need it! We go to the dentist or the doctor for a check-up and we take our car in for a service to make sure it is running smoothly, so why not make sure our relationship is on track and growing? We can do that by:

- Reading helpful books on marriage and relationships
- Speaking to other couples we trust and respect about any issues we face
- Reviewing with each other what is going well and what we would like to improve about our relationship
- Going on a marriage course or a weekend away.

The Marriage Course, created by Nicky and Sila Lee, is a great way of giving your relationship an MOT or check-up. David and I went on it two years into marriage but you can go on one however long you've been together. The thing I liked about the course is that there is *no* group work, which is a great relief to most people – you only have to talk to each other.

The course can also be helpful for couples who are struggling. It can be really hard for people to know where to turn when they encounter problems in their marriage. The temptation can be to bury your head in the sand or to try and bail out as quickly as possible. But a better solution is to seek help, to give 'us' a chance and to try and find a way back to love. If you are struggling or finding your marriage really hard I'd encourage you to give The Marriage Course a go or find a good couples therapist in your area.

the impact of 'us'

Think back to our work of art. We have explored a little more what it might look like but how do we want it to impact on those in our lives? It helps if we can be deliberate and think these through.

Impact on children (if we have them)
Children are like sponges. They learn from watching us. What do we want them to pick up from us? What values do we live out in the home? What do we want to pass on to them? What do we want to be important to them? What do we want them to have

349

learnt from our relationship? What do we want them to learn about marriage?

Impact on friends

What kind of friends do we want to be? What difference do we want to make to our friends' lives? How do we want to help our friends? How available do we want to be to our friends?

Impact on family

How do we want to be with our families? How much love and support do we want to give them? How often will we see them? How will we make sure they know that we are here for them? What will we do if they are ill, frail or in financial difficulty?

Impact on society

How can we leave our world a better place? What difference do we want to make to our society? How can we help people, animals or the planet? How can we help those who are in need or are suffering?

how are we doing?

Every now and again an artist will step back from their canvas to see how the picture is coming along. It is a great help to take a step back every year to look at our marriage and ask, 'How are we doing?'

You may want to set aside a day to do that together. Check out the work of art you're creating and ask yourselves if it is shaping up the way you would like. And if it isn't think of ways you can improve it.

At the launch of National Marriage Week in February 2005, Rabbi Jonathan Sacks said:

A good marriage is the greatest work of art that any of us are likely to achieve. And it is all the more fun because it's the kind of work of art that lives and breathes and changes and grows. Just because it is unfashionable and counter-cultural and absurdly beautiful, let us hear it for marriage, the truth of the proposition is that the love we make is the love we give away.

It is never too late to make a marriage that matters.

Tips: How to be the friend you've always wanted (for those wanting to improve)

Accept them as they are. Don't make any plans for their improvement or judge them. Help them to make their own decisions – don't tell them what to do.

Keep secrets. If a friend tells you stuff, keep their confidence. Don't be disloyal behind their backs.

Allow them to change. Keep getting to know them. Don't assume you know everything or that you know how they'll think or react.

Initiate. Don't leave them to always be the one who gets in touch or makes plans. Think of things that they might like to do.

Don't take advantage of them. Don't break plans, turn up really late or stop seeing them when a love interest comes along, even if they say they understand (they're just being kind). You'll need them to be there whether your relationship survives or not.

Be there in the hard times. Do practical things to help and don't just say it, be there for them. If someone has died or they are struggling with an illness or a difficult relationship then let them talk about it as much as they want. And be your normal self. If you aren't sure how to act, just ask them and they'll appreciate your honesty.

Have fun. Don't be moody every time you see them or constantly talk about yourself – it's boring. Have a laugh and do fun stuff together that you both enjoy. Be spontaneous sometimes and just do something on the spur of the moment.

It's good to talk! Before you text or email think about whether you could make a quick call or see them in person instead.

epilogue: the naked hedgehog

A nation that fails to learn the lessons of history is destined to repeat it.
WINSTON CHURCHILL

You must be the change you want to see in the world.
GHANDI

To build bridging social capital requires that we transcend our social and political and professional identities to connect with people unlike ourselves.
ROBERT D, PUTNAM, *BOWLING ALONE*

A look into the future

I was talking to a great friend of mine the other day (I'll call her Katherine to spare her blushes). She is an eighty-four-year-old widow who lives on her own. That could be a recipe for loneliness and isolation, but not for Katherine. She has two supportive sons, a great daughter-in-law, two lovely grandchildren and more good friends than many people half her age. She has friends of all ages and is interested and involved in their lives. She is an active member of her local church and walks the two miles there and back most days to go and volunteer (despite the pain she experiences in her legs). She goes to 'keep fit' class once a week and loves learning – whether it is how to use her computer, keeping up with the news

354

or reading her Bible. And her strong faith gives her a reason to embrace and not fear the thought of death.

But life isn't like that for many people of Katherine's age. There are plenty of elderly people in our society who live alone, with only their TV for company. Too frightened to go out, they stay shut away in the prison of their own home. They may not see a friend or family member for weeks on end. Days and days may pass without them feeling the touch of another human or hearing the voice of a loved one. Some may not have family living nearby and others may have no family at all. There is no one else to whom they can give attention and reach out to. They are left with nothing to focus on other than their own thoughts and fears.

It is depressing to think that there are people living like that in our society. More depressing still is to think what life will be like for the elderly in forty or fifty years' time if we carry on as we are now. The institutions, connections and social networks which were once taken for granted – religious or political affiliation; membership of trade unions, clubs or teams; support for charities and voluntary organisations, and community involvement – have all dramatically weakened over the last few decades and continue to do so. Greater social mobility means that more people are moving away from their original neighbourhood, family and friends. Those who move to cities often find themselves living next door to people whose names they never know. Grandchildren and close family may live miles away or even in another country. With increasing family breakdown, more and more people will find themselves estranged from family members and living on their own. With jobs for life a rarity, and as freelance, home-working and shift work become more prevalent, work connections will also become weaker.

In many ways developments in technology will continue to help keep us connected. But unless Facebook friends (or whatever the equivalent will be in forty years' time) are also friends in the flesh and live nearby they will be little actual use when we crave intimacy or feel lonely, ill or frail.

So, how can we create a different vision for the future of our society? A society where people are not increasingly disconnected but are living interdependently with each other, supporting, caring and watching out for each other?

authentic loving – changing our society one relationship at a time

During the current economic downturn there seems to have been a growing realisation that we can't find guaranteed security in our possessions, home, money or jobs. Or, if we have tried, we may have discovered that none of those can deliver the safety we crave. Financial struggle has forced many of us to reconsider our priorities and rediscover the importance of authentic relationships and social capital or community.

In his book, *Bowling Alone*, Robert D. Putnam examines the decline of social capital in America over the last few decades of the twentieth century. Writing before 9/11, the last Iraq war and the current recession, he said:

> Creating (or re-creating) social capital is no simple task. It would be eased by a palpable national crisis, like war or depression or natural disaster, but for better *and* for worse, America at the dawn of the new century faces no such galvanizing crisis. The ebbing of community over the last several decades has been silent and deceptive. We notice its effects in the strained interstices of our private lives and in the degradation of our public life, but the most serious consequences are reminiscent of the old parlour puzzle: 'what's missing from this picture?' Weakened social capital is manifest in the things that have vanished almost unnoticed – neighbourhood parties and get-togethers with friends, the unreflective kindness of strangers, the shared pursuit of the public good rather than a solitary quest for private goods. Naming this problem is an essential first step toward confronting it, just as labelling 'the environment' allowed Americans to hear the silent spring …

He could not see them coming at the time but disasters *did* strike America and also many other countries around the world. Many of us are now beginning to understand more about what is important. We are seeing that the greatest investment we can make is in social capital. If we invest in our families, our friends, our neighbourhood and our communities we are more likely to see a greater return from our time, effort and money than if we make the same investment in the property market or gamble it on the stock market. And the exciting thing is that the more we are able to do that the more likely we are to create a future for ourselves and our society where people become more connected and less isolated.

Authentic relating

Over the chapters of this book we've looked at some of the ways in which we can invest in those relationships and become more authentic in how we relate to others. We no longer have to be like the hedgehog that either hides from relationships or hurts people as it gets too close. We can learn to be more real in our connections – allowing others to know and see us and allowing them to be known and seen by us. Instead of being so independent we can become healthily interdependent – reaching out to care, support, love and share life with others. Dr Sue Johnson, in *Hold Me Tight*, writes:

> … our culture encourages us to compete rather than connect.
> Even though we are programmed by millions of years of evolu-
> tion to relentlessly seek out belonging and intimate connection,
> we persist in defining healthy people as those who do not need
> others. This is especially dangerous at a time when our sense of
> community is daily being eroded by an endless preoccupation
> with getting more done in less time and filling our lives with
> more and more goods.

We can hope that those with power in our society wake up and realise the need to invest in social capital and lead by example. We can hope that they will implement policies: that support rather than erode the strength of families; that encourage strong neighbourhoods and communities; that reward social investment as much as, or more than, capital investment; that enable children to grow up in loving environments where they learn how to relate and to think of others; that help single parents, the orphaned, the widowed and the marginalised to find support and strong connections; and that promote marriage and help couples build lifelong committed relationships.

We can hope that they realise the importance of any or all of those things, but even if they don't or won't we can still help to turn the tide ourselves. We can do that:

- When we stop, listen and help a friend in trouble
- When we make the effort to get to know our neighbour
- When we seek to rebuild or heal a difficult relationship
- When we make time to laugh and celebrate with someone
- When we give our time and our attention to those we love
- When we put down our defences and risk being known
- When we allow others to share their secrets or fears with us
- When we reach out and help a stranger
- When we refuse to allow control, selfishness or un-forgiveness to ruin our relationships
- When we offer our hospitality, share our resources and open our homes to others
- When we are quick to admit blame and apologise
- When we become a person who keeps our word
- When we lead with integrity
- When we help the hopeless to find hope again
- When we seek to understand and appreciate differences
- When we care for our marriage and support others' relationships
- When we model healthy relating to our children
- When we become involved in our community
- When we look for and pick up the golden threads
- When we do any of the things we have discussed in this book.

a relationship solution

When we do any of these things, we will make a difference to the people and the world around us.

Think of it as the 'naked hedgehog' revolution. You and I can take steps today to make the future a better place if we are willing to take off our prickles, get close, get real and get connected.

It isn't too late. You and I can be authentic – from the inside out.

And together we can change our society one relationship at a time. We really can.

Viva la revolution!

Bibliography

My thanks go to all the authors and their publishers for the quotes that I used throughout the book. I highly recommend them all. These are the chapters that they appeared in:

1. Pause for thought

A. A. Milne, *Winnie the Pooh* (London, Egmont UK Ltd) Text © The Trustees of the Pooh Properties. Used with permission.

Oliver James, *Affluenza* (Vermillion, 2007). Reprinted by permission of The Random House Group Ltd.

2. The great relationships challenge

Margery Williams, *The Velveteen Rabbit* (Egmont books, 2004).

Dr Sue Johnson, *Hold me Tight* (Little, Brown and Company, 2008).

Dr Henry Cloud, *Integrity* (Harper Collins, 2006).

3. Why a slower day isn't coming

Carl Honoré, *In Praise of Slow* (Orion, 2004). © Carl Honoré 2004.

Sue Palmer, *Toxic Childhood* (Orion, 2006). © Sue Palmer Ltd 2006.

4. Why we're made with two ears and one mouth

Gary, Greg and Michael Smalley and Robert S. Paul, *The DNA of Relationships* (Tyndale, 2004). © 2004 by Smalley Publishing Group. Used by permission of Tyndale House Publishers Inc.

Dr Henry Cloud, *Integrity* (Harper Collins, 2006).

5. Saying what you mean and meaning what you say
John Powell, *Why am I Afraid to Tell you who I am?* (Fount, 1999).

6. Real to real – building connection
Malcolm Gladwell, *The Tipping Point* (Little, Brown and
    Company, 2002).

7. Why an apple doesn't fall far from the apple tree
Louis Cozolino, *The Neuroscience of Human Relationships*
    (W. W. Norton & Company, 2006).

9. How to get over yourself
Dr Sue Johnson, *Hold me Tight* (Little, Brown and Company, 2008).

10. The challenge of differences
A. A. Milne, *The House at Pooh Corner* (London, Egmont UK
    Ltd) Text © The Trustees of the Pooh Properties. Used with
    permission.
Bill Hybels, *Fit to be Tied: Making Marriage Last a Lifetime*
    (Zondervan, 1993). Used by permission of Zondervan,
    www.zondervan.com.

11. What's the problem?
Susan Quilliam, *Stop Arguing, Start Talking* (Vermillion, 2001).
    Reprinted by permission of The Random House Group Ltd.

12. How to handle difficult conversations
Douglas Stone, Bruce Patton and Sheila Heen, *Difficult Conversations*
    (Penguin, 2000). "Sort Out the Three Conversations" from
    Douglas Stone, Bruce Patton and Sheila Heen. Copyright ©
    Douglas Stone, Bruce H. Patton and Sheila Heen, 1999 (p. 13).

Reproduced by permission of Penguin Books Ltd and Viking
Penguin, a division of Penguin Group (USA) Inc.
John Ortberg, *Everybody's Normal Till you get to Know Them*
(Zondervan, 2003). Used by permission of Zondervan,
www.zondervan.com.

13. When feelings aren't enough
C. S. Lewis, *Mere Christianity* Copyright © C.S. Lewis Pte. Ltd.
1942, 1943, 1944, 1952. Extract reprinted by permission.
Philip Yancey *What's so Amazing About Grace?* (Zondervan,
1997). Used by permission of Zondervan, www.zondervan.com.
Rob Parsons, *The Sixty Minute Marriage* (Hodder & Stoughton,
1997).

14. Reaching out
Rick Warren, *The Purpose Driven Life* (Zondervan, 2002) Used by
permission of Zondervan, www.zondervan.com.
Gary Chapman, *The Five Love Languages* (Northfield, Moody
Publishing, 1995).

15. Living in colour
Victor E. Frankl, *Man's Search for Meaning* © 1959, 1962, 1984,
1992 by Victor E. Frankl. Reprinted by permission of Beacon
Press, Boston, (Simon & Schuster, 1984).

16. How to be a leader worth following
Bill Hybels, *Courageous Leadership* (Zondervan, 2002). Used by
permission of Zondervan, www.zondervan.com.
Dr Henry Cloud, *Integrity* (Harper Collins, 2006).
Simon Walker, *Leading out of who you are* (Piquant Editions,
2007).
Julian Richer, *The Richer Way* (Richer Publishing, 2001).

17. How to date like you mean it

Mike Mason, *The Mystery of Marriage* (Waterbrook Multnomah, 1985).

Scott M. Stanley, *The Power of Commitment: A guide to active, lifelong love* (Jossey-Bass, 2005).

Nicky and Sila Lee, *The Marriage Book* (Alpha International, 2000).

18. How to make your marriage matter

Nicky and Sila Lee, *The Marriage Book* (Alpha International, 2000).

Epilogue

Robert D. Putnam, *Bowling Alone* (Simon & Schuster, 2000).

Dr Sue Johnson, *Hold me Tight* (Little, Brown and Company, 2008).

further resources

books

As well as the books I have quoted from I would also recommend the following titles:

General
Gary Chapman, *The Five Love Languages Singles Edition* (Northfield, 2009).
Dr Henry Cloud and John Townsend, *Boundaries* (Zondervan, 2004)
Rob Willson and Rhena Branch, *Cognitive Behavioural Therapy for Dummies* (John Wiley and Sons, 2005).

Engagement and marriage
Richard and Katharine Hill, *Rules of Engagement* (Lion, 2005).
Patricia Love and Steven Stosny, *How to Improve your Marriage Without Talking About it* (Broadway Books, 2007).
Michelle Weiner-Davis, *The Divorce Remedy* (Simon and Schuster, 2002).

Family
Oliver James, *They F*** You Up* (Bloomsbury, 2007).
Nicky and Sila Lee, *The Parenting Book* (Alpha International, 2009).

Work and Leadership
Rob Parsons, *The Heart of Success* (Hodder & Stoughton, 2002).
Simon Walker, *Leading with Nothing to Lose* (Piquant Editions, 2007).

courses

The Marriage Course – for married or long-term cohabiting couples
The Marriage Preparation Course – for engaged couples
(Both can be found on: themarriagecourse.org)
Undefended Leader – courses by Simon Walker (see: theleadership community.org)

useful websites and organisations

ACC – for details of accredited Christian counsellors in your area, www.acc-uk.org
Alcoholics Anonymous – to find a meeting near you, www.alcoholics-anonymous.co.uk
BABCP – website to help you find a cognitive behavioural therapist, www.babcp.com
BACP – The British Association for Counselling and Psychotherapy www.bacp.co.uk
Beat – a UK charity for people with eating disorders and their families, www.b-eat.co.uk
Care for the Family – a national charity which aims to promote strong family life and to help those hurting because of family breakdown or bereavement, www.careforthefamily.org.uk
Cruse Bereavement Care – national charity set up to offer free, confidential help to bereaved people, www.crusebereavementcare.org.uk
Gingerbread – a lone parent family organisation run by lone parents for lone parents, www.gingerbread.co.uk

Parentline Plus – offers free 24/7 parents' helpline, providing parenting advice and parental guidance, on a wide range of parenting issues, www.parentlineplus.org.uk

Prepare for Marriage – useful tips and information on courses for those who are engaged, www.prepareformarriage.org

Relate – counselling, sex therapy and relationship education supporting couple and family relationships, www.relate.org.uk

Samaritans – provides confidential emotional support 24/7 to those experiencing despair, distress or suicidal feelings, www.samaritans.org

Smart Marriages – directory of conferences, seminars, education courses, providers, school and youth courses in USA and worldwide, smartmarriages.com

The Forgiveness Project – a charity which encourages and empowers people to explore the nature of forgiveness and alternatives to revenge, www.theforgivenessproject.com

2-in-2-1 – useful information on engagement and marriage, www. 2-in 2-1.co.uk

questions for groups

If you would like to work through this book with a group you can download some recommended group discussion questions at www. hodder.co.uk

Notes

1 Quoted on Reuters.co.uk on 13 January, 2009
2 The General Household Survey ONS 2008
3 Scott Stanley & al (2005) – Centre for Marital and Family Studies,
  University of Denver
4 Harry Benson's 2009 research based on data from The Millennium
  Cohort Study